Where to, Guv?

To the memory of
Lawrence Anthony Grant
7 January 1944 – 28 June 2005

WHERE TO, GUV?

THE COMPLETE HISTORY OF THE BRITISH TAXI SERVICE

DANNY ROTH

The History Press

First published 2015

The History Press
The Mill, Brimscombe Port
Stroud, Gloucestershire, GL5 2QG
www.thehistorypress.co.uk

British Library Cataloguing in Publication Data.
A catalogue record for this book is available from the British Library.

ISBN 978 0 7524 9941 3

Typesetting and origination by The History Press
Printed and bound in Malta, by Melita Press

Contents

Foreword

'The blind leading the blind' – this taxi history is written by someone who has never driven a taxi and never will. The driving force was my father-in-law, Lawrence Grant, a well-known taxi-trade personality, who died suddenly on 28 June 2005.

I therefore start with a short biographical tribute to a lovely man. Lawrence Anthony Zeidman was born in Ware, Hertfordshire, to London East-End evacuees; they returned early in 1946.

Health-wise, he started with acute myopia and a year's near blindness in 1950–51, forcing attendance at a school for the partially sighted in, of all places, Hackney. In 1953, his parents – having added a daughter and second son – moved to Harold Hill, Essex. He thence attended a normal primary from 1953 to 1955 and, after failing the eleven-plus, a secondary modern, Quarles, Harold Hill until 1960. He achieved creditable athletic standards, notably as a half-miler, winning three gold medals at schools' events but, more importantly, being successful in White City's National Schools' meeting, where his 2 minutes 2.7 seconds equalled the then women's world record.

His father, Sydney, was a caterer specialising in wine purchasing; Lawrence participated from childhood, becoming an honorary member of the Wine Tasters' Association, Sommelier's, at 17. Following paternal footsteps, he entered South-West Essex Technical College's catering section. Two years saw his passing with distinction. However, domestic problems escalated, relationships with his parents became strained and he joined the merchant navy.

Catering qualifications enabled him to serve as senior wine steward. His first trip was with the famous Royal Mail 'A' boat *Amazon*. Another Royal Mail cruise ship, the *Andes* welcomed him later for two and a half years. Then the New Zealand Shipping Company, Rangitoto, took him to their home country; he sailed with *Corinthic* to Australia.

In autumn 1964, he returned home to work at Queensway's Finch's Off Licence. This lasted until early 1967, when he married Jasmine Lawrence, later joining London Transport, anglicising his surname to Grant.

Poor eyesight precluded bus driving, but he was accepted as a Clapton Garage-based conductor. Over two years, matters improved noticeably and by 1969, his vision, assisted by good, pebble-shaped (hence his nickname, Pebbles) spectacles, was sufficient for full-time driving, studying taxi drivers' 'knowledge'. His first trip to Penton Street saw him meet one of the most knowledgeable London taxi servicemen, examiner Mr Wicks.

Interviewing comprised two stages: firstly, one-to-one, where the candidate's general character, including any police record, was discussed. Grant could not claim Al Capone status but had once been fined 10s for carrying a friend on his bicycle crossbar aged 12. He had conveniently forgotten this when completing his application but soon appreciated police-checking thoroughness. The second stage saw all applicants – about twenty – in one room with Mr Wicks, demonstrating exactly what was expected of 'knowledgeable' drivers.

Candidates were handed a copy of the 'blue book' and were taught plotting runs, using maps, two pins and cotton. Respecting the nearest route between two points being a straight line, they had to consider streets nearest to the cotton as basis for directions. The book contains thirty lists, each including twenty-five runs, feasible in either direction (very important, particularly nowadays with many streets one-way). Additionally, it shows four secondary points around each starting position; thus drivers must know $30 \times 25 \times 2 \times 4 \times 4$, about 24,000 runs.

In addition, major points of interest, within 10 miles of Charing Cross (London's reference point, from which distances to and from provincial locations are calculated) must be memorised. Drivers must also know basic directions from Central London to all suburbs, at least within the M25.

Mr Wicks randomly picked a student, asking: 'Where were you born?' 'Ware,' Grant replied. 'I'm asking the questions!' was his reaction. 'No. Ware, Hertfordshire,' Grant explained. 'Where do you live now?' Wicks went on. This time, Grant could be less ambiguous: 'Barkingside, Essex.' Pronouncing this a 'Green badge Village', Wicks asked Grant to name all turnings, left and right, from Sandringham Gardens to the Green Gate pub. Despite this being Grant's home area, he failed, Wicks demonstrating the widest knowledge of anyone Grant ever knew.

Following this introduction, Grant's first problem was transport. Finance was short so he approached his local bicycle shop, buying a moped previously used by 'knowledge' students. In dubious condition, it broke down continually, leaving him walking home. Initially he accepted this 'job hazard', but on one occasion, stranded in Peckham Rye, he faced a particularly long trek. Approaching Westminster Bridge, he seriously contemplated tossing the infuriating machine into the Thames, quitting the knowledge quest in favour of something less arduous.

Lengthy family discussions followed, his father-in-law finally paying for a new moped, a Garrelli. Armed with renewed hope, Grant restarted. He disliked 'knowledge' work, but, accepting that there were no shortcuts, he struggled across a lake of heavy mud to make significant progress in a study course equivalent to five years in law or medicine.

Monthly tests saw Messrs Finlay, Miller (former police officer) and Rance (Blue Book authority) joining Mr Wicks on the examiners' inspection panel. As well as insisting on street and landmark knowledge, they regularly checked on character to ensure that drivers were up to the standard expected of someone deemed 'fit to be turned loose on an unsuspecting public'. Character was Mr Finlay's speciality – he sent shivers down students' spines with a heavy Scottish – probably Outer Hebridean – accent, only locally comprehensible. However, when the mood took him he could produce the Sovereign's English. His sole intention was to raise students' level beyond redemption – only 40 per cent succeeded.

Lawrence Grant's Metrocab, viewed
from various angles. (Author)

Once qualified, Grant became a black-cab driver for nearly forty years. His marriage was blessed with two children: Amanda, born June 1971 and Dean, two and a half years later. Following the death of his father-in-law, his mother-in-law Cissie Lawrence lived with them until her death in 2006. Thus a cosy-looking family of five welcomed me in July 1995. My involvement? I will confine it to incidents relevant to the Grants and my authorship of this book.

Born in the post-war birth bulge, in early 1946, I attended primary school around Northwick Park and then Latymer Upper School, Hammersmith. I took a degree in Applied Physical Sciences (early days of Norbert Wiener's 'cybernetics') at Reading University, graduating in the summer of 1967, and applied for a job in the Prudential, hoping for work on computers, my forte. The company, however, had other ideas, putting me on actuarial work. I started the examinations, reaching the Associateship in 1973 and passing my first final in 1976.

My mother's health deteriorated through the 1970s, and she died a slow, painful death of cancer in August 1977. My father suffered a stroke in the summer of 1980, and died of a second stroke in early December. I was then involved in a very nasty court case, taking several years instead of a few weeks. Inevitably, my work became affected and after several tests, the Prudential conceded that I was in the wrong job, now being more suited to 'arty' subjects like creative writing. An obvious option was to move departments, but I was well known to be a very controversial character, determined to speak my mind even at the risk of upsetting people. Rather than sack me, they gave me 'early retirement' from Christmas 1986.

By then I had reached a reasonable standard of bridge and had already been working on my first book on the game. This was published in 1987 and my twenty-third on the subject is due to come out shortly. I have also dabbled in other interests, notably the diet and nutrition industry. My book on it, *That Four-Letter Word, Diet,* was published recently.

When I met Amanda Grant, we dined out to discover that, not only was there a twenty-five-year age difference but we were also miles apart in terms of academic level and general interests, notably musical tastes. It would be exaggerating to say that we were the most incompatible couple imaginable but we were not far off. Yet with all this, we seemed to get on rather well. We agreed to meet again and the rest is history. I proposed in October 1996, and we married the following June.

The book was Lawrence's idea. He used to tell of famous passengers, Major Ronald Ferguson, Tommy Cooper and Frank Sinatra probably being the best known.

The following includes others worthy of gratitude:

Bishop, A.
Bruce, D.
Buggey, S.
Dimmock, S.

Doran, A.
Ellman, M.
Ellnor, D.
Hausenhoy, A.
Newman, M.
Parcell, D.
Peake, R.
Roth, S.
Shuster, D.
Spencer, B.
Superfine, A.
Thompson, E.
Waite, G.
Worshipful Company of Hackney Carriage Drivers

I also thank the Public Carriage Office (henceforth PCO) and several motor industry companies who have provided valuable relevant information. The National Motor Museum and similar establishments also kindly helped with time and effort. I am also indebted to previous taxi-orientated writers:

Bobbitt, M.
Georgano, N.
Gilbert, G.
Levinson, M.
Lindsay, M.
Munro, W.
Samuels, R.
Warren, P.

Danny Roth, 2015

Introduction

'Taxi! Taxi!' A well-known cry heard everywhere – even the musical *My Fair Lady* started with patrons emerging from Covent Garden Opera House, eager for transport home. But how many appreciate the history and behind-the-scenes background of this apparently simple transport mode?

Old adages indicate that only when one starts learning does one realise the alarming level of one's ignorance. When I started researching taxi history, volumes of available literature progressively increased and I wondered whether I could ever finish – researching, never mind writing.

To start with basics, one explanation pronounces 'taxi' joining our language in the eighteenth century, a German nobleman, Baron von Thurn und Taxis, running a mail-delivery-service company using a primitive device for measuring distances travelled by carrier coaches, the taximeter's forerunner.

Countless external factors are influential – each pulling in its own direction – causing limitless strings of problems. Simple illustrations will clarify. A taxicab of given size must provide adequate room for driver, passengers and luggage. Increasing the driver's room for his comfort involves reducing space for others and vice versa. The obvious solution seems to be to increase the vehicle's size, but now we run into increased manufacturing costs, maintenance, insurance and running, with larger vehicles producing lower mileage per litre of petrol. There are also increased parking problems, countless legal restrictions, which vary with government, time and place … need I continue?

I must first list relevant parameters, briefly discussing each, then, as history progresses, explain how each had its say and how the service has steered through the various minefields. The taxicab world even has its own language. The term itself might derive from Greek *taxideyo*, to travel – another explanation. Appendix 1 shows a glossary.

Vehicles themselves have changed over time from ancient history's rivercraft before the wheel's advent, to horses and motorcars. I shall outline designs, manufacture, maintenance and safety before considering fuel, ranging from hay to petrol, and distance/time measurement.

Vehicles are operated by drivers – boatmen, horsemen, taxicab drivers or 'cabbies'. I shall consider necessary qualifications and how he (i.e. he or she) has performed and behaved over time. Drivers can be self-employed but often work for companies, each having their story. Passengers vary from fitness fanatics to those with special needs, blind and disabled. I shall contrast treatment of various users, from attractive young ladies to sprint-champion bikers and from drug dealers to entertainment stars or senior politicians.

I then need to consider environment – qualities of river, track, or road – how to handle various weather conditions from temperature extremes to those of ice, flood and dryness. In addition, I look at off-road conditions, drivers' facilities for food, washing, etc., unions and welfare organisations.

Administration includes financial balance sheets, which tabulate collected fares, including tips, against costs, fuel, maintenance, insurance, tax, uniform where applicable, advertising and communication – lists are endless against a background of economic troubles, inflation, interest rates and so on. These all deserve books to themselves and then there is legality. Laws vary not only with time and place but also apply to financial elements and taxi design, general driving, licensing standards and qualifications.

Thus taxi history is effectively a series of stories, mostly running parallel but frequently crossing paths. It is therefore impractical to work chronologically without awkwardly jumping between tracks every paragraph. I discuss general periods and within each, tell a number of stories while emphasising places at which paths cross.

It will be convenient to consider six periods, noting some inevitable overlap, particularly legally:

> Up to 1834
> 1834–97 Victorian era
> 1897–1918 when the motor gradually took over from the horse to the First World War armistice
> 1918–45 interwar period and the Second World War
> 1945–61 immediate post-war period
> 1961–present day, modern era from the appearance of minicabs

I also consider the future, bearing in mind that lotteries or football pools may be considerably more reliable.

1

Early Days:
Up to 1834

As indicated, if licence permits description of rivers as 'roads' and boats as 'taxis', vague evidence dates back to 4000 BC when Ancient Egyptian boats carried passengers along the Nile. More confidently, advancing to 2000 BC, Cairo's Museum boasts boating exhibits.

Further clues emerge from considering the necessity for some sort of taxi service. Cities of significant size existed from 3000 BC; however, most were small and densely populated and local journeys could usually be walked, the slow pace of life demanding little hurry. Only the late Middle Ages saw cities grow to the degree that occupants lived and worked more than walking distance apart, necessitating transport. Most had populations below 5,000, possible exceptions being London at just under 18,000 around 1100, approximately doubling by 1400, and Paris with 6,000 in 1300, increasing to five figures a century later. Around then, only Ur of the Chaldees was more heavily populated, perhaps 25,000 to 30,000 with sardine-style crowding.

However, towards 1600, trade, commercial development and city growth necessitated and brought about marked changes for urban dwellers, notably expanding around harbours and along rivers. In Britain, Renaissance and Reformation periods brought in, for the first time, industries like herring fishing, iron and steel, and cloth production to cities. Cultural mobility increased significantly as long-distance travel enabled craftsmen, philosophers, artists and others to spread their talents in centres of government, industry, learning and entertainment. Increased populations and land-area use, building of large residential properties, streets, bridges and the establishment of parks and gardens, characteristic of the late sixteenth century, resulted in higher growth rates.

These dramatically exceeded those of previous periods as suburbs were absorbed, necessitating public transport. However, environmental conditions needed improvement. At least up to the seventeenth century, roads were terrible – cobblestones being frequently punctuated by pits, trenches and mud. Thus, unless it was inconvenient to use the Thames, then easily the best route, it was probably quicker to walk than use wheeled transport. At best, this would be extremely uncomfortable, passengers feeling as though they were progressing on very eccentric elliptical wheels.

The Spanish Armada year, 1588, saw a thanksgiving service for deliverance of the conflict's survivors held in St Paul's Cathedral, horse-drawn carriages being laid on for congregants. The coaching company's licensees paid £50 per annum, then considerable, for the privilege of running their service.

With fuel-powered motorised transport still three centuries away, the principal form of land transport was equestrian with the key name Hackney. The term may originate from the fourteenth century with several explanations. One states that horses, bred in pastures in the East London borough of that name were led through (appropriately named) Mare Street to Smithfield Market. Another quotes the ancient Flemish/French term *Hacquenée*, a spotted, patched or 'dappled' grey or dark-coloured ambling nag, customarily ridden by ladies. The breed was developed in the eighteenth century, crossing thoroughbreds with large-sized Norfolk Trotters, an important example being mid-eighteenth-century stallion shales. About 14–15 hands high, these horses have heavy muscles, wide chests and impressive bodies with arched necks. They display high-stepping flashy trotting and, highly strung, must be handled with experienced care by qualified trainers.

Carriages and coaches, usually waiting outside inns and taverns, were then also named Hackneys and, although hardly describable as either sleek or comfortable, they boasted the sturdiness necessary to run on the adverse road conditions of the day. The first record features the Earl of Rutland ordering a coach in 1555. However, sixty-odd years passed before further examples emerged. The 1620s saw coaches operating and in 1633, one Captain Baily, a retired sea captain or 'matelot', who served under Sir Walter Raleigh on South American expeditions, bought four coaches and employed drivers, appropriately equipped with livery. They stood in London's Strand next to St Mary's Church and outside the Maypole Inn. This was the earliest recorded ply for hiring (nowadays 'cruising'). Areas congregated by Hackneys, nowadays termed 'stands' or 'ranks' were named 'standings', and first appeared in 1634.

The year 1639 saw the Corporation of Coachmen licensed to ply for hire in London. Early coaches were usually two-seaters, pulled by one horse. Most originally belonged to noblemen, who had sold them off on falling into disrepair. Their poor state on acquisition earned the nickname 'Hackney hell carts'. By about 1650, there were over 300 larger versions, still two-seaters but driven by two horses, the driver mounted on one. They were described as 'caterpillar swarms of hirelings' congesting traffic in narrow streets. A 1654 parliamentary Act officially limited the number permitted around

London and Westminster to 300, authorities relenting to 400 in 1661, then 700 by 1694. Around 1650, Cromwell's era, the Worshipful Company of Hackney Carriage Drivers was established, recognised as a City of London Livery company from 2004.

Another parliamentary Act, passed in 1662, specified that horses (stallions, geldings or mares) must be at least 14 hands high. Nowadays, horses below 14 hands 2in are legally deemed 'ponies'.

Hackney drivers seldom owned their coaches, preferring leasing. A well-known lessor was Thomas Hobson of Cambridge who earned immortality by placing horses he wanted used in the first stall, effectively giving drivers 'Hobson's choice'. Cab operators were mainly from the equestrian business, typically livery stable keepers or 'jobmasters', who, in addition to cabs, ran hearses and coaches for private purposes like mourning. Probably best known was Thomas Tilling, supplying horses to London's Fire Brigade, Members of Parliament, the Salvage Corps, and tram companies among others. Most other operators were smaller companies.

Of the comfort improvements attempted, most notable was the 1660s introduction of glass windows. They had appeared much earlier on private coaches, the best-known belonging to the Spanish emperor Ferdinand III, providing his wife with a glass coach from 1631. However, they were liable to break, as vehicles bounced on uneven road surfaces, and were expensive to replace. Diarist Samuel Pepys, reported paying £2 for a single pane, a huge amount of money in 1668.

As taxis became more significant transporters, specific legislation was inevitable. Industrial legal participation can be traced back at least to King Richard I's accession in 1189. However, the Hackney was first to come under serious transport legislature. In 1634, Charles I, objecting to traffic congestion and to Hackneys impeding the path of royal and aristocratic carriages, tried to reduce numbers by introducing competition – sedan chairs.

These were already popular amongst the continental well-to-do but unknown here until the King, accompanied by his favourite, George Villiers, Duke of Buckingham, travelled to Spain in a failed attempt to arrange a marriage with their King's daughter, the 'Infanta'. Charles was impressed with sedans and insisted on their introduction here. Buckingham was first to be carried on London's streets – the King's present. One Sir Saunders Duncomb was given royal exclusive rights to rent them out. The chair was originally carried on the bearers' shoulders (considered slave labour), but it was unpopular in England until a century later when a newly designed version arrived, portable at arm's length – now the carriers' arms pointed downwards. Either way, they hardly alleviated congestion.

Hackney operators protested (the usual welcome to newcomers – minicabs suffered similarly 300 years later) and Hackney numbers carried on increasing regardless. Nonetheless, rivalry was bitter and by 1711, when Hackney licences were increased, firstly to 800, later to 1,000, some 200 sedan licences had been granted by Hackney Coach Commissioners, increased to 300 in 1712. Despite their being more expensive,

Is a mile against Hackney's 8d, and slower, being restricted to the bearer's walking pace, the sedan was popular, offering the advantage of having tough fellows as carriers, who, for a small tip, would guarantee passenger safety against pedestrian robbers, muggers or, as they were known, 'footpads' (unless bearers cooperated with criminals; now the chair would commonly be set down while they enjoyed a refreshing tankard).

In 1635, a Royal Commission was established for Hackneys' regulation. The King insisted on licensing drivers. His proclamation of mid January 1636 allowed up to fifty Hackney carriages to ply in the London area but barred them from the Cities of London and Westminster unless they entered the area intending to take passengers at least 3 miles outside, in practice to country homes. Aldermen were expected to enforce the limit. Also no private individual was allowed to keep a coach in City confines unless he had four fit and able horses available for His Majesty's war service. He further complained that Hackney coaches broke up street pavements and increased demand drove up prices of hay and other dried animal food, 'provender'.

However, modest police numbers made enforcement difficult. Nevertheless, all this threatened the industry and distressed Hackney men petitioned in June 1636. They requested that 100 be allowed to form a corporation for unimpeded plying. They argued that full-time operators in London scarcely numbered more than 100 anyway and that traffic congestion was actually caused by coaches hired out by speculative shopkeepers. Petitioners offered £500 per annum for this right but the King refused. Two years later, they 'improved' the offer by volunteering to keep fifty men and horses readily available for military service. That was also rejected but the Hackneymen ignored the King, escaping unscathed, primarily because he had other problems, notably desperate money shortages, leaving him dependent on unsympathetic Parliamentarians. In 1639, licence was granted to the Corporation of Coachmen.

From 1654 and the start of Cromwell's rule, Parliament placed Hackney legislation with the London Court of Aldermen; they made by-laws, restricting Hackney numbers in the London/Westminster area to 200 or 300 (historians differ) and also, as before, requiring licensees to have four horses available per Hackney. Around then, Cromwell also established The Fellowship of Master Hackney Carriages or 'Coachmen'. The coachmen, Civil War Roundhead combatants, were licensed at £2 annually. However, political and religious disharmony forced him to disband it in 1657. Nonetheless, taxi driving had now become a recognised profession.

The coronation year 1660 saw King Charles II forbid, by proclamation, street plying. Apparently little notice was taken; diarist Samuel Pepys proudly recorded breaking the rules from the first day. In 1662 the King appointed commissioners to oversee registration and licensing of coaches, the permitted number rising to 400.

This new Act replaced that of 1654. Restrictions imposed typically included one that no licensee could have another trade and that horses needed 14 hands minimum height, ponies being deemed insufficiently strong to pull heavy and cumbersome coaches. The Cavalier Parliament also taxed each Hackney 20s plus a registration fee and a £5 licensing fee for street damage, sewer repairs and by-way improvements. However, this was discontinued from 1679, there being no sitting Parliament to renew legislation (until re-imposition in 1688, following the first major trade enquiry led by Sir Thomas Stamp). The permitted number now rose to 600 until new 1694 legislation added a further 100.

The year 1679 saw early signs of the 'Conditions of Fitness' concept on Hackney coaches, referring specifically to drivers' seats' size. Wording mentioned the 'perch' of every coach to be 10ft minimum, to have cross-leather braces and be strong enough to carry at least four persons. With the rule applying to all new and second-hand coaches, many nobility cast-offs now serving as Hackney coaches, needed modification. However, the *insignia* of former owners were kept on the doors. From 1654 to 1714, Hackneys displayed registration numbers on *both* coach doors. Subsequently, they were displayed on a metal plate nailed to the rear door – something that holds today except that computer-generated, forgery-proof plastic versions are used.

Following the Great Plague of 1665, an authoritative decree or 'ordnance' was enacted, under which Hackney coaches carrying passengers to shelters and/or hospitals for the infected – 'pest houses' – needed five days' airing before further use. The Great Fire of London in 1666 resulted in many streets being rebuilt and widened for easier manoeuvrability. Drivers could now sit on coach boxes rather than riding horses. Larger coaches could now be used, including many nobility discards.

Strangely, this has been repeated recently: discarded Rolls-Royces are often used as hire cars. Users enjoyed the 'status' of riding in vehicles formerly belonging to 'betters'. In 1685, some women donned masks and hired a coach displaying a well-known aristocratic crest to drive through Hyde Park. On seeing several rich and famous people riding in private coaches, they started a stream of abusive behaviour. The resultant complaints led to Hackneys being banned from the park for two years. Following several more instances, the ban was reinstated in 1711, this time lasting until March 1924 when ex-cabbie Ben Smith, now a Labour MP, hired a cab, driving there for a 'lap of honour'.

With Hackney coaches flourishing, more companies wanted to join, increasing pressure for further licences. However, 'who you were' rather than your capabilities took priority. For consideration, prospective licensees needed a sitting MP's recommendation, implying that friends, associates and former servants not only dominated but appreciated monopolistic advisability of limiting numbers. Inevitably, bribery was rife; licences (standard charge £5) changed hands for £100 – like stadium-ticket touting. After standardisation under William and Mary in 1694, Parliament took control and the Hackney Carriage Office, along with five commissioners answerable to Treasury Lords, was established to control trade regulations. The Ways and Means Act of 1710 was one example. (Actually, the purpose was funding war with France; one account quotes £20,000 needed for trade organisation over seventeen years while collected fees totalled £82,000).

That year's licence fee was legally increased to £50 with twenty-one years' validation. However, much illegal plying continued, notably in night-time London. Unlicensed men exploited a loophole by moving to towns, typically about 20 miles away, then entering the area 'plying as stagecoaches'. When they reached London's streets, they could ply in direct competition to legally licensed coaches – similar to taxi-minicab warfare. If anything, violence then was more intense. There were numerous complaints against Hackneymen who used tactics like impeding customers from entering shops and picking fights with argumentative tradesmen; occasionally even aristocrats were involved. Thieves' attacked coaches, knifing the back open, after which passengers could be robbed of anything, even wigs.

Nevertheless, opposing forces operated. Generally, authorities showed greater interest in honesty than in drivers' and horses' ability and, from its formation in 1698, the Society for Promoting Christian Knowledge published specially written moral pamphlets ('tracts') applicable to worker groups whose morals and behaviour were poorly viewed. These also applied to sailors, innkeepers and soldiers. London's City Mission has worked in this area ever since.

The year 1695 saw the first Commissioner for Licensing appointed, numbers increasing to 1,000 by 1768. That year saw King George III create a commission regulating Hackney coaches. Its functions included approval of locations for standings, licensing of caddies or 'cads' to water the horses, care of Hackneys in drivers' absence and passenger assistance. Coachmen had to give way to 'persons of quality and other coaches belonging to "gentlemen"', being fined £5 for indiscretions. A further 100 licences were issued by 1805 but complaints of poor late-night theatreland availability abounded.

The early nineteenth century (possibly 1823) saw French cabriolets make their London debut, their name being shortened to the (many thought) vulgar-sounding 'cab'. Eight were licensed initially, four more joining later. Painted yellow, they stood for hire in Portland Street. They were popular with the public, but in-force regulations granting exclusive rights to Hackney owners inevitably hindered their expansion. Hackney owners opposed their rivals, predicting a limited future. However, in 1805, nine licences were granted to a couple of MP's. Several Hackney operators, observing the popularity and success of their fast-travelling competitors, impatiently petitioned to have their licences transferred to cabs. However, cab operators were men of high social standing, using their considerable influence for maximum obstruction. Consequently, such transfers were not granted until 1832; soon afterwards several hundred cabs rode London streets.

Two new Hackney cab versions then appeared. Spring 1823 saw twelve purpose-built but cumbersome Hackney coaches operated by David Davies of Mount Street, Mayfair. Originally named 'covered cabs', this introduced a curtain protecting passengers against wind and rain. A later improved variant, two-wheeled and lighter, earned the nickname 'coffin cab', being shaped accordingly. Their rank was near the Oxford Circus end of Great Portland Street. Painted yellow and black, they became very popular, charging two-thirds of competitors' fares. Other trials had poorer success.

One, in 1823, was an enclosed four-wheeler, named Clarence after the Duke (King William IV from 1830) but also known as the 'growler', detailed later. Reasons are debatable, candidates ranging from the noise it made as it traversed irregular cobblestones to their drivers' temperament.

William IV's reign saw major legislative overhaul with 1831's London Hackney Carriage Act. This ended 177 years of transport history, during which the Hackney carriage was the only public transport form recognised apart from the sedan chair. The Act cancelled many previous regulations (applicable to Hackneys as distinct from stage coaches), abolishing the Hackney Coach Office and transferring licensing power to the Commissioner for Stamps (in 1838 this was transferred again to the Commissioner for Excise). 'Stagecoaches' were so called because originals were Hackney carriages travelling in stages – short distances along a fixed route, picking up passengers at set stopping points, nowadays termed 'stops'. They were the precursors to modern omnibuses.

Numerical limits on operating Hackney carriages' were lifted. Responsibility for issuing licences approved by the Commissioner, collecting revenue, making by-laws regulating conduct of proprietors, trade, etc. and offence and dispute adjudication passed to Metropolitan Police magistrates. In 1838, licence issue became the responsibility of the Registrar for Public Carriages, appointed by the Secretary of State. In 1850, when that office was abolished and the Public Carriage Office established, a Commissioner, an MP, acting under the Secretary's authority, assumed all registration duties – taxicab and rank licensing, regulation in the Metropolitan Police Area and City of London, and lost property redemption or disposal. Area division details are in Appendix 9.

The PCO opened in April that year in Great Scotland Yard, Whitehall Place (annex of New Scotland Yard, from which it was nicknamed 'The Yard'; some say 'The Bungalow'), subsequently moving to 109 Lambeth Road in 1919, then 15 Penton Street near King's Cross from 1966. (It has, however, terminated many of its maintenance activities since March 2007; nowadays cabbies take vehicles to SGS Maintenance). Around then, registered cabs under regulation numbered around 4,500. Office management and control remained unchanged up to 2000 (19,500 taxis then licensed in the areas and 23,000 drivers), but from early July that year it became a government agency, parting from the Metropolitan Police Service. Control then passed from the Department of the Environment and Region to the 'Transport for London' section of the new Greater London Authority, directed by the new Mayor of London. He has powers under the Greater London Authority Act to dispense with outdated regulations like the 6-mile limit; further details in Appendix 2.

It was anticipated that future years would see it take control of regulation of unlicensed minicabs and hire cars. Minicab licensing became legally compulsory from the summer of 2004. Plans anticipated licensing under three headings: operators, drivers and vehicles. The major change forecast was that, whereas originally considered a separate entity, taxis would hence be deemed part of an integrated transport system, including buses and the Underground.

Sadly, many records disappeared in the two moves. Early days saw horse-drawn cabs as the only recognised form of Hackney carriage; appointed inspectors were required to have intimate knowledge of vehicles, equestrian diseases and associated problems to be able to issue certificates of fitness as per 1843 legislation discussed below.

Defining the area under these authorities, the original London Area Act was enforced from 1829, the formation year of the Metropolitan Police, taking over traffic control from appointed parish officers – 'beadles'. Amusingly, while the intention was 'improvement', complaints about hour-long delays were frequent with notorious police arm signals misunderstood by frightened horses. Originally, the area covered was defined as the Cities of London and Westminster but in 1831 this was redefined to a 5-mile radius around the General Post Office. In 1838, the radius was doubled and from 1843 to 1895, to the City and Metropolitan Police District.

Previously short-stage coaches could only legally operate on fixed routes beyond the area of the Bills of Mortality, defined as that within which return of parish deaths were drawn up as a 'Bill' and accounted for by the Worshipful Company of Parish Clerks. The area extended east–west from Whitechapel to Marble Arch and north–south from Islington-Hackney to Southwark. Within it, 1,200 Hackney coaches had plying licences whereas short- and long-stage coaches could only collect passengers at a central point, dropping them outside the area. This arrangement had stood since the Elizabethan era closed in 1603, but now London streets were open to everybody. Major bus companies were formed, eventually merging as London Transport. Other notable names were Thomas Tilling and Goode and Cooper of Brixton, lasting until the 1970s.

So … cab or coach? Clearly cab travel was faster but at the expense of comfort and safety. Cab drivers were markedly less safety-conscious than their counterparts, keen to show off speed, even if that meant frequent collisions with lamp posts or other vehicles. Horses fell regularly, usually propelling passengers on to the street, putting many off. Customers were restricted to youths and those who thrilled in risk-taking. Dress-conscious men – 'dandies' – used to flaunt their manliness by boasting of accidents. Criticisms were thrown in both directions. The coach drivers wondered why anyone was prepared to risk their neck for a few minutes' saving, while cab drivers derided coach horses' 'walking' pace.

Such public conflict had begun around 1832 when a paper entitled *The Cab* started but proved a literary rather than trade journal, capitalising on current cab popularity. The trade waited until the mid 1870s for its own journal, *The Cabman*. By about 1900, several others, devoted at least partly to the trade, had arrived and departed, notably *Cab Trade Gazette*, *Cabmen and Omnibus News*, *Hackney Carriage Guardian* and *Cabmen's Weekly Messenger*.

The Act of 1831 also regulated drivers and licensing; hours and days of work were limited; a code of behaviour forbade refusals, abusive language and reckless driving (alcoholic or otherwise). Drivers were also instructed to avoid blocking traffic and to be honest, charging passengers correctly and returning lost property. They had to request on-board passengers' permission before accepting additional clients.

Refusing and bilking (runaway cheating) passengers have plagued the industry to the present. It's mistaken to think that offenders were poverty-stricken or other low-grade individuals with no conscience about a free ride. In 1695, nobody less than the King and Queen, William and Mary, hired all London's Hackneys to take their entourage home to London after landing at Margate from a trip abroad. The charge came to £2,000 but only a modest payment was made. The remainder is still outstanding!

In 1832, Edward W. Boulnois introduced a new small, box-like cab, a two-wheeled, enclosed version, the driver sitting on top and in front of his passengers, sitting facing each other. Their door was rear-mounted, a serious design fault; a dishonest passenger could easily alight quickly and run off. The cab, originally termed 'backdoor cab', 'duobus' or 'minibus', became known as the Bilkers' cab and soon disappeared. A further version was named 'Victoria' cab shortly after she ascended the throne in 1837. This was a lightweight four-wheeler with a low-sweeping cabriolet-type body and collapsible hood, seating two passengers with an elevated driver's front seat. Sometimes known as 'fly' cabs, these were popular with ladies.

Around then, came the brainchild of designer Mr Harvey of Westminster, the tri-bus. He had been licensed since 1814 but now introduced refinements. With room for three passengers, the driver's seat was offset, allowing him control of the passengers' door. Two additional frontal small wheels were added so that if the horse stumbled or fell the cab would land on them rather than awkwardly pitching forward. Finally, there was even a quarto-bus, designed by Mr Oakey, but those aside, the hansom and growler virtually monopolised the scene until internal combustion engines arrived around 1900.

2

The Victorian Era: 1834–97

The introduction of hansom cabs came in 1934. Joseph Aloysius Hansom (1803–82), originally from York, grew up in Leicestershire, taking apprenticeship in his father's building business. He later became noteworthy as a young architect, designing Birmingham Town Hall. Sadly, this venture proved financially disastrous so he turned to another business, cabs. The hansom cab, originally known as the 'Hansom Safety Cab', was patented that year. A square frame ran on two huge 7ft 6in wheels with a front driver's seat and room behind for two passengers. The design aimed for maximum speed consistent with safety, the centre of gravity being as low as practical so that cornering spelt minimum danger. The weight was also minimised for comfortable pulling by one horse for greater economy. (Larger four-wheeled coaches needed at least two.) Early variants seated two passengers (three at a squeeze) with the driver on a sprung seat. Weather protection was afforded by the cab exterior and by folding wooden doors, which enclosed feet and legs, providing a barrier against splashing mud. A door-mounted curved fender warded off stones thrown up by horses' hooves.

In 1836, John Chapman arrived. Initially a clockmaker and lacemaking machinery manufacturer, he subsequently became an authority on Indian finance and an aeronautics trade pioneer. As a London cab operator with the Safety Cabriolet and Two-Wheel Carriage Company, he helped rectify faults with five prototype designs. Smaller wheels were used with the driver's seat moved back to improve balance. He now entered through a frontal folding door. A trapdoor and sliding roof window afforded easy driver-passenger communication. A cranked axle, passing under the vehicle, was originally used, later replaced by a straight axle, even if that meant cutting away part of the body beneath passengers' seats. This cab, already popular in London from 1836, survived until motorisation. In 1873, further improvements were made by coachbuilder F. Forder, who then successfully introduced it abroad.

The Safety Cabriolet and Two-Wheeled Carriage Company purchased Chapman's patent in 1837, remaining active for about twenty years. It put out fifty new cabs, subsequently incorporating Hansom's patents and Chapman's improvements into a new 'Hansom Patent Safety' Company. Using Hansom's name, with Chapman probably more appropriate, proved an expensive commercial mistake. Design problems still abounded. The framework, weighing about 4cwt, or just over 200kg, was unsprung so that if the cab hit an obstacle the horse could not proceed; either the weight was thrown forward on to his back or forces could act vertically so that the weight was now on the belly band. It was also difficult for passengers to squeeze out past large, often muddy wheels.

Inevitably, imitations soon appeared, prosecutions being showered on copiers. However, despite the plaintiff winning consistently, this proved to be 'good money after bad', offenders being of little or no substance. Typically, £2,000 spent on legal action 'earned' £500 in damages or compensation, leaving the company little alternative but to abandon exclusive rights to use 'Hansom Patent Safety', which appeared on all cabs of this type thereafter. Users were usually unable to distinguish between genuine and fake, but drivers were well aware of the distinction and treated pirate drivers contemptuously, calling them 'shofuls'. The word, variously spelt, is Jewish 'slang' for worthless or counterfeit material, rubbish. Jewish drivers, employed by the original company, so described rivals but it eventually became slang for hansom cab.

The 1840s saw growlers appear. Four-wheeler Hackneys, around from the mid 1820s, had been popularised by the General Conveyance Company from 1835. This example, back wheels larger than front, seated two passengers in an enclosed area with room for a third on a box beside the driver. They were slower but more robust than hansoms and greater capacity made them favourite for heavy-luggage carriers. This was secured by a rear rail, as proposed by designer Tommy Toolittle. Its considerable noise, odour and tough springs, which gave a ride resembling one over endless strings of closely-placed sleeping policemen, earned its nickname of 'maid of all work'. By contrast, a future Prime Minister, Benjamin Disraeli, proved a hansom fan with the friendlier description: 'Gondola of London'.

Growlers mostly worked between railway termini. But railway authorities allowed only limited numbers on external ranks, and then only on payment of 'privilege fees'. On occasions when supply failed to meet demand, staff reserved the right to call in extra outside cabs – 'bluchers' – after a Prussian Field Marshall Battle of Waterloo combatant known for always being the last to arrive on the battlefield.

Dispute was inevitable but railway companies argued that their rules ensured respectable cab standards, allowing them greater control over drivers. Snobbish discrimination suggested by that first point caused particularly hot rebuffs. Cabbies argued that privileged proprietors kept their best cabs away from stations, fearing knocking about by heavy luggage. One major proprietor insisted that it cost 12.5 per cent more to maintain privileged cabs than others. Furthermore, station interiors were dark; with passengers more concerned about quick departure than cab quality, they were ideal places to send modest-standard cabs. Il-feeling persisted until the privilege system was abolished in 1907.

During this period, Hackney popularity also plummeted. The public became increasingly intolerant of carriages' filthy condition and drivers' hostility, dishonesty and recklessness. (Even with honest charging, most considered them too expensive). The 1840s saw barely 400 in London, public pressure intensifying for firmer legislation. Within a decade, they virtually disappeared, a handful remaining until 1858. Hansoms and growlers markedly increased overall cab population. Typically, 1855 saw London's licensed cabs numbering just below 2,800. This increased towards 4,300 by 1860, further increases following. However, while hansoms dominated London, provinces thought otherwise. Typically, in 1880, Manchester had about 100 hansoms, with four-wheelers exceeding 360; Newcastle, still further behind, had as many two-horse cabs as singles. Many seaside resorts preferred Victorias.

As old Hackney coaches retired in some disrepute, one bitter critic was Charles Dickens. One London magazine published an article mentioning wet straw, broken windows and cushions on which shoes had been cleaned, fever and convict carrying to deportation ships. Another mentioned a 'great lumbering square concern of dingy yellow colour like a bilious brunette with very small glasses but very large frames'. It talked of panels ornamented with faded coats of arms – dissected hat-shaped – red axletree, green wheels and old grey-coat box-coverings. Even horses were verbally abused.

Notwithstanding Dickens' literary expositions on the period's poverty, population and wealth grew, as did consequent cab demand. The industry responded in 1855 with around 2,500 licensed cabs, increasing to about 4,300 within the next five years. Hackney coaches and carriages were still being produced with new designs always welcome. Over this period, there had been many attempts for design improvements of both two- and four-wheeled cabs. Typical examples included Harvey's New Curricle Tribus, appearing from 1844 with a rear entrance. The driver's offside seat allowed him easy door opening/closure. It could thus carry three passengers and be converted to a single-horse variant. It had frontal, rear and side windows and thus appeared an improvement on the hansom with increased weather protection. However, possibly overweight, it never caught on. Others included Evans, whose principal feature was under-springing of shafts, and Felton, a vague hansom copy.

Early July 1868 saw the Society of Arts offer gold and silver medals for the best coach for two, open and enclosed, and similarly the best carriage for four. Response was minimal, the offer being abandoned until 1872. That year, cab proprietors, previously reluctant to incur entry expenses, indicated greater interest with cash prizes offered. The Society agreed, withdrawing medals in favour of £60 first prize for the most improved cab of any description. The runner-up would receive £20 and the next two £10 each. The committee specified that cabs had to be working for at least three months and be ready for exhibition by 1873. Panellists included representatives of the aristocracy, services and the trade.

Sixteen entrants left them unable to agree an outright winner, sharing the prize money between Mr C. Thom of Norwich, Mr Lambert of Holborn, Forder and Company, coachbuilders of Wolverhampton, and Messrs Quick and Mornington of Kilburn. The four 'winners' were presented to the Prince of Wales (later Edward VII) at Marlborough House. His Royal Highness, a man of decision, ordered himself a Forder. The Forder cab's principal improvement feature was the straight axle. The driver's seat was also raised to 7ft above ground level, his weight counter-balancing the shafts' for perfect balance. Thus maximum weight was taken off the horse for higher speed and manoeuvrability. The following years saw Forder hansoms adopted extensively in London, the Society feeling justified that its pecuniary offer had earned credit.

This success prompted the Royal Society to hold a special exhibition in October 1875, at Alexandra Palace. A prize of £200 was offered to the best cab and the driver claiming the longest employment stint with one employer. To qualify, the winner had to be free of charges of cruelty to his horse, drunkenness, reckless driving or similar misdemeanour. The press, notably *Punch* magazine, felt sure that finding a winner would prove impossible! However, Forder won again with their 15–17mph hansom. Nevertheless, since 1843, as well as Harvey's patented seat attachment, several others had patented improvements; most notable was Clark's 1868 folding-hood invention.

The London Improved Cab Company proved most successful. Their depot at Gray's Inn Road, Holborn incorporated shoeing forges and repair shops. From Chelsea's stables, they operated about 300 cabs over a decade to 1894. Also solid rubber tyres were introduced on Forder cabs owned by the Earl of Shrewsbury and Talbot. These were recognised as among the smartest around London with their distinguishing trademark 'S. T.' surmounted by coronets above windows either side. Inclusion of such tyres implied silent cab motion (manufacturers were known as Noiseless Tyre) so small bells were attached to horses, warning pedestrians of approaching vehicles. Like most successful innovators, His Lordship earned himself considerable unpopularity with rivals, feeling obliged to change to rubber tyres themselves at considerable expense, although they earned benefits of smoother rides and treble wheel life. While the business's 'cab' side was financially unsuccessful, patenting rubber tyres for other users compensated.

Other hansom variants included the four-wheeler 'Court cab', the driver returning to the normal rear 'hansom' position. It appeared from the late 1880s for about fifteen years. One other prototype from Joseph Parlour, first exhibited at the 1885 Inventors' Exhibition and subsequently developed by John Abbot of Bideford, was the 1887 'Devon' cab. This seated four passengers (two facing two) with two small rear doors either side of the driver's seat. However, few were manufactured and it was commercially unsuccessful. Similar comment applies to the Imperial Brougham, which had a movable seat and doors opening both ways, and to Floyd's, having a forward hood ('calash') with front and side windows, which could be lowered in a curved line against adverse weather. This luxury was at the expense of considerable extra weight. The handful produced, decorated lavishly, were used privately by the wealthy. There was also the Prince's cab, boasting lighter weight and good side ventilators with patent windows, and Birmingham's bow-fronted Marston cab in 1889. Finally, a three-wheeled version was proposed in 1900 carrying four passengers, with the cranked rear axle designed to keep the body low; this, combined with the angled front door, eased access.

In 1894, Mr Thrupp of Maida Vale similarly attempted growler promotion. He offered prizes for four-wheeled cabs, insisting that candidates had to carry at least two passengers with luggage; the hood had to fold with the driver seated in front. Judges primarily sought durability with accuracy and simplicity of design and construction. Thirty entrants arrived at Baker Street's Cambridge Bazaar, but this form of transport was facing sunset, motorisation impatiently awaiting its cue.

The year 1860 had seen the introduction of the internal combustion engine, Étienne Lenoir patenting a two-cycle version in Paris, crucial to the industry's future. In 1878, Germany's Nikolaus Otto built the first four-cycle version. Then 1885 saw the German invention of the four-cycle spark-ignition gasoline engine by Karl Benz and Gottfried Daimler, patented in 1886, with Rudolph Diesel patenting another compression-ignition combustion engine seven years later.

Vehicles using the Benz/Daimler were already running in the early 1890s, with cabs plying in Stuttgart and Paris from 1895. Soon both the hansom and growler faced replacement, 1905 seeing numbers dropping by 600 annually. Clearly equestrian days were numbered; even petrol was in doubt. Electric cabs were already seen in Paris and Chicago before 1900. However, legal requirements, detailed shortly, worked against them. That year, several new names emerged, notably Simplex, which lasted a couple of years. There was also the Straker–McConnell 14/16 horsepower (hp) and a German Dixi hansom. A further hansom variant, manufactured by Lloyd and Plaister, hardly lasted. Achieving PCO approval proved problematical and even when licence was granted around Christmas, most working for the Motor Hansom Company needed remodelling in landaulet style.

Another important participant was Henry Cook. He had bought a hansom and three horses in 1868, stabling them along Montague Mews, Baker Street. His success, detailed later, was considerable and, two years later, he moved to larger premises in York Terrace, Regent's Park, continuing to prosper, at least until motorisation.

The year 1833 saw the first major legal change. Licensed taxi trade, the world's oldest regulated public transport system, became deregulated. Thus limits on Hackney carriage numbers, established since 1710, were lifted, universally opening the market, with the only firm stipulations being on drivers' health and fitness – disciplines still standing.

From 1838, trade control passed from the Home Office to the Treasury. Basic authoritative functions – licence issue, (which, that year, was transferred to registrars appointed by the Secretary of State) revenue collection, proprietors' conduct regulation, trade and drivers' discipline – were moved several times over the years; this was one example. Through Metropolitan Police auspices, it remained in charge until the Department of Transport takeover in 1984, the Metropolitan Police having acquired powers slowly and haphazardly.

In 1839, further legislation introduced the 'privilege system'; agreement stipulated that, for a driver's 1s daily fee, the cab authority or 'master' would guarantee that a dozen cabs (in practice growlers) would be assigned to Euston's London/Birmingham terminus. Other railway companies soon followed. However, this caused considerable animosity among cabbies excluded from the deal.

A further London Carriages Act, passed in 1843, combined with the earlier Act and laid down the basis for all future legislation applicable to demand-responsive vehicles. Coaches and horses required regular inspection for maintenance, fitness and health. (Previously, coaches discarded by nobility were merely given cursory glances for roadworthiness by four 'inspectors', 'experienced' as valet, land agent, gardener and butler!) More important, it clarified a decades-long legal wrangle, driver/owner relationship. This was now summarily laid down as one of servant and master respectively and responsibility for damages caused by a driver's carelessness and/or neglect lay with both, irrespective of leasing arrangement. However, while this applied to passengers, drivers were liable for property damage. The Act also directed that drivers wear metal badges, displaying registration numbers, which still holds today.

The Metropolitan Police Commissioner was empowered to establish cab standings but all his proposals were criticised. For several years, officers refused to regard policing the trade as strictly police work and in 1850 (during which all registrars' powers were transferred to him, acting under Secretary of State authority) the new commissioner, Sir Richard Mayne, took over control with little enthusiasm, describing his job as 'his most obnoxious ever'. Traffic congestion problems continued to intensify as best illustrated during the Great Exhibition of 1851. Journeys through the London area were time-consuming and dangerous because of accidental and/or criminal interference. The absence of fixed fares opened doors to bargaining and bullying behaviour by coach conductors, frequently described as 'cads' for their treatment of foreign visitors. Thus, legally, the century's second half began in most unpleasant disharmony.

In 1853, a new Act allowed Hackney coach owners a weekly duty reduction from 10s (from 1715) to 7s. Deference was also made to Sunday Observance Lobbyists by the introduction of a six-day-a-week cab at the proportionate rate of 6s. Approximately a quarter of London's cabs decided on this basis, displaying themselves with coloured licence plates with identity numbers above 10,000. Duties were collected until their abolition in 1869's Metropolitan Public Carriages Act – relevant extracts are in Appendix 3.

However, the Act's principal feature, effectively consolidating legislation of its 1843 and 1850 predecessors, was that, as indicated, it gave absolute control of the PCO to the Commissioner of Police. The trade was incensed, the press sympathising. *The Sunday Times*, for example, protested over an individual being given such power, trade representatives adding that they considered police responsibility extended to people and their property but not to Hackney carriage administration.

Worse followed when the government decided to reduce the basic cab fare, then 8*d* per mile, to 6*d*. The first day, 26 July, saw the disruption limited to withdrawal of service from the Houses of Parliament, drivers refusing to take MPs home, using 'unparliamentary' language (the mind boggles). Drivers' employers fully sympathised, striking spreading to wider areas but the police contradicted. As blacklegging reared its ugly face, they took no action against unlicensed cab drivers plying. The turmoil continued for four days until strikers were sufficiently alarmed to abandon their inaction. Finally, however, the authorities conceded an increase in cab radius from 3 to 4 miles and cab tax reduction from 10s weekly to 1s per day.

Detailing fares, books giving regulation figures for sample journeys had been published for some years, the most comprehensive probably emerging in 1805, giving, amongst other information, 10,000 examples. Police statements on fares are in Appendix 4. Despite this, driver-passenger altercations were frequent, women being particularly vulnerable to overcharging. However, on the other hand, one book on Hackney Coaches, by James Quaife, mentioned several charitable drivers often undercharging passengers. That aside, the press was generally heavily anti-driver, usually with justification. In 1825, one London news correspondent, signing himself Jehu, described coachmen as 'extortionate', proposing a primitive meter, 'pedometer', a simple distance-measuring device. He maintained this would be as effective against distance-related fraud as a watch would be against a similar time misdemeanours. The cost, under £2, would save endless bad-tempered arguments.

However, his idea was not completely new. During China's Ch'in dynasty, around 200 BC, a vehicle called a *giligulicha* (literally 'counting mile drum car'), a two-storey single-axle cart, which seated around a dozen passengers, was pulled by three horses. On the lower storey, a wooden man-like figure carried a drum and struck every li (distance covered by six minutes' marching, perhaps 500 to 700 yards, opinions varied). On the upper storey, a second such figure struck a gong every ten li. More recently, evidence dating back to ancient Rome features a runner with a bag of small stones proceeding alongside a hired chariot, discarding one every few paces, measuring distance travelled by counting his remainder at the end. For time measurement, Romans used regularly marked candles.

The year 1847 saw initial trials of taximeters, or 'Patent Mile Index', distance-measuring devices attached to Hackney coaches. Placed inside the cab for easy passenger view, these were clock-like dials, 'hour' hands showing completed miles and 'minute' hands displaying fractions. They worked through a connection to the rear axle by a specially calibrated gear train, fully enclosed to prevent tampering.

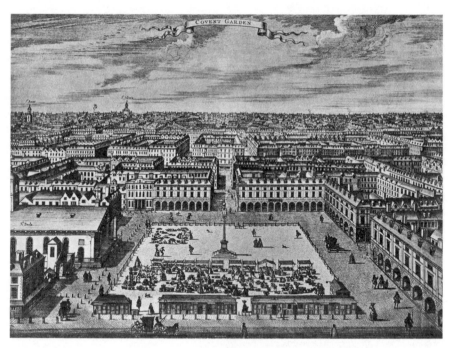

Covent Garden with carriages in around 1720. (Library of Congress)

Accident in a Georgian cab. (Library of Congress)

Horse-drawn cab of T. Tilling, London (Library of Congress)

Satirical cartoon of a Georgian sedan. (Library of Congress)

Taxis at the Bank of England, c. 1897. (Library of Congress)

Elaborate carriage in Oxford Street. (Library of Congress)

Hansom cab by the Royal Albert Hall. (Library of Congress)

Cab stand, Trafalgar Square. (Library of Congress)

Horse-drawn cabs in the street at the Strand. (Library of Congress)

Whistler sketch of a Hansom cab. (Library of Congress)

It was not adopted universally until some seventy-five years later; the same applied to a similar Kilometric Register of 1858. Drivers resented income regulation by mechanical devices. Detailing fares and collection during this period, 1867 saw a minimum fare of 1s introduced, covering the first 2 miles of any journey. Thus short journeys became more profitable to cabmen at passengers' expense. From 1870, regulations compelled owners to display cab-fare tables inside their vehicles. In principle, fares have always been set by Parliament, initially a function of distance and time with additional charges for 'extras' — more passengers, luggage measuring over 2ft (60cm) and journeys taking place at specified times — late evenings, Sundays and Public Holidays. Fares for journeys outside the Metropolitan Police area are subject to driver/passenger negotiation. Taxicabs thus showed basic standard legal charges, exact money being expected. If a large note was offered, they were entitled to take it, sending change to the passenger's home address. Sending money through the post must be dangerous and ill-advised at the best of times. It is doubtful whether this 'law' was ever adhered to seriously. Then came the delicate question of tipping.

Legislation dating back to 1830s Hackney Carriage Acts prohibited tipping; it was illegal for passengers to give drivers extra money or for them to accept it. In practice, knowing it is impractical for taxi servicing to survive without tipping, police have never enforced this. Strict enforcement — probably difficult anyway — would imply drivers' needing more realistic wages, necessitating higher fares. Consequent demand drop would put the industry between the devil and the deep blue sea. It has therefore always been acceptable and customary for passengers to add a modest amount, typically 10 per cent, to the fare in gratitude for safe journeying, assistance regarding luggage and general courtesy. Safety is always considered paramount as best illustrated in the Locomotives Act of 1865, (nicknamed the 'Red Flag' Act), stipulating that mechanically propelled vehicles were subject to maximum speed of 2mph, requiring a man walking in front with a red flag to give ample warning of oncoming.

The amount will always be a bone of contention between driver and passenger. Until meters became standard, the cabman would normally hire a cab and horse from a proprietor at fixed daily rates; thus his first goal was to recover his initial 'stake'. Typically the early 1890s saw him pay 16–17s, necessitating driving at least 25 miles to break even. Regular users often tipped generously, but country visitors and many women, from everywhere, feeling already overcharged, gave nothing. Here many may have been justified; some cabbies treated passengers as mugs, behaving disgracefully, notably when 'under the influence'; in one early twentieth-century court case, the presiding judge described the term 'cabbie' as a 'word of contempt'.

Cabbie-women relationship problems have taken several forms over the years. To quote two well-known pronouncements, The Daily Mail in late 1900 indicated that, thirty years back, it was a heinous social sin for young ladies to hail and drive alone in a hansom (even if considered a great thrill compared with a growler or motor cab). This opinion had disappeared by the time of publication. Later, one H.C. Moore, writing in

1902, spoke of old ladies who would not enter a hansom and would sorrowfully shake their heads on seeing their granddaughters doing so. The other extreme was covered in Hackney carriage legislation – drivers were forbidden from using vehicles as brothels. However, they were also forbidden internal central rear-view mirrors, leaving them blind to activities behind.

So where is the moral-immoral line drawn? The standard illustrative story features a courting couple. He knows that she has recently undergone an operation on her genital area. Suddenly she says: 'Would you like to see where I was operated?' He replies: 'Oh, rather!' 'All right, then,' she continues, 'Stop the taxi'. The taxi grinds to a halt. The lady points to the east. 'There you are; that's the hospital over there.' The line is finely drawn and the driver who fails to distinguish between the genuine innocent girlfriend and the prostitute, who uses the cab as cheap alternative to a hotel bedroom, can court trouble regarding deformation of character.

Before anti-vice laws came in, street prostitutes were picked up by police, electing to accompany them to the station by taxi rather than face public humiliation in being marched there by two officers (one could often be bribed; it was difficult with more). New laws have forced prostitutes off London's streets, changing, in particular, the face of the 'red light' West End. Nowadays, they are found in apartments, striptease or drinking clubs, 'photographic' studios (anything but) and similar buildings. Advertisements using photography and language likely to attract sex-starved men appear in local shop windows and similar.

The year 1870 saw the formation of the Cab Drivers' Benevolent Association. The previous year had seen mounting drivers' unrest, primarily because of friction with police. Many drivers felt ill-treated. Marlborough Street court alone oversaw twenty cases weekly. A backing-up fund was established to help drivers suffering sickness or other grievances and widows and orphans of those deceased through illness or accident. Several famous names figured among benefactors, notably the Marquis of Townsend, The Dukes of Norfolk and Rutland and the Earl of Shaftesbury. Royal patronage was received years later from Prince Edward, subsequently Edward VII.

Returning to tipping, following poor or absent additions, overcharging was frequent, but even that failed and May 1894 saw Cab Drivers' Unionists ask proprietors for a daily reduction of 3s. Proprietors' reactions varied; some minor players conceded but major names refused. Angry cab drivers held a mass meeting at midnight in the Novelty Theatre, massive attendance forcing an overflow meeting outside. A strike, called for the following day, was less than solid. Privately owned cabs displaying a notice 'Fair-price cabs' joined those who had won their way. Nevertheless, for nearly a month, 9,000 cabs were inactive but with little effect, merely proving the popularly held view that 12,000 cabs in London was, apart from late-night theatre time, excessive.

On 11 June that year, Home Secretary Herbert Asquith revised rates payable by driver to owner, varying with vehicle type and season. He judged that summer months would enable drivers to secure more business and the rate, applicable to first-class hansoms for 4 June to 15 July, was 16s per day. Later, from 20 August to 21 October, it was reduced to 10s. Those were not guaranteed and subject to revision. Rates applicable to four-wheelers with iron tyres, pulled by two horses, were slightly lower but rubber tyres cost 1s extra. One-horse drivers paid a much lower rate but this proved to be a false economy, cabs making markedly slower progress. The public, notably late in the day, added insult to injury by avoiding cabs pulled by obviously tired horses. Undeterred, cabbies were back two days later.

Further fare problems arose as new, hopefully improved models appeared. Similar cabs were, by law, charging similar fares, leaving proprietors problems in that if they invested capital on new projects they were prohibited from charging higher fares needed to recoup their outlay. Only the consolation of higher tips might benefit owner-drivers – hardly guaranteed. The authorities were sympathetic, trying to encourage higher standards – in 1869, they allowed proprietors to set and display their own fares table. This had some success but fixed fares were reintroduced in 1871, passengers having shown limited interest in novelties, apparently preferring the 'devils they knew'.

In 1891, German inventor Wilhelm G. Bruhn produced a new meter welcomed in several capitals, notably Berlin, Stockholm, Paris and Vienna, but others were furious; typically Frankfurt cabbies threw them into the River Main.

The Act of 1853 also introduced compulsory cab inspection; only those deemed 'fit' were granted licences. Procedures saw examiners take a cursory glance and if satisfied, take a pot of yellow ochre paint, stencil and shaving brush and inscribe a crown surrounded by a wreath, showing the month and year with the word 'approved' and the Chief Commissioner's initials. This had a disappointing effect on standards; cabbies could easily transfer the approval plate from approved cabs to potential failures and even introducing a second dated stencil was hardly effective; cheating proprietors found ways to transfer that too.

Unsurprisingly, more success was achieved when the Commissioner was empowered to establish cab-construction regulations. Typically, from 1858, cab windows needed fitted knobs; straps and iron frames were required on roofs for better luggage security. By the 1870s, such orders were codified into published 'Notices to Proprietors as to Conditions for Obtaining a Certificate of Fitness'. These proved important regarding future design and quality.

From the mid-nineteenth century, drivers needed testing on every vehicle type used to demonstrate adaptability with varying hand and foot operations and push or pull hand brakes. After many customers' complaints regarding drivers' geographical ignorance, the 'knowledge' test was introduced from 1866. Drivers now had to demonstrate adequate knowledge of London streets, important landmarks and places of interest – hospitals, clubs, railway stations, hotels, parks, theatres and other entertainment centres, law courts, restaurants, education establishments like schools, colleges and universities, government and administrative buildings, major sporting venues and places of worship.

This caused controversy; proprietors, who wanted squads of spare drivers on their books to cover illness and special events while minimising their payroll, considered the test too stiff. Against that, qualified drivers, keen to maintain their pay by forcing 'spares' out, thought it too easy. As mentioned earlier, all drivers, whatever their hours, had to be licensed (details in Appendix 5) but in practice little attention was paid to driving standards until parliamentary introduction of tests in 1896.

Further problems centred on bilkers' legislation. Until 1879, the offence was officially criminal but, in practice, drivers found it nigh on impossible to press charges successfully. The Summary Jurisdiction Act removed the criminal element, unpaid recovery being deemed 'civil'. Thenceforth, until 1896, drivers had no practical redress against bilkers who typically 'alighted for change' and disappeared. Under the new Bilking Act, offenders could face a £2 fine or fourteen days in jail. Where a fine was payable, drivers were awarded a proportion as compensation. Nonetheless, many bilkers escaped, leaving drivers to accept losses. Even if bilkers were caught, the badly drafted Act left drivers coming out poorly. Drivers have therefore always been reluctant to release passengers into buildings with many exits.

Provincially, a significant proportion of cab drivers owned their vehicle and kept two horses and sometimes a third to cover illness or injury. However, even that only partially eliminated risks of bankruptcy. Proprietors owning more than one cab obviously had to employ extra drivers, procedures differing geographically. In London, drivers, described as 'bailees' (trusted with goods), hired cabs from owners for a fixed daily sum, hoping to exceed it in fares and tips; provincially they were paid employees. Rates varied seasonally, rising to 35–40s during early summer when social-calendar events like the Epsom Derby and Lords' Eton v Harrow cricket match generated heavy demand, but dropping dramatically to 11s from August to November once aristocrats had resumed their country seats.

Cab legislation was principally local-authority responsibility but some uniformity was generated in 1847's Town Police Clauses Act. This established basic guidelines for uniformly applicable by-laws. Up to 1884, authorities were answerable to the Home Secretary, who, in practice, took relevant advice from the Metropolitan Police Commissioner. Subsequently, responsibility passed to Local Government Boards. They were empowered to limit cab numbers operating locally but an 1894 survey found only seven, of sixty-two surveyed, standing firm. Leeds was one, restricting to under 160 cabs, including fifty hansoms. However, a realistic comparison must note that their proportion of cabs to population was 1 to 2,300 against London's 1 to 50.

Cab drivers formed associations, trade union forerunners, late in the nineteenth century, typically, around 1879, the Wheelchairmen and Hackneymen Cab Drivers and the Amalgamated Cab Drivers' Society. The first provincial branch started in Brighton. Many companies operated Hackneys, distinguishing themselves by different uniform or 'livery' and carriage colours. The practice had started in Paris where typically Compagnie Générale painted their carriages blue while Abeille painted theirs 'Paris

Cabman' green. However, decades passed before black – the only durable paint – was replaced by other colours.

Another provincial innovation was the cab shelter. Off-road facilities were unpopular, the public finding them obstructive, particularly disliking stands without washrooms. Records go back to 1859 when one appeared in Edinburgh. Liverpool started ten years later; however, the expensive brick building was considered a traffic obstruction. A wooden version appeared outside Birmingham Town Hall in 1872, London joining in 1875. A cabmen's shelter fund was established to provide services around the metropolitan area, a leading promoter being *The Globe's* editor, Captain Sir George Armstrong, sponsoring the first in Acacia Avenue, St John's Wood. Armstrong was keen to give cabmen meeting places away from public houses, strictly teetotal, allaying the cabmen's reputation, rife since Victorian times, of heavy drinking. Writing in magazines like *London Labour* and *London Poor*, a Mr Mayhew described cabmen as 'of intemperate habits'.

A Cabmen's Shelter Fund was established in 1875, to run drivers' shelters, initially of hansom cabs, later Hackney carriages (then termed 'black cabs'). Up to then, drivers were disadvantaged, debarred from leaving cab stands with vehicles parked there. They could neither visit washrooms nor enjoy hot meals, not to mention obvious unpleasantness in inclement weather. Driving to pubs was only a partial solution, forcing them to pay somebody to watch the cab against theft. Several dignitaries, including the Earl of Salisbury, volunteered to establish funds for cab-stand shelters. Famous subscribers included the Prince of Wales, the Duke of Westminster, who provided one around Maida Vale, and Sir Squire Bancroft, actor-manager of Her Majesty's Theatre, Haymarket, providing another outside the theatre. This later moved to Leicester Square and subsequently to its current Russell Square site illustrated in Appendix 20.

Shelters were small green huts, limited to horse-and-cart size because they stood on public highways. From the fund's foundation to the First World War, Central London numbers topped sixty before dropping to about a dozen. At their peak, one, in Piccadilly near the Ritz Hotel, attracted society hierarchy. That era, prior to the advent of nightclubs, saw virtually nowhere to eat or drink in the small hours and aristocratic revellers congregated in what cabbies called 'high ground' and patrons (whose principal sporting interest was racing) called 'Junior Turf Club'. Shelters were staffed by attendants, expected to sell food and non-alcoholic drinks. A kitchen and limited food were provided; other food was provided by the cabbies themselves, attendants being expected to make a living from sales without explicit salary. Shelters were provided with tables and chairs (mostly donated by benefactors), and newspapers and magazines (normally donated by publishers).

The Edwardian era to the mid 1920s saw regulars, including Lord Derby, Russia's Grand Duke Michael, financier Jimmy White, portrait-painter Jon Sargent and several Royal guards, usually accompanying girlfriends. A good fish or meat dish cost half-a-crown, cabbies allowed a shilling discount. Teetotal rules were treated with scant respect, champagne being smuggled in. Gambling and swearing were also strictly (theoretically) prohibited.

Many shelters were destroyed during the Second World War without replacement. Others were pulled down as one-way streets were established or simply for lack of updating finance. Nevertheless, thirteen still exist, run by the Cabmen's Shelter Fund – all Grade II listed buildings (locations in Appendix 20).

Regarding cabmen, latter nineteenth-century years saw the first of two periods of mass Jewish emigration from persecution in central and eastern Europe. This first came primarily from Russia, escapees from Czarist purges. The second (including my parents) were eluding Hitler's gas chambers from the late 1930s. Both faced terrible job-market discrimination. However, many young and middle-aged men joined the more welcoming cab trade. They introduced their terminology, much originating from Yiddish. Principally medieval German, this language includes many words from Hebrew, Polish and Russian. In Polish/Russian, light open carriage, horse-drawn cab, translates as 'droshky', German equivalent 'droschke'. In 1841 a horse dealer, Alexander Mortier, originally from Dessau, moved to Berlin and established a horse-drawn transport business there, importing horses and carts from Warsaw. Residents there often used small Russian coaches known as *troiken*. The singular term *troika* later corrupted into troske and subsequently *droschke*.

The turn of the century saw dramatic vehicle-industry changes. With equestrian days numbered, the first hint of 'speeding up' was 1896's repeal of the Red Flag Act after which motorised cars (the 'motor car' was still some way off, the public being dubious about this most expensive 'unknown') could be driven without its 'leader'. RAC members celebrated with a run from London to Brighton, the 'Emancipation run', still held annually, customarily on November's first Sunday, welcoming vintage cars.

3

The Turn of the Century: 1897-1918

The four decades following 1860 saw further massive cab-number surges, exceeding 11,000 by Christmas 1903, including just under 7,500 hansoms and nearly 4,000 growlers. Congestion, notably in central areas like Strand and Piccadilly necessitated restrictive rules. Typically, 1899 saw cabs banned from these thoroughfares, many hansom drivers having to spend hours on rank until hired. In 1895, a Home Secretary's committee of enquiry was appointed to consider this and associated problems; its findings are in Appendix 6.

The London Electrical Cab Company, based at Juxon Street, Lambeth, was formed around Christmas, 1896, the general manager being an electrical engineer, W.C. Bersey. Starting with share capital around £150,000, they elected a governing board from a comprehensive spread of current transport interests. H.R. Paterson was director of goods-carrying company Carter-Paterson. From the coach-building world, Hon. Reginald Brougham (descendant of Lord Brougham) and H.H. Mulliner participated. J.H. Mace was a director of the Daimler Motor Company Ltd. The Hon. Evelyn Ellis, instrumental in repealing the Red Flag Act, was a pioneer motorist and director of The Great Horseless Carriage Company; this company was contracted as builder, fitting them with Mulliner bodies and 3½hp Lundell electric motors. A novelty was inclusion of both internal and external lighting – overdoing things for some passengers, feeling highlighted as 'stage actors'.

The first non-horse cab vehicle appeared in September 1897; late 1898 saw seventy more joining, the Prince of Wales taking an early ride. After the Boer War and Queen Victoria's 1901 passing, the new king's reign, with his womanising reputation and association with tradesmen and others considered 'low-grade' heralded a period of moral-standard decline, industrial acceleration and other major lifestyle changes.

The year 1898 saw Frederick Simms become the first Briton to acquire rights for Gottlieb Daimler patents; he was elected chairman of the Taxameter (German spelling) Syndicate Ltd. His letter to Edward Bradford, Metropolitan Police Commissioner, requested the recipient to examine the taximeter device, with a view to London cab standardisation. Started by the lowering of a red flag, the machine calculated fares via a road-link, measuring distance travelled while the cab was moving, and a clockwork-style device, to measure time elapsing while stationary.

Bradford was interested but the PCO (Chief Inspector Dormer) indicated two legalistic problems. Firstly, no current legislation compelled drivers to start the meter. Secondly, if fares were disputed, meter readings were not considered legally binding. Only the distance between two places, tabulated in the Commissioner's 'Authorised fare-book', was permissible. Bradford was, however, prepared to allow Simms a try, provided meters were run at authority-specified legal tariffs (1s for the first mile) rather than the scale originally suggested (6d for short journeys). Trials failed abysmally, cabbies, with full union support, refusing to invest in meters. Within six months, the idea disappeared.

Distance-time conundrums caused considerable problems. London cab Acts had been written with horses as 'standard' and hiring in principle being time-based. The idea would continue for motors, but the big difference was that, while horses tired, motors could continue indefinitely, being obvious favourites for long journeys. Inevitably passengers, hiring motor cabs with an hourly basis, complained of being charged excessive fares shown on the distance-based meter. Then there was risk of fraud. The PCO had no explicit records of which cabs were meter-fitted. London General Company's files suggested that far more of their cabs were fitted with meters than suggested by PCO records. With no legal requirement in force regarding fitting or type, trouble loomed.

Following introduction of mandatory meter recording and plate numbers, fitting taximeters to all cabs became legally standard, and July 1907 saw 'taxicab' appearing in standard dictionaries.

Bersey's Humming Bird was presumably named after its electric motor sound. Perhaps 'loud bang' was more appropriate with the first licence issued on 5 November. With a yellow/black livery, this managed a top speed of 9mph with a 30-mile range. Hopefully electric cabs, being half the size of their horse-drawn predecessors, would ease traffic congestion. Designs were influenced by preceding horse-drawn cabs, this one resembling a Clarence four-wheeler. Bodies were built initially by the Great Horseless Carriage Company.

Mid August that year saw the first batch – twenty-plus – emerge from London Electric Cab Company's garages. Like 1823's David Davies cabriolets, they were painted distinctive yellow and black, and received a mixed welcome. Many other drivers and the proprietors' London Cab Trade Council protested at the licensing. They feared that if they became popular, members would have to buy large numbers at considerable expense – a similar 'keep up with the Joneses' scenario to the Shrewsbury rubber tyre problem. Furthermore, they anticipated difficulties for horse cabbies to switch to motors. Stablemen ('ostlers') and yardmen would lose their jobs with new cabs likely to attract different classes of driver. New incumbents, with mechanical knowledge requirement, would feel entitled to higher wages. This had some truth but the *Daily News* held the view that motor cabbies were among the smartest and that the more intelligent horse drivers would want to change.

An illustrative example was one Mickey More. Known as 'the Demon Driver' after sixteen years of hansom experience, he described horses 'moving in unstable equilibrium with feet treading on lines so that if one stumbled others would come down with it'. He added that horses were weak in the head, short-lived and continually coming to grief. Of course, he failed to appreciate that just as horses could tire so could batteries. Drivers were reluctant to accept long-distance journeys, particularly late in the day ,and abuses abounded. One classic example saw a driver, hired at Oxford Circus for Hampstead, claiming that his power had gone after a few hundred yards. He demanded payment for the short journey whereupon power miraculously returned and he drove back to town.

Nevertheless, the Metropolitan Police Commissioner expressed satisfaction at the new arrivals, emphasising interior roominess, good mechanical control and reduced size. The 1906 regulations for Construction and Licensing of Hackney (Motor Carriages) laid down by the PCO at Scotland Yard are in Appendix 7. The 10,000-strong London Cab Drivers' Union also gave enthusiastic approval. Favourable press reports included the *Daily Telegraph* speaking of speed, comfort and quietness. Several famous names were also keen, notably music-hall stars George Shirgwin (white-eyed kaffir) and Minnie Palmer (who bought herself a petrol-driven Daimler.)

Problems soon arose, however, with several defects appearing after six months' continual use. Tyre wear far exceeded expectation – designers had not realised that carrying up to 40cwt was a different proposition to a hansom's 8cwt. Initial smoothness soon gave way to vibrations, notably on starting, and the accumulator box slid about, knocking the cab floor. The rear-wheel shoe-brake action was also criticised. April 1898 saw the early batch replaced by an updated version, fifty-odd being built by the Gloucester Railway Wagon Company. They reduced vibration problems by placing the body on a new spring set, a separate set being earmarked to support motor and accumulator. A new larger accumulator enabled a higher maximum speed of 12mph. The new version was complimented on quietness and smoothness, earning the nickname 'electrical Pegasus' from some press quarters. However, new problems soon surfaced with marked noise increase and breakdowns frequent enough to discourage drivers. Also expensive batteries needed frequent replacement. The most publicised mishap saw a driver lose control in Hyde Park Gate crashing to cause extensive property damage.

Further trouble saw urchins pinching lifts by climbing on the back, resulting in the motor trade's first fatality. Late September saw one Stephen Kempton perched on the rear springs in Stockmar Road – appropriately in Hackney. His coat became entangled in the driving chain, fatally crushing him. Earlier that month, there was a near disaster in Bond Street for 25-year-old George Smith. Heavily drunk, he drove his cab on the pavement into a shop. He was convicted of drunken driving and fined ... £1. The magazine *Autocar* commented that it was even worse for drivers to be drunk in charge of motor cabs than horse-drawn versions. Breathalysers were still decades away.

By August 1899, the cab fleet had grown to seventy-seven but the company had had enough hassle, selling them off and ceasing trading. Electric cabs also failed, running costs way exceeding those anticipated. The worst offenders were the electricity needed for recharging batteries (so prohibitive that the London Electrical Cab Company established its own generating plant), tyre wear and accumulator maintenance. The company kept several cabs for general hire but were moving towards private hire, hoping to lease cabs daily, weekly or monthly, arguing that this would reduce above costs, private work being less strenuous on vehicles. There would be further saving with Scotland Yard licences no longer needed. Here there was some success, Prince Henry of Orléans being a notable customer. There had been modest Anglo-French exchange. Some Berseys were available in Paris and at least one French electric cab, the Krieger, came to London. The magazine *Autocar* described this as cruder than the Bersey but conceded the advantage of handbrakes over Bersey's shoe brakes.

Hopes were for 320 cabs operative within twelve months. However, following adverse publicity, some rival cabbies, fearing for their livelihood (even inventing stories of accidents, breakdowns and injuries) protested strongly. By December 1898 plans had been shelved, leaving only seventy-one in service. Achieving a daily mileage around fifty, they completed about 200,000 miles between them.

Drivers originally paid 6s daily for hire but this proved uneconomical; the rate was increased to 12s 2¼d (i.e. 30p to 61p decimal) as then applicable to hansoms. Combined with disastrous accident rates, this decreased interested driver numbers. August 1899 saw London Cab Company's debenture holders sell all the company's plant and cabs to protect their financial rights. With all equipment specialised and therefore of little use to others, money realised was modest, ordinary shareholders being left empty-handed. No buyers, willing to take over the company as a going concern, were forthcoming and a serious accident proved the last straw. Consequently, amid terrible press publicity, electric cabs were withdrawn. A handful, owned by small proprietors, continued for a further nine months to the summer of 1900 but by then few electric cabs were running anywhere. A handful running abroad hardly lasted.

With the motor novelty worn off, the public returned to hansoms and growlers. They resumed their monopoly up to 1904 but petrol-driven motor cabs were already in the wings, having made their debut in 1899 in Paris. Private motor cars were rapidly making their mark with 2,000 in 1900, growing fourfold four years later.

August 1903 saw the London Express Motor Service Company of Walbrook, East End, announce fifty new entrants – French-built Prunels – the first licensed cab in London, referred to as 'London's New Hansom Cab'. Formed in January 1902, Henry Remnant was manager.

The year 1903 saw the licence granted and although Express withdrew their Prunels briefly from October 1904, successful operations were progressing by 1905. Their first appointed driver was James Howe of Hammersmith; despite rival claims, he is deemed the 'first motor-cab driver'. Keen to become a motor-trade pioneer, he sold his horses and cabs in 1894. By August 1933, his forty-nine years' cab-driving service was recognised by a special commemorative badge, presented by then Police Commissioner Lord Trenchard. Today it hangs alongside other PCO memorabilia.

Initial excitement proved unfounded and by December's licence approval only a prototype was running. It had a French-built engine chassis and a hansom-style body built by Henry Whitlock and Co. of Holland Gate, London. Essentially a two-seater but with the driver in front, it allowed room for a drop-seated third passenger. A further feature – then novel – was a rear enclosed luggage boot. The effectively hybrid hansom received unfriendly press, the well-known engineer Henry Sturmey being an outspoken critic.

Two further experimental motor-driven hansoms appeared during 1904. In May, the Metropolitan Police Office at Scotland Yard, responsible for cabs, signed plying approval for petrol-engined vehicles. However, slow progress saw only three motor cabs running regularly by Christmas. Vauxhalls (most notable among several motor-orientated companies formed around then) also offered a three-cylinder motor-driven hansom during the summer of 1905. Lord Ranfurly, former New Zealand governor-general, now chairman of Metropolitan Motor Cab and Carriage Company, ordered for five such vehicles. They were run by the Metropolitan Motor Cab and Carriage Company, based in Sussex Place, South Kensington. Drivers were keen, but passengers became very nervous with neither driver nor horse visible in front. With brake controls positioned at roof level beside the driver's 'crow's nest' seat, the whole arrangement looked very insecure. *Commercial Motor* magazine spoke of frightened passengers seeing impending trouble 'rushing towards disaster' without being able to observe drivers' intentions. One model was redesigned, putting the driver further forward but with little success.

By March 1905, all had been withdrawn, Vauxhalls disappearing. The Automobile Cab Company of Chester Gate, Regent's Park, also withdrew motor hansoms within the year. One model was built with the driver sitting over the engine but, by spring 1906, all had gone as the Metropolitan Motor Cab Company turned to French-built Heralds. They scarcely lasted, withdrawing from 1908.

General reluctance to replace horse with motor proved the principal reason for allowing French dominance. The legal position had to mirror the times. Necessity for new regulations had to be outlined, the PCO's Chief Inspector Bassom being responsible.

Legislation applicable to horse-drawn taxis had been statutory for centuries but 1903's Motor Cab Act first detailed licensing applicable to drivers and vehicles. The following year saw the Motor Cars (Use and Construction) Act in which brakes, lights, tyres and steering first appeared. Bassom, however, was convinced that rules laid down were insufficiently stringent, insisting at least on consistency with previous legislation, i.e. the 1896 and 1898 Locomotive Acts. Obviously, safety was the first priority and the prime insistence was that tanks carrying liquid fuel should be manufactured from materials ensuring adequate strength and placement to avoid overflow on to the vehicle's wooden parts, minimising fire risk. Thus electrical wiring needed firm insulation. Incredibly, these had been neglected in 1904's Use and Construction Act. Thus two body types were permitted – the hansom and landaulet (or brougham); brief legislative details are in Appendix 7.

That period saw horse-drawn vehicles (gradually but not without hiccoughs) superseded by the motor cab. Competitive pressures began to affect hansoms and growlers from about 1906, hansoms leading the way off stage. Their numbers had fallen more dramatically compared with the four-wheeler by the Great War's commencement and by 1927, there were only twelve licensed in London against over 100 growlers, preferred by old country ladies who could ill-afford motors but needed capacious vehicles for luggage. The handful of survivors notably hung around Jermyn Street and St James areas, occasionally picking up sentimentalists or young couples seeking 'novelties'. Old traditions die hard, however, the last horse-cab driver handing in his licence in 1947. Kensington Palace's London Museum displays a 1912 model.

Heralds were hansom two-seater style in appearance but more user-friendly – the driver's seat being adjustable for easier passenger access. The fleet of fifteen was London's largest around 1906, but the following year saw them withdrawn as departure proved awkward. These cabs were difficult to identify and consequently, advertised on tariff cards, worked from ranks usually designated by management. Herald went out of business that year.

The Automobile Cab Company operated three Ford cabs from spring 1905. They were conversions from landaulettes (miniature variants of German four-wheeled landaus – covered carriages with tops divided into two sections, front and back; the back being let down or thrown back while the front was removable; some use alternative (technically masculine) spelling: landaulet). They earned licences the following year for three ex-horse drivers, Messrs Crow, Chambers and Clarke. Ford, while dominating the car industry, contributed little to cab trading, but, as detailed later, they produced a provincial cab in 1932, subsequently trying the V-8. They also provided engines for Beardmore, bodies for Winchester and parts for Metrocab.

The period from 1905 to November 1918's armistice saw more than forty motor rivals. The best known included Renault (certainly dominant), Napier, Panhard (more accurately Panhard-Levassor), Unic, Belsize, Fiat, Sorex, Wolseley and Hayes. Interested firms are detailed below:

Adams (subsequently amalgamated to Adams-Hewitt): The Adams 'Pedals to Push' model, introduced by the Adams Manufacturing Company of Bedford, participating from 1907 to 1911. Their model was unique by the day's standards, body placed over the engine, leaving the vehicle only 10ft long; one horizontal cylinder with pedal-operated gears.

Adler: A German firm operating about 1900–40. From approximately 1907, they introduced a 12hp cab under auspices of coachbuilders Morgan and Co. here but few appeared.

Albion Motor Car Company: based in Glasgow's Scotstown suburb; interested to 1915.

Argyll: operated from 1908 and was nicknamed 'Mustard Pot' (bright livery so coloured). Argyll had tried a cumbersome model (unique engine placement) in 1906, introducing it with a demonstration run from Glasgow to London. However, no London licence is evidenced and like Humber (discussed below) engine inaccessibility proved critical. They originally used a 16hp model but for London's market, they preferred convention. The newer version saw some forty vehicles in London service by late September 1908. The combination of the 12–14hp engine, clutch and gearbox in a single self-contained unit, easily removable for maintenance, was outstanding. Also introduced were two extra cricket-seats for additional passengers facing rearwards. Engines proved uneconomical but fifty chassis were exported to the USA.

Ballot Cab: operated by Express Motor Company (affiliated to French company Express de Paris); about 100 appeared. Another organisation, the Quick Motor Company, added a handful more, painted distinctive white.

Belsize: Principally combating French invaders was the 'all British' Manchester cab Belsize. The company, founded by Marshall and Company in 1901, took its new name from Clayton's suburb's Belsize Works. Its ¾ landaulette style was rare for the period and reputation was partly earned by reliability but possibly more through patriotism, despite its old-fashioned appearance. Belsize traded until about 1915, resuming after the armistice with a 20hp four-cylinder variant.

Brouhot: introduced in Paris from 1907. The company traded for a decade but from 1911 concentrated on agricultural machinery.

Calthorpe: sadly details unavailable.

Charron: an important name; their taxi was added to General Motor Cab Company's fleet as De Dion-Bouton.

Cottereau: sadly details unavailable.

Darracq: French. Like Renaults these sported a characteristic coal-scuttle engine cover. About 450 were supplied to London-based purchasers in 1908. Of these, about 250 were owned by London General subsidiary United Cab Company. London and Provincial took a further 100. Nine more were owned by a garage in Central London's Old Jewry; one other by the Stanhope Motor Company of Gloucester Gate, Regent's Park. The remainder (nearly 100) were owned by the London General Cab Company itself, joining the fleet of nearly 650 Renaults and nearly forty Wolseley-Siddeleys. This group was built by the Wolseley Tool and Motor Company of Birmingham. London General added more than 200 additional two-cylinder, 8–10hp models to its fleet despite their being deemed 'difficult to drive' and 'needing humouring'. Thus, in 1907 they were the world's largest fleet owners.

Four-seaters became the norm in 1908, cabmen rejecting two-cylinder troublemakers in favour of new four-cylinder 10–12hp models. London United ordered 250. These worked to late 1913 before gradual retirement.

Delahaye: sadly details unavailable.

Dixi (DPL, Dawfield-Phillips): from 1907; two-cylinder engine mounted under floorboards, midway between front and rear axles and a single-chain final drive.

Electromobile: Ford (converted several cars for cab use)

Fiat (F.I.A.T. of Bologna): The four-seater boasted ample luggage space for 330lb weight and, for the period, a remarkable top speed of 44mph. A signalling device was installed, enabling driver/passenger communication regarding speed and direction. Based in Lupus Street, Pimlico, their initial fleet, fewer than forty, rapidly increased to 400 following their move to St Pancras Road, King's Cross. Altogether more than 2,100 1908 models were produced, serving Paris and New York markets – more details later.

Gamage-Bell: A.W. Gamage was High Holborn's clothes store and Horace Bell was former manager of General Motor Cab Company. They designed and built several bodies on varying chassis, including those from BSA (originally Birmingham Small Arms Trade owned by industrialist Bernard Docker), Renault and Napier, with 15hp engines from several suppliers, notably the French De Dion and Lacoste et Battman.

Gladiator: discussed under Vinot below.

Gobron-Brillié: sadly details unavailable.

Hillman-Coatelen – Hillman: Coventry-based company arriving late on the scene. Luis Coatelen came under Hillman's umbrella on marriage to a William Hillman daughter. Early production was confined to large private cars but they later toned down to 12–15hp vehicles, converted for cab use from 1911. However, Louis Coatelen designed a more conventional 10hp variant, manufactured in Nottingham's Beeston factory (of better vehicle-finish reputation) and approved in London. Hopes for further expansion were dashed; disastrous trade returns saw Beeston closed (Coventry kept alive for private cars). London's cab production terminated in 1912.

Humber: the period's biggest motor-vehicle manufacturers, starting with a 'cab-over' design variant (similar to Argyll) in July 1907. The first licence was granted the following autumn and several hundred appeared, reputed for comfort. Two models: the standard two-seater type was cheapest on the market, being operated in London by Humber Cab Company of Holborn Viaduct; noteworthy for its roof's considerable luggage space. It proved particularly popular with owner-drivers or 'mushes'. The term originates from Canada; some lexicographers suggest Gold-Rush origin, prospectors said to be 'mushing along'; others maintain derivation from French-Canadian fur trappers' call to dog-packs to push or 'mush' on. An early owner was one W. Withey of Surrey; his grandson Alan becoming famous as a vintage-cab restorer.

The following years saw them introducing more conventional designing. The 'de Luxe' had a short wheelbase, with the driver sitting above the engine: no London approval; provincial town work only. The company fleet numbered nearly fifty with thirty-plus more owner-driven. By 1910, the design was dropped and they restricted themselves to a forty-strong fleet of conventional cabs. Sadly, engine inaccessibility for maintenance proved its undoing.

George Hurst: earlier joining forces with Simplex manufacturer Lewis Lloyd but independent from 1900, manufactured modest numbers of 12hp two-cylinder cars, following with 24hp four-cylinder cars. In 1906, he joined R. Middleton to produce a 40hp six-cylinder car, selling under the umbrella name of Hurmid. The 12hp two-cylinder cars were approved for cab service and although the company folded in 1907 they were active until about 1910.

Leader: was a product of the Nottinghamshire company Charles Binks & Co., based in Apsey. A few were in London between 1905 and 1910.

Lotis: discussed later.

Marlborough: manufactured by T.B. André, who took over British concession for French company Malicet et Blin.

S.A. Marples: coachbuilder, building cab bodies on their proprietary chassis in 1907 for London Improved Cab Company.

Masco: built in 1907 as 'Mascot'; had Forman engine.

Napier: The Napier Sunstar of 1908 was a popular two-seater landaulette built by Wolverhampton's Star Engineering Company. Although appearing slightly old-fashioned, this was favoured by livery-stable keepers ('jobmasters') for private day hire. The 1909 Napier was built by the Napier Cab Company. D. Napier and Son Ltd, starting in Lambeth, had moved into a new factory at Acton Vale; operators were neighbouring W. & G. du Cros Company. This proved the most successful cab of that era in both London (with 900 licensed, 700 two-cylinder versions, the remainder four-cylinders) and provincially; there were also huge export orders to Commonwealth countries. The du Cros reputation was further enhanced by driver courtesy.

Nic: sadly details unavailable.

Pullcar: manufactured by Motor Cab Company of Preston, selling two- and four-seater versions (front-wheel drive with hansom-style large rear wheels); chains attached to front wheels.

Star: important motor manufacturing name to late 1930s. Started with 12hp, four-cylinder model; soon preferred more popular two-cylinder 9hp variant, used to about 1910.

Squire: sadly details unavailable.

Straker: sadly details unavailable.

Thames Ironworks, Shipbuilding and Engineering Company Ltd: based in Greenwich and Millwall; built cabs for Motor Cab Syndicate of Cannon Street; interested only until 1910.

Vabis: from Scania-Vabis of Sweden. They converted cars for taxi use from 1909. Their founder, Arthur Denonville, encouraged purpose building from 1922 but their prime customers were Benelux countries, leaving little British market impact.

Vinot: Introduced by Gates Bros. of Wimbledon; good reliability record; sales all over Britain.

However, most finished cab trading by Christmas 1911. The principal reason was the Home Secretary's insistence on a fare ceiling, resulting in companies' finding cab-running uneconomical. Also a poor economic climate, consequent demand slump and several strikes hardly helped.

Regarding electrics, vehicle technology started around 1800 when Volta invented the primary cell (most primitive battery) generating electricity by chemical reaction. The problem was recharging, only achievable by replacing the active elements. Sixty years elapsed until Gaston Faure invented the secondary cell through which a current could be passed to generate portable renewable electric energy. During that period, actually 1833, American blacksmith Thomas Davenport appreciated electromagnet potential. He invented and, four years later, patented the first electric motor.

As mentioned earlier, electric vehicles were suggested in the 1880s and for approximately two decades, seriously competed with internal combustion and steam-powered rivals. Queen Alexandra used a Columbia. Only the early 1900s saw improved engine technology and cheap fuel spell the end of electricity's challenge. This century may see electricity return.

During that first decade, there were still a few electric cabs but they were more popular with private-hire firms leasing for given periods. Success fell below aspirations; in 1908, the British Electromobile Company of Mayfair – works base in Lambeth – manufactured a solid-looking vehicle, a large, capacious, heavy four-seater, on a chassis from Greenwood and Batley of Leeds. Initially, fifty were ordered during the autumn of 1908. The body came from Gloucester Carriage and Wagon Works. They were operated by the Electromobile Taxicab Company, hopefully replacing growlers as heavy-luggage transporters.

They intended to put 500 into service but only twenty actually appeared, minimising the threat to growlers. Of those, ten survived to 1920, using the Gillingham cab rank near Victoria. Their eventual withdrawal was largely due to poor range – barely 45 miles against the average 55-mile shift, decisive against motor rivals' unlimited range. Motor cabs were considered much more serious challengers to hansoms with the latter's limited seating and modest luggage capacity. Four-seater versions appeared from 1908, mostly on four-cylinder chassis. Additional seats faced rearwards for many more decades.

In Coventry, Rover launched their Motor Cab Company in 1907. Waving the British flag, they announced promotion of 500 cabs for Liverpool, Manchester, Glasgow and other major cities in addition to London. Weekly production barely reached twenty, leaving their ambitions appearing optimistic but it was a start, possibly snowballing. A sales agency was established in London's Victoria Street. By Christmas, over 10,000 cabs were around, just over two-thirds motorised. Of the motors, two-thirds were General's Renaults. The following year saw the PCO grant approval to double-figured numbers of new names and more than 2,800 new vehicles gradually eliminated hansoms. The year's end saw different cab types number eighteen, six owners sharing nearly 2,500. French makes dominated, Italian Fiats having a significant minority interest. Outside the big six, nearly 170 owners ran fewer than 330 cabs between them – several owner-drivers had a few minuscule fleets.

Also a commercial vehicle builder, Dennis constructed several taxis before discontinuing in 1913. All submitted designs to P.C.O., about forty-five British and foreign companies earning licences. This proved the initial rush of blood anticipating a sizeable market. Later, say 1920–30, there were only a dozen, the following decade seeing reduction to just four.

From 1908, four cylinders became normal although Renault stayed with two through the Great War and persisting until 1930. Early on, most designs were of modest size and power – seldom over 2½ litres and 20bhp but commonly drivers sat over 10/12hp two-cylinder Fafnir engines – with three-speed gearbox and shaft drive. Exceptions were Albion, who used chains, and Pullcar as above. They were unique with pneumatic front wheels but solid tyres on the larger rear wheels, the original intention being use as an attachment to horse-drawn cabs (or delivery vans). Actually few appeared. By 1909, once motor hansom fashion had passed, Pullcars were given equal-sized wheels with four-cylinder White and Pope engines.

Taxi literature says little regarding satisfying demand. How many taxi journeys involve one (typically businessman or shopper), two (the married couple), three or four (the family or friendly group) or, where possible, even more and how do figures vary over time periods – working day, weekend and holiday season, and place – city centres contrasted to suburbs and rural areas? There are occasional references to (pre-First World War) four-seaters being London's norm with two-seaters preferred provincially but no published statistics exist. Yet this consideration is critical.

However, logistics must be considered. Typically, early motor cabs had to be two-seaters, being built on chassis of short wheelbase and low power. As just mentioned, 1908 saw four-seaters become the norm with the advent of four-cylinder chassis. Additional passengers were normally accommodated on rear-facing jump seats. Subsequently, many cabs had all four passengers facing forward but traditional cabs have two rear-facing seats to this day.

General Cab Company's Renaults illustrate this perfectly. They were initially licensed to carry two passengers only. However, space beside the driver easily accommodated a third. Many drivers taking advantage were prosecuted for 'breaking rules'. Feeling that cabs were wastefully being used below capacity, their solicitor wrote to the PCO's Superintendent Bassom in August 1907, encouraging authorities to grant licences for up to four passengers – two originals, one beside the driver and a fourth squeezed in on the inside seat. Bassom refused, insisting on safety being paramount – cabs lacked both space and power for extra loads. He emphasised that, typically, intoxicated passengers seated beside the driver might interfere with controls, endangering occupants and others.

Two distinct fare tables, distinguishing between two- and four-seaters, were therefore deemed necessary. It was stipulated that an extra 2d per passenger above two was applicable only to four-seaters. The period's distinctive fares, listed in Appendix 4, were most unwelcome. Companies were stifled in their efforts to generate profit with work strictly metered and could only get round it with private hire, charging their own rates. They now faced competitive elements and seasonal fluctuations, sharp at the best of times.

Parliamentary authorities, appreciating the problems, added a new Act – 1907's London Stage Carriage Act, enacted February 1908. The necessity to carry meters, as enforced the previous summer, was reinforced by stipulation of subjection to Police Commissioner approval and sealing by the PCO and National Physical Laboratory, responsible for accuracy and fraud prevention. Furthermore, a passenger could not be carried beside the driver (that 'seat' still called 'box' from equestrian vocabulary). Fares for journeys under 6 miles (or one hour) had to be accepted. £2 was payable per vehicle licence.

The privilege system of 1839, now deemed unnecessary, was abolished in central London but maintained in certain suburbs. Thus work became available to motor cabs. Larger four-seater vehicles were soon seen congregating in station forecourts. Controversial issues of this kind were discussed in Fred White's *Hackney Carriage and Taxicab Gazette*. Cab drivers commonly met in St Martin's Street Cabman's Club – Leicester Square area – discussing problems.

Anyway, there was general movement from two-seaters to four-seaters around 1910, the only exception coming from Frank Morriss, (well-known as capable car-maintenance assistant to Edward VII at Sandringham), who experimented with steam cars. He planned to import American Twombly (Nutley, New Jersey) cycle cars, fitting them with two-seater bodies for use here. Sadly the Twombly Car Company terminated business in 1915 and although Morriss imported other American cars post-armistice, he contributed nothing further to taxicabs.

Trouble soon loomed over the extra 6d charged by motors (and growlers) for carrying more than two passengers. In contradiction, the London General Cab Company had put notices in cabs instructing passengers to pay the meter charge only. Consequent confusion prompted motor-cab drivers to a token strike. Worse still, drivers thought that these notices forbade them from accepting tips (passengers may have thought similarly). Fortunately, offending notices were quickly removed.

For motors, several operating companies were involved, notably General Motors, United Cab, National Cab, Express Cab, Fiat Cab, The West End Cab and Sharp Brothers. Smaller fry, some starting earlier, included Ford, building their Model B taxi but few appeared, hardly lasting. They were operated by Automobile Cab Company, originally planning to order 200. However, the London Manager of Ford, unhappy regarding financial reliability, refused to accept such a big order. Actually only three white-painted taxis surfaced. His judgment was vindicated when the company folded in

1910, its reputation already tarnished by drivers who did not use taximeters, tending to charge passengers according to wealth-indicative appearance.

Consequently, the company turned to France, ordering forty. Thirty were proudly paraded on Thames Embankment between Charing Cross and Waterloo late in October 1906. Amid blazing publicity, they displayed a large letter A for the company's initial; however, the manager announced replacement, avoiding confusion with private cars. Sorexes sadly lasted barely two years.

Others included the Rational, from the London Motor Company of Manor Road, Chelsea, with improved design, even with chassis apparently dated by 1905 standards (as were solid tyres, pneumatics appearing a year later). Design and manufacture was by Heatly-Gresham Engineering, based originally in Brassingbourne, Cambridgeshire (later Letchworth, Hertfordshire). Owners were RAC members, Mr Heatly being a founder. Its red livery and doors gave a distinctive impression with the structure affording modest weather protection. The first British-built petrol-engine cab licensed boasted a top speed of 18mph, completing 1906's 53 mile London-to-Brighton run in three hours. There was a fleet of thirteen (although only eleven were licensed). Lack of orders resulted in Rational folding in 1906 but reliability saw most of the fleet's survivors serving until autumn. Only then were they superseded by French Brouhots, introduced in Paris from 1907. The Thames cab, the Dawfield-Phillips front-wheel-driven Pullcar and the Adams Hewitt single-cylinder taxi were all withdrawn by the year's end.

However, new operators now appeared: W. & G. du Cros of Acton, West London. The late nineteenth century saw patriarch Harvey du Cros establish a strong financial position in the rubber industry, having invested in, and later becoming chairman of, Dunlop. He associated with Darracqs, acquiring British rights for Mercedes and Panhards. Further motor-industry investments included Austin and Napier. Two of his six sons, William and George (W. and G.), gradually took over from 1908.

Financed by Mr Francis Luther, they quickly established a fleet of over 1,000 Napiers and Panhards, distinguished by W. & G.'s logo on yellow bonnets. This gave the impression of 'their' make whereas, on the manufacturing side, they built everything but cabs (called them 'hiring landaulets' anyway) – vans, lorries, buses, and ambulances. From July 1910, drivers observed discipline by not smoking without passengers' permission.

Hansom operators like Henry Cook weathered the storm for some time, courtesy of 6,000 drivers working for larger companies. Protesting against spying by countless inspectors, whether standing on rank or cruising for fares, they struck. Their absence enabled Cook to augment his cab fleet, working three shifts round the clock. However, even he suffered a setback in 1916 when a strike protested at drivers' having to buy their own petrol at 8d per gallon. That lasted six weeks until employers acceded to demands for free petrol and increased commission; but the damage had already been done, many garages having suffered forced closure.

As indicated, the motor's arrival – notwithstanding vehicles' having to traverse unsuitable roads – spelt equestrian departure. Market forces worked throughout the country, more rapidly in London than provincially. Changeover bore inevitable problems for varieties of transport mode. The period 1820–40 had seen popularity for steam-powered buses, although this idea never caught on for cabs. (The only known example of steam-powered cabs were second-hand Stanleys in 1920s New Zealand). Police were hopelessly ill-equipped to handle the situation as escalating traffic congestion propelled accident rates into five figures.

Additionally, the 1906 Conditions of Fitness posed problems for those wishing to convert motor cars for cab use. Manufacturers faced high hurdles in compliance – engines had to be placed further back or 'aft' on chassis, which was mostly extremely difficult. By the time success had been achieved Renault dominated, leaving home manufacturers unable to sell. By the year's end, Louis Renault, having outbid a rival offer from Panhard, had completed negotiations for a contract with the municipality to deliver 1,500 taxis. Renault was popular with drivers, having established a reputation for reliability, with excellent weather protection. They wore long overcoats, hats and breeches in fashion with horse-drawn predecessors. Following an order for 500 by Camberwell-based General Motor Cab Company early in 1907 and another 600 joining later that year, Renault dominated both capitals for many years. From their start, late in March that year, taximeters were fitted, ahead of legal necessity in July. Sadly, their two-cylinder 8–9hp engines gave insufficient power, the company gradually replacing them with Unics, discussed shortly.

Thenceforth, the term 'taxi' was in common use. Drivers were recruited, meters being described as 'ziegers' (strictly translated as 'indicators' or 'pointers' but often nicknamed 'Jewish pianos'.) The company was severely criticised as unpatriotic, financial support coming from France, the Compagnie Générale des Voitures. Financial connections with France ran into the mid 1930s, although by then the two backing companies, the Banque d'Alsace Lorraine and the Compagnie Générale de Exploitation had both called in Parisian receivers.

With the French having escaped requirements under Conditions to the degree of violating the 32in minimum between front springs, home resentment was understandable. A letter was written by Henry Sturmey (mentioned earlier), and a cab-trade deputation was sent to the Metropolitan Police Commissioner at Scotland Yard. But cries fell on virtually deaf ears, the Commissioner insisting that the 500 Renaults were experimental, deserving rule relaxation for a fair chance, even if that left home challengers well behind. Nonetheless, in practice there was some relaxation but valuable time had already been lost in trying to establish a significant market hold.

Sturmey founded *Automobile* magazine, but in 1906 he left for a rival publication, *Motor*. He also contributed to a third magazine, *Motor Traction*. That magazine's editor outspokenly criticised the 25ft turning circle; possibly his views were stimulated by Sturmey, keen on entering cab trading. Sturmey believed that Conditions of Fitness, notably the turning circle and 32in front-spring spread, although probably well-intentioned for greater stability and turning ability, were impracticable and that the Society of Motor Manufacturers and Traders (commonly SMMT) had objected.

The implication was for the engine to be pushed back, causing several companies great hardship (although, by now, a number of British companies, like Humber, Adams and Argyll, had found solutions). Sturmey's contention was featured in a controversial discussion following presentation of a paper to the RAC in early 1911 by a member, J.S. Critchley, entitled *The Evolution of the Taxicab*. Critchley was a famous motor engineer, his name figuring among founder members of both the RAC and SMMT. However justified Sturmey's objections were, Scotland Yard ignored them.

Sturmey, already involved in motor manufacture – the American Duryea – up to 1904, introduced, in 1908, his own vehicle, the Lotis. He met the turning circle requirement with a very short wheelbase and the engine placed under the driver's feet. This was the first cab to have luggage space beside the driver. Production continued until 1912.

The motor cabs' advent also had far-reaching effects on financial and proprietary positions. Prior to about 1895, fewer than 15 per cent of London's cabs were owned by big proprietors – no large garages or stables. Mostly, there were one-man businesses, each cabby taking individual responsibility for equipment maintenance and horse upkeep, even regularly sleeping on adjacent straw piles.

Although horses were still going to be around for some years, the position was dramatically reversed. By 1911, no fewer than 75 per cent of all London cabs, horse-drawn or motors, were in the hands of just twelve companies, with as many as 4,000 cabs under the roofs of only four of those. The most notable survivor was General Motor Cab Companys, incorporated as a cab garage that year. With initial capital of £250,000 the company's workforce of 1,500 cabs soon increased to 2,300. Competition between garages was intense and, in many instances, drivers were tempted to leave one company for another with offers of improved financial rewards and possibly a new cab. The company survived by amalgamating with the British Motor Cab Company and later the London General Cab Company. Cab-type competitive pressure was also high. Many had already withdrawn but about two dozen remained, notably Renault, Unic, Fiat, Napier and Hayes.

In October 1898, a PCO Licensing Branch report discussed problems regarding cabstand monopoly. (The relevant legal document, establishing stands, was laid down in 1894; illustrated in Appendix 8). A illuminating case involved a New Cross driver, Frederick Coman, who was summoned by police for plying outside his allocated standing place. With the case considered of paramount importance to the trade, the defence council took advice from local proprietors. It was stipulated that a Mr Jones of New Cross had the privilege of supplying cabs to the South-East Railway Company station at New Cross, thereby having monopolistic advantage. Outside, on the southbound, 'up-town' arrival side, there was a five-cab rank and Mr Jones used his ingenuity to acquire that stand on top of his monopoly. He placed five of his own cabs there, keeping two more inside the station yard. If a cab were needed, one of these two would drive up, signalling to the rank occupant to take the fare, thereby keeping the rank full. Coman, under the impression that he had the right to use the stand, duly awaited his chance by standing behind the last cab on the rank. However, police were watching; they had received complaints about the monopoly but up to that stage had remained impartial. The judge ruled that no advantage should be granted to a driver on the basis of employer identity. Mr Jones' method was considered out of order, the summons being dismissed.

Five years later, a Royal Commission was established, studying London's traffic problems. Submitting in 1906, their recommendations proved helpful, notably in reducing accidents. PCO administration was divided into twelve district passing stations (listed in Appendix 9) whose responsibilities ranged from public-carriage inspection and Hackney-carriage-standing viewing to handling enquiries and complaints. Inspectors visited areas regularly and from 1920 were given motorcycles – initially Douglas solos but from 1924 Charter Lea combinations. They were assisted by variously graded sergeants. Station sergeants, with an assistant group, would check mechanical or equestrian fitness. Another took responsibility for drivers, conductors, proprietors, licences and lost property. Subject to Assistant Commissioner's approval, they could be promoted to inspector rank either by passing a two-year course examination at an approved Polytechnic Institution or by motor-engineering examination success with the City and Guilds of London, the latter deeming ordinary or honours level acceptable.

For drivers, four tests were laid down, still surviving, as follows:

> Medical – alcoholism evidence resulting in immediate exclusion;
> Knowledge – London geography;
> Scotland Yard examiners' driving test; and
> Past life and character.

Medical testing can be conducted by the driver's GP. However, if queries arise, police are entitled to demand a second examination by their own specialist. Candidates especially will need satisfactory eyesight and hearing standards and be free of potential heart trouble and epilepsy. There is no stipulated upper age limit but in practice, although several elderly gentlemen applied during Edward VII's era, nowadays few drivers over 50 contemplate starting a taxi career. However, once drivers have earned licences, they need only pass annually from age 65. In 1930, over 100 drivers were over 70; one over 80.

Turning to 'the knowledge', encyclopaedic familiarity with city and suburban areas classes cabbies above rivals, hire-car and minicab drivers. It is divided into two: firstly important buildings – railway stations, police and county courts, principal clubs and hospitals, hotels, squares, theatres and other public buildings like town halls. Subsequently, this list was extended to cover cinemas, museums, Mansion House, the Stock Exchange, Bank of England and Livery Companies. Important sporting venues – football and greyhound stadia – were added later. Secondly, the routes: initially the area to be covered in detail was defined as a 6-mile circle around Charing Cross. Drivers had to clearly distinguish places with similar names – a particularly potent problem for foreigners with little or no English – Kensington Park Gardens and Kensington Palace Gardens, Kensington and Kennington and Croydon (Surrey suburb) and John Bell and Croyden (Wigmore Street Chemists) being obvious examples, not to mention countless pubs called 'The Red Lion' and other identically named meeting places. Additionally, there are buildings, typically religious centres like temples, mosques, monasteries, convents and Quaker houses, which are not advertised and must be recognised by familiar appearance rather than map knowledge.

As London expanded, the knowledge required increased dramatically. In 1907, six months' study was required and even then three-quarters of Hackney carriage applicants never completed the course. Nowadays, it's two years to cover the 800-square-mile area. Not only size but factors like road works, traffic jams, marches and demonstrations, festivals, like Notting Hill's Carnival, pop concerts, major sporting occasions, one-way streets and bomb scares, are all included.

Over the years, study methods have altered little, the time-honoured tradition being for learners, or 'butter-boys', to take needle and cotton on a map, work out the shortest 'crow-fly' distance between any two points, then find the shortest available street-route between them. When following the route on bicycles or, later, mopeds, they note important buildings, other landmarks and parking facilities *en route*. Familiarity with one-way streets and systems is crucial – particularly nowadays as they become increasingly common – as well as dead-end streets (cul-de-sacs).

To help knowledge study, police supply a 'Blue' Book (actually pink nowadays) giving 468 prototype routes or 'runs'. Interestingly, the first is from Manor House to Gibson Square. Scotland Yard oversees the book's production, with clerical work completed by an appropriate Civil Service department. The PCO assists by conducting tests – oral examinations or 'appearances' – at eight-week intervals, later reducing to four or even three. For Central London, there are further tests fortnightly.

Standards expected are noted worldwide and foreign government delegations, notably Chinese, have arrived to learn about discipline. Those ready for testing apply to New Scotland Yard and are asked several trial questions. According to performance, candidates are instructed to return, typically after a week or month. A second test follows, concentrating on previous weaknesses. On being deemed 'satisfactory', the candidate is 'passed'. There are two grades: drivers considered competent to work throughout the Metropolitan London area are awarded a green badge, a yellow badge award only requiring knowledge in a specific London area. Yellow-badge holders bitterly resent their 'green' counterparts intruding on their areas to pinch modest amounts of work available. In practice, about a third of test applicants are successful. Therefore a cabbie's greatest asset is a phenomenal memory, well illustrated by a licensed cabbie, Fred Housego, winning an early series of TV's quiz *Mastermind*.

The successful geographer then takes a driving test. Nowadays standards required are considerably higher than applicable to the normal Department of Transport driving test, absent in 1900. This is taken in a taxi. It normally takes time to get used to this. Three failures rule a candidate out completely, leaving his knowledge efforts wasted. In practice, many fail their first attempt but pass the second. Over many years, Scotland Yard records indicate that taxi drivers are the roads' safest.

Finally, the character test primarily refers to brushes with the law; serious criminal convictions debar candidates automatically. Even lesser indiscretions like cycling without lights can be critical.

Standards caused hostility between cabbies and rivals. Returning to the period currently discussed, this was evident between Cab Drivers' Union members and new motor drivers; they were immediately expelled if they took up a motor cab. Throw-outs formed their own union, the Motor Cab Drivers' Protection Association, in 1907. Sadly, their first meeting was attended by unwelcome horse cabmen, breaking up in disorder. However, by 1909, it was appreciated that elderly horse-cab drivers were in an embarrassing position, their services becoming obsolete. Some corrective action was taken by the *Daily Mail*, who, having received a letter from Lord Rosebery, highlighting the problem, started a helping fund, considered a charity. The popular cab drivers' magazine *Motor Traction* opined that beneficiaries had little alternative but to accept.

Young drivers were welcomed by the motor cab trade and Friswells, a well-known motor firm, offered to train twenty-five to drive, free of charge. There was a relatively lukewarm welcome for the middle-aged; however, they were allowed to buy their own cabs on hire purchase and be their own masters. Many such older drivers, having formerly driven horse cabs, proved easier to teach than the less experienced.

Further changeover problems surfaced; typically in February 1909, a motor-cab driver deputation arranged to meet the Home Office Permanent Under-Secretary and the Metropolitan Police Commissioner, complaining of police harshness, typically revoking the licences of drivers convicted of offences in equestrian days. They felt similarly about the limit of three driving-test attempts, adding that rules regarding time allowed on ranks left drivers insufficient mealtimes. They received a sympathetic hearing but the Secretary spoke of considerable general public annoyance regarding *feeling* or actually *being* knocked down by cabbies. The following year saw new regulations, most notably regarding mealtimes. A driver, seeing other cabs on his standing, could approach a policeman, who would give him a card, signed by the Metropolitan Police Commissioner, stating that the cab was unavailable – meal break. The driver would place the card on the meter, allowing half-an-hour's parking on a reserve rank.

In 1910, the London Cab Drivers' Union was formed, caring for motor-cab drivers, now a majority. The big problem then was market saturation. Despite there being fewer cabs around than in 1900, work was scarce, drivers complaining bitterly about waiting up to three hours for a fare. Why? Passengers could be divided into three major categories:

Firstly, the well-to-do or 'upper crust' used them for shopping and theatre; *Motor Traction* magazine welcomed their interest, describing taxis as 'democratic cars being used by *all* classes of society'. This was sadly mistaken as working classes could ill-afford them; drivers considered poor areas a waste of time.

Secondly, travellers crossing between London termini; because of their greater suitability to this type of work, growlers, outlasting hansoms, were now still active. Station authorities were reluctant to allow 'potentially explosive machines' on their premises, fearing higher insurance premiums.

Thirdly, the middle-class businessmen: this last group, albeit relatively small, rapidly switched to trains, buses and trams, hence the drop. The National Motor Cab Company, largest operator of Unic cabs with a fleet of 250 bright red vehicles, faced the facts, converting many into Broughams or delivery vans.

Since 1922, taxi drivers have been a subsidiary of the Transport and General Workers' Union, which has a cab drivers' section. Over the period to the present, several similar organisations have been formed, notably the London Taxi Drivers' Association, in 1967.

Turning to fare payment, a company, using alternative spelling Taxameter Syndicate Ltd, introduced meters in 1898, fitting them to hansoms and growlers in provincial cities like Leeds, Manchester, Liverpool and Bradford. The first half-dozen London cabs trying it from mid March 1899, were stationed outside the Hotel Cecil in the Strand (later Shell-Mex House). Meters registered several readings: for the passenger, distance covered, appropriate fare and extras regarding luggage and waiting time; for drivers, number of journeys, miles covered and total daily earnings. Availability was indicated by a metal flag, replaced by an illuminated meter sign from 1959. However, most hansoms up to 1905 saw little reason to use it – 'devil you know' mentality.

However, in 1906, the General Motor Cab Company tried them on Renaults and thence hansom drivers became interested, anticipating public attraction to 'fair play'. When meters were made compulsory on motor cabs, despite being optional on hansoms and growlers, many owners thought it competitive to adopt them. Relevant regulations stipulated that motor cab fares would be 8*d* per mile against 6*d* for horse-drawn cabs. There were obviously no laid-down rules on tips; two pence per shilling was common. A relevant popular music-hall song included the line 'You can do it in style for eightpence per mile'. In 1907, there were some 720 motor cabs around; by 1908, it had increased fourfold. Progress of cab numbers of different types over the period is shown in Appendix 10. As hansoms rapidly departed, cabs were sold off as firewood for £1 each. Once the railway station insurance problem was resolved in 1910, the death knell sounded for growlers too, numbers decreasing to well under half up to the Great War. By the armistice, they had virtually disappeared, although nearly seventy were still around in 1930, the last licence granted in 1943. However, *total* cab numbers dropped significantly during the period, illustrating improved efficiency.

The year 1910 saw Edward VII's passing after reigning over *la belle époque*, the beautiful age or era; he had acquired a reputation as something of a peacemaker – at least on industrial fronts. A period of gradually increasing prosperity and advancement gave way to one of economic depression and domestic turmoil. The taxi industry suffered accordingly, facing disasters of the oncoming war in a precarious position.

For the time being, meter-cab introduction heralded new payment methods. Rather than paying owners initial fees for cab use – typically 12s per day in the 1890s – drivers paid about £2 2s weekly plus a percentage of recorded earnings, allowed to keep 25 per cent of the meter reading plus all extras and tips. Initially, they paid for petrol at market rate but from 1911, a fixed rate was agreed, effectively evening out market fluctuations. However, cab driver unionists strongly objected to what they deemed a 'German Toy', considering users as 'wee blacklegs'. Meters disappeared within two years, drivers doing better without them, overcharging as far as possible, notably when passengers were women or others thought unlikely to stand up to bullying arguments.

Still, financially 1910 heralded the introduction of new taxation laws. So far, private motor-car owners, on top of a road fund licence, had to pay £2 17s annually to the Inland Revenue for vehicles weighing over one ton. Hackney cab owners, however, could earn exemption by paying annual tax in advance. Problems arose in the 'London Season' – late spring to early summer, May to July – when many proprietors deemed it more profitable to lend vehicles to private hirers while surrendering their Hackney licence plate. Where this applied, an allowance of 7s 6d was granted for cabs only licensed for a part of the year. London Motor Cab Proprietors' Association representatives protested. Writing to Home Secretary Winston Churchill they clarified resentment of lightweight cabs' exemptions while cabs licensed for public hire, which had to be stronger, and therefore inevitably heavier, were subject to levy. Owners were already required to pay a 15s annual licence fee to Scotland Yard, thus feeling ill-treated by the surcharge.

In the event, it was David Lloyd George, then Chancellor of the Exchequer, who resolved matters with his 1909–10 Finance Act. Now car owners were required to pay an annual Road Fund Licence according to an RAC-calculated sliding scale. This was intended to standardise manufacturers' product ratings in contrast to previous methods loosely based on brake-horsepower. Consequentially, the two-guinea (£2 2s, £2.10 decimal) fee was no longer required.

The public enjoyed the novelty of the motor cab and undoubtedly the pleasant atmosphere helped to generate the view that motor drivers were better mannered than their equestrian predecessors. Early on, therefore, tips tended to be higher, but, once the novelty wore off, they dropped again; dismayed drivers felt the need for action, demanding higher wages (effectively higher fares and/or a petrol tax rebate).

Earlier, the Home Office's 1853 Act had determined scales of extras but allocation between owner and driver had been negotiable. In practice, horse drivers kept them as there was no way of recording details. In 1907, the Home Secretary laid down a fare scale of 8d for the first mile and 2d for every subsequent quarter and thenceforth there was the taximeter. Details of taximeter distributors are in Appendix 11. It was now mandatory to show full fares, *including* extras; henceforth owners felt entitled to claim them to offset running costs.

Inevitably, dispute followed until resolution in 1911 when a government committee was established, owners and drivers being invited to report. Major problems of pre-Great-War cab trading must now be discussed; observe that much is relevant nowadays – albeit with different absolute figures. Owners demanded an increased fare for the first mile from 8*d* to 10*d*, emphasising the following:

- Gross takings had decreased markedly over the previous twelve months so that after paying drivers 25 per cent commission there was insufficient money for running expenses, notably tyres.
- Extras were currently going to drivers; owners felt entitled to 75 per cent.
- Owners did not receive full percentage of earnings, to which they were entitled, on long-distance runs where fares were agreed following driver/passenger bargaining.
- Meter-tampering was frequent and increasing.
- Lazier drivers, content with modest earnings, were not operating cabs to expected standards.

Against this, drivers had their complaints:

- Their promised earnings of 7s per day had not been maintained; they felt entitled to a guaranteed minimum; some wanted 10s.
- Taxi driving placed strain on health; consequently drivers had to pay increased life-insurance premiums.
- They suffered further financial losses through breakdown, bilking, false calls and tips expected at garages. The magazine *Motor Traction* was unsympathetic here, arguing that tips were an inducement for others to do work on cabs which drivers ought to undertake themselves.
- They had to take out two 5s licences per annum, one from London County Council, one from the Police.

The Committee made several recommendations, so far not legally enforceable:

a) Tariffs should not be increased.
b) All extras should go to drivers.
c) The driver's share of fare takings should be 20 per cent of the first £1; 25 per cent thereafter.
d) Owners should supply drivers with petrol at fixed rate, 8*d* per gallon, independent of market variations within 20 per cent either way; effectively inside the 6½*d* to 9½*d* bracket.

e) No limit on numbers of taxis.

f) One of those two licences should be abolished.

Despite the recommendation in b) above, the London Motor Cab Proprietors' Association announced, in November 1911, their intention to appoint observers, ensuring that 75 per cent of takings were handed to owners who claimed that the decision would cost them £45,000 over four years. One realistic driver said that owners would never collect extras unless a policeman was carried on each cab's running board. Regarding extras, the big bone of contention centred around the rule that, when passengers exceeded two, drivers could charge an extra 6d per passenger. Trouble loomed when four-seater cabs operated and inconsistencies arose regarding cost calculation over the horse/motor period. Early motor-cab owners had worked on the basis of equestrian costs (1s hiring charge) and found a turnover reduction when 8d taximeters were introduced. Their idea was to recoup losses by claiming extras defined above. At that time, there was no statutory rule stipulating who should benefit. Drivers were unhappy, insisting on their entitlement to this money; matters had come to a head a month before, in October, when a National Cab Company driver, refusing to hand over extras, was dismissed.

Dispute was inevitable and the London Cab Drivers' Trade Union called a meeting, deciding to strike. By 3 November, 7,000 cabs were inactive, and more than twice as many drivers, cab washers and mechanics joined. The Government established a committee of enquiry but the Home Secretary refused to allow fare increases despite London rates being markedly below provincial equivalents set by local authorities. *The Times* indicated that they thought Churchill was arguing that cabs were the principal form of transport of parliamentarians (their 'bus) and that fares should be accordingly generous.

They were back within a week, having won the right to keep extras for a 'hiring fee' of 6d and the petrol price dropped from 9d to 8d per gallon. Fifteen hundred owner-drivers had not joined the strike and were issued with permits by the Union to ply with a flag or 'pennant.' However, police ordered their withdrawal, infringement of 1886 by-laws forbidding cab advertisements. A lifting attempt was made, a solicitor, Mr Rex Woods, writing to Scotland Yard in May 1910 on behalf of his hansom-cab-owning client. He suggested that those modestly sized and in good taste would do no harm while enabling drivers to earn a shilling or more. Feeling that cabs, while hired, were the 'property' of the passenger who should be exempted from a barrage of advertising, Chief Inspector Bassom ruled for complete prohibition.

With new rules on extras seeing four-seater-cabs earning more than their two-seater counterparts, drivers favoured larger cabs; sadly owners still had to pay higher overall costs with the larger vehicles falling into a higher tax bracket. Their application for fare increase to 1s per mile was turned down by a Churchill-led committee; larger cab fleets thus gave way to owner-drivers and small-fleet operators.

This applied to London but Glasgow owners were allowed to charge 1s for the first mile and 3d per quarter thereafter, rates doubling between midnight and 6 a.m. and increasing by 50 per cent on Sundays. Impatient London proprietors increased the price to drivers to 1s 1d per gallon. Furious drivers argued that fares and thus income were under government control (petrol obviously being critical) and refused to pay; a Lambeth meeting called for strike action. Cab Drivers' Union President Alfred (Titch) Smith explained that, while they accepted the arbiters' ruling that drivers would have to pay more, they could not bear overall cost increases. He spoke of cheaper, if not free, petrol.

Newspapers backed the union's slogan 'Why should labour have to pay for action of capital?' The Times suggested that fare increases were justified to reflect fuel cost. Drivers suffered while oil companies lavished 20 per cent dividends to shareholders and sold petrol to bus companies at half cabbies' rates.

In March 1912, an arbitration court ruled that all extras and 25 per cent of the meter reading should go to drivers. The court also confirmed that the petrol price of 8d per gallon should stand for one year. Motor Traction commented again, claiming that this would encourage drivers to overload vehicles, causing excessive wear on parts, notably tyres, for which owners would be liable.

In practice, petrol price (contractual, the public did not necessarily pay similarly) rose dramatically in 1913 – from 6d + 1½d tax to 11d + 1½d tax. Drivers actually had to pay 1s 1d per gallon, resulting in a daily loss of 1s. Motor Traction this time sided with drivers, emphasising that they were the only ones obliged to pay the government 1 shilling per pound on all earned income to stay employed.

Consequently, they suggested a slight fare increase but the government refused. Two frictions resulted. January of that year saw 5,000 major-company drivers striking. Smaller firms kept their drivers, as well as owner-drivers, active by keeping petrol to 8d per gallon. This worked well, pay for extra work becoming available more than offsetting the loss on petrol. The strike lasted two months but was effective only in that London's cab population was reduced to 40 per cent of normal, horse-drawn cabs earning a final, if unspectacular windfall.

Eventually, cab companies offered a compromise price of 10d per gallon but drivers refused to pay anything and employers had to settle for 8d. The drivers' victory sounded the death knell for large companies. Fiat had already started to sell cabs on 'pay by instalment' bases, others soon following. The Great War accelerated the process but black clouds had been gathering anyway. Large fleets did not disappear completely but many were reduced to well below half.

This decline was followed by increasing numbers of owner-drivers. Numbers had been modest in equestrian days but, from about 1908, many bought their own vehicles, effectively becoming their own bosses, working as they pleased. Their own union, formed in 1910, the Motor Cab Owner-Drivers' Association received favourable press, Motor Traction describing them as 'smarter and more courteous' than company-employed or 'journeymen' rivals. Discussing finances, the magazine reported in 1911. It laid down cab cost as an initial deposit of £50–100 plus three annual payments of £150. Allowing for day-to-day expenses – petrol, tyres, repairs, fees to authorities like Scotland Yard and London County Council for licences – annual expenditure totalled about £350.

These figures emphatically ignore anxiety and worry suffered by owner-drivers. After repairs, they had to watch police examiners searching vehicles with toothcombs. Everything from engines to felt linings around windows and doors were scrutinised for slightest traces of rust or similar offenders. There would then be road tests – drivers would circumnavigate the block while examiners would test latches and door handles for firmness and correct position. They then jumped up and down in case seats collapsed. Trained ears would then be listening to engines for unusual noises. Commonly, drivers needed new back axles, brake linings and exhaust pipes. Additionally, there was meter accuracy, penny-perfection expected. Meters belonged to manufacturers who hired them out and, in principle, were responsible for maintenance (although drivers could legally buy their own, they were well-nigh impossible to obtain).

Thus, if drivers worked 300–310 days per annum (discounting fifty-two Sundays and major festival holidays like Christmas and Easter but ignoring summer holidays), total receipts plus tips gave annual income of about £495 leaving £145 profit, about £2 16s weekly. Journeymen made slightly less, £2 2s.

Public opinion sympathised with drivers but meetings and negotiations had achieved nothing by Christmas 1912. Three months' inaction followed, costing £40,000 in strike pay and £1 million in owners' lost revenue. The Union was renamed London and Provincial Licensed Vehicle Workers' Union. However, Churchill turned down higher fare demands, leaving everybody suffering in the economic misery. Typically W. & G. du Cros reduced their fleet, redesigning some cabs as vans and reorganising the Acton premises to accommodate parcel depository. The General ran up £500,000 debts and were unfit to face the effects of striking. Fiat's British Motor Cab Company and London Improved Cab Company all closed before the Great War.

Left without vehicles, many drivers found it difficult to buy cabs, drivers having to take several tests to satisfy variable PCO regulations. Owner-drivers with one vehicle had to work a dangerous seventy hours per week. The beneficiaries were Mann and Overtons, selling 4,000-plus Unics (appropriately the only cab manufactured in 1914) up to the war.

J.J. Mann and J.T. (Tom) Overton figured prominently in twentieth-century taxicab history. The Overtons were originally Surrey farmers, the late nineteenth century seeing Tom Overton, visualising a motor-engineering career, visiting Paris to study. There he met J.J. Mann, originally Mancunian. Mann established a motor-car agency in 1898 – buying and exporting cars (from Germany as well as France) to his London agency based in Mortimer Street.

This retailing business was taken over in 1899 in conjunction with several Overton family members, notably Tom's brother Will. It became a limited company in 1901, operating initially from Mortimer Street but later, in mid December 1904, moving to Victoria Garage in Lower Belgrave Street, Pimlico. Their main interest was importing, primarily Daimler, Hotchkiss and Mercedes cars into Britain, Mann often driving himself. Early on, they had overall sole agency. The Hotchkiss agency was transferred to Mann and Overtons in March 1905; the Mercedes' ended that year.

The beginning of the period 1905–14, often referred to as 'the Golden Age of British Motoring' saw Overton working in London and Mann in Paris, closely watching the equestrian–motor changeover from two angles. There were already 6,000 motor cabs in London by 1904 in an otherwise equestrian-orientated transport environment. Motor cars were thought only for the wealthy but clearly, if they proved themselves, large orders would follow.

They also established links with the Paris-based French car firm Georges-Richard, who had established a reputation with, among other things, victory in the famous Gordon-Bennett race of 1904–05. The French directors managed to convince Mann and Overton that French cars would sell well in Great Britain, granting them sole agency. Georges had left in 1904 to work single-handed and later, during 1905, the partnership split, leaving Maxime to form a new alliance with Brasier. Richard-Brasier produced Brasier cabs as well as Unics. The Brasier, selling from 1908 to 1913, was 10–12hp vertical twin-engined with three-speed transmission. Georges acquired financial backing from Baron Dr Henri de Rothschild, starting a new model, the Unic. The baron's land in the north-western Parisian suburb of Puteaux provided ample new factory space to produce vehicles for Paris taxicab fleets.

The Unic proved more powerful than the two-cylinder Renault as run by newly formed rival London General Cab Company, also being more reliable and serviceable than many competitors. Complete with attaching power train, these were driven from Paris to London by J.T. Overton for coachwork and body fitting. Thereafter, taxi trading became Mann and Overtons' principal interest. After their agency acquisition, the City and Suburban Motor Company bought four 10/12hp two-cylinder vehicles, which they added to their existing fleet of Richard–Brasiers, adding twenty-five more a year later.

Hammersmith-based National Cab Company joined in, ordering 250, all painted bright red. They appointed a new fleet manager, 23-year-old W.O. Bentley, who learned motor-industry basics, earning fame later in luxury cars.

Unics made their mark at the Town Motor Carriages' Competition organised by the Automobile Club in mid October 1906 at York Road, Waterloo – garage of the Wolseley Tool and Motor Company. Entrants also included two 12hp Richard-Brasiers, direct from Mann and Overtons, featuring in Class A, restricted to vehicles below £600. These were fitted with limousine-style bodies, manufactured by Belvalette and Bagley/ Ellis. A third model was entered by The City and Suburban Motor Company; its body was from the French company La Carosserie Industrielle. All three performed well, the last earning a silver medal in the 'Public Vehicle' class. Argyll also entered – a 16hp cab driven from its original Glasgow factory, thereby enhancing its reputation for sturdiness and reliability built since inception in 1901. This compact example was from 1905, the driver seated above the engine. The design was orientated to carrying heavy luggage, providing a modern replacement for growlers, working primarily around larger railway stations. Sadly, the 30ft turning circle ruled out London acceptance.

The highest-placed vehicle in Class A, however, was American. The Carl Oppermann Electric boasted a hansom-style body fitted by Cleaver Brothers. With smooth starting, quiet running and minimal pollution being obvious criteria, it outclassed rivals. Strangely, this was never licensed for cab use here, the company folding within twelve months.

Unic was awarded first prizes for bodywork, quiet and smooth gear-changing and running and for passenger comfort and access. It also gained second prize in its class for manoeuvrability and fourth for ease of cleaning bodywork and machinery and oiling. So commenced Unic's cab-trade contribution, lasting from 1907 to 1932. First operators were the City and Suburban Motor Cab Company of Kensington, the first recorded London purchase being a 10/12hp model for which a Mrs Brown of Russell Square paid £468 1s 8d. After Unic imports ceased, the company, in 1906, obtained permanent concession for Austin cab sales. Since then, they have supplied about three-quarters of London's cabs.

Thus, with business well placed in the market, Tom Overton continued expansion, establishing offices in Dublin and New York. For financial help, the company turned to Motor Specialists, formed for that purpose in November 1907. (In 1965, it became Mechanical Investments Ltd, a later descendant being London Taxi Finance Ltd.)

Competition visitors also included Cab Drivers' Trade Union secretary Will Wright. He appreciated that motorisation was the future; even if many were reluctant about a dubious investment, he organised classes and seminars improving driving skills and mechanical knowledge. He also appreciated the significance of two directors of the General Motor Cab Company Ltd, namely an MP, Hon. Davidson Dalziel, and Mr Edward Cohen. This company got much of their capital from their French counterparts, the Compagnie Générale des Voitures. They also started site clearance in the Camberwell–Brixton area. A parade of old houses made way for steel joists covered with red and yellow bricks – a purpose-built three-storey garage for cab construction and maintenance.

Shops for the chassis, motor repair and body were established to service 500 new cabs ordered from France. Original orders were for two-cylinder Charrons, but these proved below standard so an updated version of the one-cylinder AG Renault (produced by a Parisian sister company) was preferred.

In May 1905, an agreement was signed with Unic Automobiles Ltd to purchase chassis to satisfy 1906 PCO Conditions of Fitness requirements. This, combined with the Green-badge privilege for London geographical knowledge, made London taxicabs the world's envy.

The Fulham-based United Motor Cab Company acquired assets of City and Suburban during winter 1907. In 1908 more than 200 Unic 10/12s were bought, Mann and Overtons providing Dodson landaulet bodies; thus London's Unic proportion significantly increased.

Sadly, Mann's deteriorating health forced his resignation from the board; he retired, dying the following year. Tom's brother William and Herbert Nicholls eventually replaced him. The company supplied cabs to, among others, two of the largest operators, the General Motor Cab Company (principal investor was Associated Newspapers Ltd) and the United Motor Cab Company based in Walham Green, West London, both operating French-built models. The General bought 500 Renaults during 1907–08. The United bought 224 Unics and 250 Darracqs over that period and autumn 1908 saw the two merge as London General Cab Company, boasting a fleet close to four figures. Nearly 100 more Darracqs were bought to replace Renaults, which had been converted to four-seaters but lacked power. Several Charrons were added.

Other interested operating companies included Fiat Motor Cab Company with 400 Fiats, the London United Motor Cab Company, who had 250 Wolseley-Siddeleys, of two- and four-cylinders and the London and Provincial Cab Company with another 100 Wolseley-Siddeleys.

They showed their mettle typically with a run of over 1,000 miles around Great Britain in a Marshall 79, then a remarkable feat. The Marshall was the precursor of the Belsize cab, a 14–16hp model introduced in 1907 and becoming popular from 1908, albeit sold by other dealers.

Later, in March 1910, Mann and Overtons took larger premises (previously stables, converted for motorisation) in Pimlico – Commercial Road (subsequently Ebury Bridge Road) near Victoria Station, thenceforth concentrating on taxis. Two months later, an agreement was signed with Unic Automobiles Ltd regarding new four-cylinder 12–16hp chassis, specially designed to meet Conditions of Fitness. Expansion continued nine months later, adding further premises in Lower Grosvenor Place, SW1. Showrooms and offices were established there, leaving scope for Commercial Road's site to establish body-building assembly lines.

Austin worked on cabs from 1906. Herbert Austin arrived on the automotive scene in 1895. A 30-year-old works manager of Wolseley Shearing Machine Company Ltd, he became interested in internal combustion engines and horseless carriages, fascinating for many late-Victorian engineers and scientists. Over the winter of 1895–96, he started work on improving the 'accepted' design attributed to one Léon Bollée. Austin had seen this in Paris but modification was a non-starter. French design rights had already been bought by a British company, leaving him little alternative but to restart from scratch.

The year 1899 saw the death of Wolseley and the company building its first four-seater car designed by Austin. Various design advances emerged over the next four years until Austin left Wolseley in 1905, founding his own company. J.D. Siddeley (later of Armstrong Siddeley) replaced him.

Returning to 1906, the major prototype problem was the turning circle, set at 25ft, enabling vehicles to U-turn from centrally-placed ranks. Their first presentation to the

PCO was therefore rejected. They solved it by mounting the engine beneath the driver, centrally placed with luggage space either side, exhibiting the result at Olympia's 1907 Motor Show. The engine, clutch and gearbox were all mounted on a subsidiary frame, suspended at three different points with rubber buffers to give complete insulation against disturbance from road contact and maximum lock without track loss. The snub-nosed bonnet completed a compact appearance.

Thus Austin's original cab earned PCO approval, appearing later that year. Ten were run by the Taxi de Luxe Company of Kensington, but 1908 saw a newer model with more conventional layout and a 15hp engine. But during winter 1909, following changes in Conditions of Fitness regulations, cab bodies had to be removed from chassis for rigorous police inspection, being legally immobilised on failure. Coachbuilders usually completed the necessary repairs but at great expense, time- and cost-wise, to operators. A more conventional version was introduced in that, although the basic style remained, the engine was placed further forward with a neat shining sheet-metal panel fitted to the window's upper half behind the driver's head. This sliding partition served for driver-passenger communication – improving on predecessors' speaking tubes. In addition to the roof rack, it had folding shelves for extra luggage. Urban Taxicab Company of West Kensington ran a fleet of ten such four-seaters in green and white livery. A variant, slightly differently styled with a soft sloping canopy over the driver's head, was licensed for Edinburgh from 1910.

That year saw luxury 1908 model variants appearing as Austin landaulets with brown and brass mountings and black-striped panels. Doors were fitted with coach-style handles and a hinged top-half screen combined with anti-splash shield on the driver's nearside. Subsequent variants displayed a changed cooling system, the pressure-tube arrangement or 'thermosyphon' replacing simple-pump circulation. Taxi de Luxe of Hammersmith were operators. However, Urban soon returned. In 1911, their newest version cast the cylinders separately with a longer piston stroke, crankshaft bearings being increased from three to five. A more sophisticated pump circulation replaced the thermosyphon. However, apparently, none lasted beyond 1918.

Turning to facilities, early models were Spartan; hansoms offered meagre improvements, Fiat and Beeston Humber going modestly further. Darracqs used their engine exhaust gases as heating fuel for foot warmers; electric lights and tubes for oral communication appeared on other cabs. In 1909 Fiat had an indicator, passenger-operable, to let drivers know desired speed and direction. Overall, smaller operators appeared to boast the smartest cabs and one London example, Charles McBean of South Kensington, had eight Unic cabs in two different shades of green, decorating vehicles with interior mirrors, ashtrays and fresh flowers.

Regarding luggage space, legality was important. As indicated, in 1908, the PCO ruled that no passenger should sit beside the driver. In many cabs, this was impossible anyway but some, notably Humber, Rover, Marples, Argyll, Unic, Renault and Ford had an adjacent seat, which needed removing. Thereafter new designs have respected this order, leaving space for luggage. Lotis cabs, manufactured by Sturmey Motors Ltd of Coventry, were the first built with platforms of just over 9sq.ft, specifically designed to accommodate it. Previously, notably on growlers, cabs had fitted luggage racks. For weather protection, several models had canopies covering driver and luggage; others experimented with glass windscreens. That was until in May 1910, when the Commissioner of Police expressly forbade these as 'not being in the public interest'. He discussed further reduction in drivers' visibility in 'pea-soup' fogs, then common. The ban stood until 1934 when full glass screens were permitted but, even then, they had to be fitted with devices to wipe water away – nowadays 'windscreen wipers'. Finally, 1910 saw the introduction of the roof sign 'taxi'. Prior to that April, horse-drawn cabs had displayed no specific identification but now Panhard proved the pioneer, others soon adopting the feature, which remains.

With the majority of cabs and meters foreign, unsurprisingly patriotic outcries came from horse-cab traders, parliamentary questions being asked. However, company managers were almost entirely British and although French cabs retained their popularity for two decades, British makes like Napier, Argyll (Scotland's largest motor-car manufacturer) and Belsize were slowly competing, the biggest sales expansion being provincial. Premises were established by Mann and Overtons in Manchester in January 1914, Liverpool joining five months later. Sadly, trade with Unic Automobiles was curtailed by the Great War, the purchase of 250 chassis during autumn 1912 proving well timed.

Cab profusion led to inevitable market saturation; the bubble, expanding from around 1907, reached bursting point about three years later. Supply exceeded demand, the public turning to cheaper and more efficient rival modes of transport – bus, tram, surface train and underground tube. Petrol prices had rocketed by 70 per cent, the full impact seeing drivers facing a 20 per cent plus income drop. Trade recession saw them suffering long idle periods between fares. Consequently, fleet operators had to cut costs by laying off drivers and disposing of many vehicles – some to owner-drivers, others for delivery-van conversion.

By that year, several larger names, notably Reliance Cab Company and Express Motor Cab Company had wound up. The London General balance sheet displayed credit of £1,700, a meteoric drop from the previous year's nearly fifty times as much. In addition, several entrepreneurial motor venturers, who had jumped on the bandwagon, made countless expensive mistakes through trade ignorance. Certainly around two thirds of motor cab drivers were former horse cabmen who knew their way around but their administrators had little experience of depreciation allowance in a heavy traffic environment, fuel costs and matters regarding drivers' retaining extras.

Experience showed that, while early two-cylinder cabs ran relatively cheaply but suffered heavy depreciation, later four-cylinder versions had higher fuel consumption but, being more sturdily built, depreciated less dramatically. Drivers liable for fuel but earning no 'depreciation' benefit obviously preferred the two-seater.

Other efforts were made to circumvent fuel problems. Pimlico's British Motor Cab Company pioneered a device that, after the cab had started using petrol, enabled it to switch to paraffin (costing under 10d per gallon against petrol's 12d) once engine temperature had risen to an appropriate level. Drivers agreed to resume work on conversion completion. The effect, however, was minimal. Striking only finished when W. & G. du Cros agreed to follow suit. They employed 1,000 drivers, running 600 vehicles and had witnessed smaller companies succumbing to union pressure not to pass on petrol-price increases to drivers. But the damage had already been done. Garages of Fiat, de Dion Bouton and Universal Cab Company never reopened and 1914 saw those of The National Motor Cab Company and Waterloo Cab Company having to close.

Now Napier cab supplies ran out. Francis Luther, mentioned earlier – a leading figure in Coupé Cab Company – reappeared, obliged to look elsewhere for cab manufacture. He had formerly held British concession for Austro-Daimlers and following an earlier visit to Austria, he had won rights for an aero-engine, originally designed by Ferdinand Porsche, a friend. He now arduously sought British manufacturers. He was pointed towards leading Scottish industrialist William Beardmore and soon visited him in Glasgow.

Beardmore had formed his company, basing it on the former site of Arrol-Johnston's Company at Underwood, close to the Glasgow suburb of Paisley. This followed a take-over of Aidee Motors of Motherwell, vehicle manufacturers. His cab-trade involvement commenced. Luther and business partner George Allsworth suggested a cab for London use. Beardmores had considerable free capacity in their Paisley Underwood Works, then virtually unused. This seemed ideal for cab manufacture, due to start in late summer 1915. Luther took over section management later. Contact was made with Superintendent Bassom who was pleased to advise on design specifications, thereby avoiding Conditions of Fitness trouble from inception. However, as war escalated, the factory was used exclusively for shell production, cab work being suspended until peacetime. Beardmore's war contribution and other ventures earned him a peerage (Lord Invernairn) in 1921.

However, though an outstanding engineer, his poor management training proved critical. He had little success post-war and borrowing for further ventures proved disastrous in a high-interest environment, leaving him unable to service debts. The 1929 Wall Street Crash proved decisive and, following Bank of England intervention, he retired, dying in 1936 at the age of 79.

4

Two World Wars: 1918-45

By 1914, nearly 8,400 motorised cabs contested a highly competitive London market, forty-five manufacturers having had designs accepted. But war brought inevitable shortages on at least two fronts. Military-aged men were called up – 10,000-plus cabbies in 1915 alone, about a third of the nation's force – and many never returned. Conscription, from February 1916, removed more. Deserted cabs were largely neglected, a few helping injured or convalescent servicemen. They benefited free of charge as did several younger women, mainly upper class, volunteering as nurses. Others worked in the explosives industry where picric acid was involved resulting in skin turning a canary yellow. Women, thus nicknamed, earned well, affording taxis when available.

Petrol was scarce, necessitating rationing from July 1916, and each licensed cab, driven by one driver, was allowed 1½ gallons daily, later increased to 2 gallons. Cabs commonly driven round the clock by two drivers, day and night, were allowed 2 gallons from commencement. So taxicab supply declined but demand increased when private-car owners felt obliged to garage their cars to hire cabs on a weekly basis, reducing drivers' need to ply for hire. Demand intensified as buses became progressively overcrowded, with soldiers on leave and well-paid munitions traders using taxis. Authorities urged the public not to use them unless necessary. Additionally, spare parts were difficult, if not impossible, to obtain.

Secondly, regarding the railway-station toll, 1d was authorised after the relaxation of the motor-cab ban in station precincts and drivers reluctantly paid until August 1917, when the charge was doubled, after which they refused to enter the area. The public did not suffer unduly; they were encouraged to travel with minimum luggage and could easily instruct a porter to hail a passing taxi. The toll was lifted in December.

Thirdly, war stress strained driver-public relations, unpleasant incidents occurring regularly. One well-publicised altercation saw a driver refusing to take a wounded soldier; he (the driver) dragged him 20 yards and then assaulted him. Peace was restored, years later, with taxi drivers organising two annual events, one taking disabled war veterans, notably Chelsea Pensioners, on the London Trades Outing; the other, when underprivileged children were taken to the seaside on the Norwood Outing.

The year 1928 saw London Taxi Driver's Fund for Underprivileged Children officially starting, twelve drivers taking local orphanage children to London Zoo for the day. Nowadays, the charity organises trips to Paris Disney for a few days. The winter of 1972–73 saw Princess Alexandra take the salute at the fiftieth outing for disabled army/navy ex-servicemen, 200 drivers giving up a day to take them to Worthing. Earlier, the taxi trade had spent over £1,000 on a mechanical bath for Roehampton Hospital's disabled ex-soldiers and sailors. It has also become customary to carry blind people or uniformed nurses free.

Fourthly, drivers risked running out of petrol and being unable to refill, lacking individual petrol licences, and might have to leave the cab, causing obstruction. Consequently, drivers tended to favour customers wanting short journeys. Regulations forbade the petrol-shortage excuse and although drivers were not obliged to stop when hailed, if they did and talked to customers, they had to take them, at least within the 6-mile limit.

Strictly speaking, drivers are not obliged to pick up anybody, even with their 'for hire' sign on. This is because, legally speaking, drivers are only deemed 'plying' while vehicles are stationary. However, on stopping, they are deemed 'available' and must accept fares unless journeys will obviously exceed 6 miles' distance or one hour's time. This was originally laid down in deference to horses, likely to become thirsty and/or tired on longer journeys. Thus laws need updating, forgetting equestrian considerations. But legality moves slowly and its mentality is illustrated even nowadays – seatbelts are compulsory for all drivers but taxi drivers are not obliged to wear them when working; if they do, they are deemed not for hire. Drivers wearing seat belts will probably be heading home.

This might have given a temporary equestrian reprieve, if only because horses' food supply had been less seriously affected. In practice, this did not materialise; partly at least, because as many cabs were inactive for lack of drivers as for petrol shortage. By Christmas 1917, just over thirty horse cabs in London numbered scarcely 3 per cent of the total.

At least two arguably drastic rectifications were suggested. One was to relax driver-qualification standards; the other to welcome women, the PCO allowing them to take the Knowledge for the first time. The first was bitterly opposed, *Motor Traction* magazine arguing that standards were already too low, not to mention extra dangers during darkness hours when black-outs were imposed. Possible female participation was raised as early as 1908 but then the PCO specified that 'Licenses to act as Hackney carriage drivers are not granted to females.'

However, rules are there to be broken! One enterprising lady, Sheila O'Neill, drove a cab for businessmen in a 'semi-private' capacity. Cheekily, she mounted, on her bonnet, a small metal figurine displaying a policeman signalling 'stop'! In February, 1917, despite vigorous opposition from the Commissioner of Police and male cabbies' representatives (opinions unrepeatable), moves were made to welcome women. A threatened strike never materialised, very few women applied for tests; those who did, failed. Nowadays, accepted women drivers represent only 1 per cent of London's cab force.

Many expected hostilities to end by Christmas 1914 but fighting escalated and with it munitions priority. In France, Unic's factory in Puteaux concentrated thereon, UK cab imports stopping completely and leaving Mann and Overtons cabless. Napier had already stopped manufacture of 15hp chassis in 1914; seemingly cab manufacturing either side of the Channel was a non-starter.

Financially, October 1917 saw owners request a fare increase to 1s for the first mile and 3d per quarter-mile thereafter. The Home Secretary refused but offered a 6d initial hiring charge, favouring shorter journeys. Companies rejected it, assessing this as only worth 6s daily per cab. Drivers also argued that higher fares would result in lower tips, further insisting that, because of high petrol costs and other war privations, they would not work without free petrol. This left owners fighting on two fronts. A minority of drivers, working for larger fleets, struck for six weeks from November 1917, many more leaving to work in munitions factories. Drivers got their way, the petrol charge being abolished in 1918. Strike action also won abolition of railway-station charges. However, still feeling entitled to compensation, owners attempted to introduce a 'drivers' charge' of ½d per mile. This led to another strike; a Court of Arbitration deemed the charge 'unjustified'.

Larger companies thus felt unable to continue. Many economy-minded employees became owner-drivers, leaving the remainder, described by *Motor Traction* as 'lacking in skill and/or manners', out in the cold. Typically, The British Motor Cab Company, already in serious financial difficulty from January 1918, claimed that even an increase from 8d to 1s per mile would be insufficient rectification. The Home Secretary had promised them that, if they abolished the petrol charge (as indeed they did), he would allow the proposed increase but failed to keep his word despite likelihood of public objection. Over 700 of their cabs were inactive from February that year, remaining so until November's armistice amid terrible ill feeling and frustration all round.

The old dictum: 'the cure is worse than the disease' was arguably applicable in that armistice hardly proved a light at the end of the tunnel on several counts. Many lean years for the trade – manufacturers, owner-drivers, fleet proprietors and qualified workers – followed. With youths called up, older drivers had to run poorly maintained, worn-down vehicles. Pre-war had seen about 7,260 cabs on the road. No new cabs were manufactured during the hostilities and, as explained below, those built immediately afterwards cost double that of similar pre-war predecessors, way beyond returning servicemen's pockets. They found their old cabs sold or in long-term storage. By armistice, cab numbers had reduced considerably, some say by about 3,000 down to scarcely more than 3,800, some even less, drivers outnumbering available, serviceable cabs.

April 1919 saw the British Motor Cab Company discontinue cab operation, stating their intention to sell off reconditioned and overhauled two-cylinder Renault cabs together with their meters and three necessary licences – driving, road fund and Hackney carriage. They also offered large spare stocks. Hire-purchase companies tried to help, permitting owner-drivers to buy such cabs for a single payment of £180 or a staggered series totalling £200. The scheme was primarily angled at ex-servicemen who wanted to become owner-drivers, but private motorists who wanted modestly-powered, reasonably-priced landaulets were also encouraged. The company had also saved about 450 older cabs. Repainted, these had been fitted with taximeters and were, at least in the company's opinion, roadworthy, although not passed by the PCO. Each was sold off to demobbed drivers for £120. Remaining cabs were converted to light delivery vans. Large taxi fleets were history.

In May 1919, Alfred Smith filed a complaint with Scotland Yard: new regulations left over 1,000 discharged soldiers, all properly licensed, unable to find employment. Scotland Yard replied that they were not strictly enforced – they had even permitted the British Motor Cab Company to run 100 'non-qualifying' cabs but those had never appeared. They added that only a couple of months earlier Ford Motor Company had requested permission to operate 500 such cabs and had received it, primarily because of the shortage. No further correspondence was received. The Union argued that the shortage was, in part, artificial; one large garage in London was holding back 600 pre-war cabs and another in Tooting had a further 200 pre-war Darracqs and Vinots, selling them – about two weekly. The Darracq, passed by the PCO, went for £300 (fractionally discounting on the new price – exorbitant for vehicles nearly 10 years old). Vinots – not passed – were offered for £200.

Consequently, second-hand cab prices rocketed, usually way too high. Potential salesmen took full advantage with many companies finding it lucrative to recall 'officially mothballed' vehicles. Two-cylinder Renaults, distinctly past their sell-by date, still sold for £180 (£200 on HP). Vinots from 1910 were subsequently renamed 'Gladiator' and others were in dreadful states of disrepair and hardly, if at all, roadworthy. Fiats, Darracqs and Unics were inspected and those in a better state were overhauled, given a fresh coat of paint and sold at ludicrous prices, sometimes – as with Palmers of Tooting – 7- to 8-year-olds at more than new models. Even older (9- to 10-year old) models were fetching £300 – only just below the brand-new cab's price! Of the remainder, some, considered terminally unfit, were converted into delivery vans with others sold to private citizens as 'reliable' family cars; most were satisfied. Other older vehicles – even those failing Certificate of Fitness requirements – were sold off at £120. Horse cabs made a modest return with nearly 350 around London in 1923, marking the first London cab's centenary.

An important change to Conditions of Fitness requirements intensified cab short-age problems – insistence on 10in clearance. Most cabs already in service – 5–600 – failed to comply and stood idle. Owners felt justified in requesting a waiver, pleading 'special circumstances' in an attempt to save themselves exorbitant costs of redesign, and thus survive financially.

Around then, Ford offered a two-seat-cab Model T variant. Scotland Yard refused, probably on design grounds, the transverse-leaf front suspension being already banned on British cabs. History might have been different had this inexpensive model been accepted, Ford's influence likely rivalling Austin's. As it was, in principle, Bassom, to his death in 1924, flatly refused to bend his rules, even refuting argument that they should be modernised to reflect motor vehicle technological advancement. Authorities were slow to replace him and clearly no changes would materialise quickly, leaving 'expect-ants' with little further interest in London's market.

Fares were increased in March 1920 to 1s per mile and 3d per quarter thereafter plus an additional 6s per hour waiting time. But, as indicated, this hardly improved on locking the door after the horse had bolted; the damage had been done in terms of company closures. Fare increase, originally demanded in 1911, was already outdated. Consequently, trade sank into decline, proving unable to meet increased demand of Londoners trying to return to peacetime routine. That increase was particularly pronounced late at night, notably during victory celebrations. One leading restaurant encouraged custom by ensuring that patrons would have taxis available, even late at night; cabbies were offered free meals from 11 p.m.

Regarding taxi drivers' unions, history had illustrated difficulty in organising societies but the National Federation of Hackney Carriage Proprietors was founded in 1921. Their publicity medium was *Steering Wheel* magazine. Sadly, the organisation folded in 1926 but the magazine survived, becoming the trade's leading news outlet, giving drivers useful information on London landmarks, other tourist data and entertain-ment reviews. It celebrated its golden jubilee in 1971, the Queen joining many leading sportsmen, politicians and entertainers in sending congratulations. The only contem-porary rival was the Taxi Drivers' League's *Taxi World*. Sadly, both league and magazine, after flourishing for about six years, were abandoned before the Second World War . The Taxi Drivers' Association was formed years later.

With many manufacturers withdrawing from London's cab scene – no new large British manufacturers entered between 1918 and 1929 – doors were wide open for new cabs; Glasgow-based Beardmore, mentioned earlier, were ready. September 1919, the year of company establishment, saw them introduce their Mark I or MK I, nick-named Grand Old Master at the London Commercial Vehicle Exhibition.

Thoughts of a taxi designed to meet modern trade requisites had already seen drawing-board stage from four years earlier, but final approval for new cabs was only granted by Superintendent Bassom around now.

Rugged terrain and modest-standard roads provided ideal ground for testing new vehicles. The MK I prototype drove over 1,000 miles of Highland steep hills, hairpin bends and dubious surfaces, the 10in clearance and 25ft turning circle proving their worth. Having satisfied Scotland Yard's requirements, Beardmore established a subsidiary, Taxicab and Motor Company, with £250,000 base capital. Under the selling slogan 'For comfort and speed, it's all you need!', used for decades to come, they had, by New Year 1920, supplied 1,120 cabs on cash or HP terms – HP was welcomed by owner-drivers who could pay while they earned.

Marketed at just under £800, its price reflected recent inflation. Subsequent reduction to £675 hardly impressed – suburban houses fetching about half. Salesmen tried to justify the price by plugging overall quality and modern technology, supposedly outweighing heavy, old-fashioned appearance. Beardmore sold its cabs to London from offices in Great Portland Street, with servicing at a Hendon depot.

With many modern sophisticated designs, it proved popular with London's drivers although minimal side protection was disadvantageous, the windscreen and canopy only helping frontally. This was typical of problems facing yesteryear's cabbies. Many worked from garages placed under railway arches or similar, often rat-infested. There were few, if any, washing or cleaning facilities, vehicles being liable to break down spontaneously. Many models had no nearside door and only a half-door offside; drivers needed overcoats and scarves.

Despite goodish sales in a difficult economic environment, the MK I had a short life, and it was soon deemed as antiquated-looking as many pre-war rivals. An improved version, the MK II, or 'Super', with a modernised body displaying refined wing edges – was arguably expensive at £625 but the price was justifiable by quality and low long-term running costs. The new cab, based on a modern 30cwt truck chassis, was initiated in 1923 by Underwood manager Angus Shaw. It was produced until 1926. The MK III Hyper Cab followed later.

Beardmore also produced cars but limited success soon led to financial difficulties. However, being the only British-owned cab manufacturer, it was felt that, at least, this business section had to be maintained. Thus the Treasury guaranteed a substantial loan – £350,000 – under the auspices of the Trade Facilities Advisory Committee. But such financial support was offered only on the condition that Underwood works was run separately from other activities.

The directors Francis Luther (now managing), George Allsworth (assistant) and John Girdwood (secretary) agreed, accordingly forming Beardmore Taxicabs Ltd, conducting cab sales and Beardmore (Paisley) Ltd organising finance. Leasing of Underwood works enabled MKIIs to be produced with minimal financial worry.

Other companies joined over the following years; in autumn 1920 was Olympia's Motor Cycle and Commercial Motor Show, where Belsize, Unic and Fiat, with their 1.8-litre engine model, numbered among exhibitors. With Belsize and Unic, new models resembled their pre-war cabs. Belsize never made a significant post-war impact and folded in 1925. Unic restyled their bonnet and made their radiator V-shaped in line with private-car fashion. In terms of deliveries from France, it started slowly but, following a parliamentary question, a special Board-of-Trade licence was granted, after which imports accelerated. Fleet operators and owners were particularly impressed with spares supply and back-up service efficiency. Fiat's IT was, however, completely new, being designed specially for London taxicab work. Modern features included disc wheels, contrasting rivals' artillery style. It had modest success here but did far better in continental cities.

Also several taxis, established as sidecars, were exhibited. Two well-known motorcycle manufacturers, Campion Rex BSA and Excelsior, offered good examples, Campion seating passengers side-by-side, Excelsior preferring staggered arrangements. The first appeared in Glasgow in December 1920, fares undercutting ordinary taxis' by about a third. In 1921 Nottingham purchased a fleet of Campions; other sidecar taxis appeared in Birmingham, Leeds, Margate and Brighton. With the earlier mentioned fare increase having been imposed in London, the capital's population wondered why they couldn't join in. The Ministry of Transport summoned a departmental committee. Their report of January 1921 recommended rejection, primarily on safety grounds, arguing that taxis had to withstand accidents better than private cars. Clearly flimsy sidecars would fail badly. Sidecars consequently left the provincial scene rapidly.

This was a disastrous year generally. War funding was expensive but once hostilities ceased, many anticipated peacetime prosperity so that returning soldiers could enjoy 'a land fit for heroes to live in' (Lloyd George). Prospects initially looked good but few realised that war demands had caused incalculable economic strain. The economy collapsed; unemployment skyrocketed, leaving dole queues, begging and soup kitchens 'normal'.

The early 1920s saw several other competitors enter or re-enter the field. Some, notably Fiat, had limited respect for the Conditions of Fitness then ruling, presumably dreaming that authorities would 'soften up'. Their IT was replaced in Italy by several more modern vehicles, but none satisfied and with Fiat unwilling to make necessary changes they were soon out of London. March 1921 saw SKAM (Skam Motors, Uxbridge Road, West London) introduce their new cab. After prototype approval, it was tested over several thousand miles but was not an immediate success. It did, however, reappear over a year later in autumn 1922 as the 'Kingsway' (Holborn's main thoroughfare) but at over £700 disappeared – too expensive.

In 1922, Vulcan introduced a 2.2-litre T-head taxicab but it hardly lasted; they abandoned production in 1928, going into receivership three years thence. Unic also reappeared, attempting to update their pre-war cab. Working on 1910s Edwardian, they introduced gate-change gearboxes with modern radiators. However, McKenna duties levied from September 1915 on imported luxury goods rocketed prices beyond purchasers' pockets (Reginald McKenna was Asquith's Chancellor). Intentions were temporary but apart from a short mid-1920s suspension period, they lasted until 1956.

Early peacetime years saw Mann and Overtons move premises from Pimlico to Battersea Bridge Road but then discontinue body manufacturing, probably lacking space and/or funds. Also manufacturing rights were apparently sold to Dyer and Holton in Brixton. In 1922, they lost concession rights to sell Unic commercial vehicles and cars; United Motors, under Ernest Mepstead, took over.

W & G (modestly-successful pre-war Napiers and Panhards) also re-emerged but were now in grave financial trouble. Their Acton premises had been acquired by Darracq and cab manufacturing was transferred to Turpin Engineering Co. Ltd, a subsidiary of Standard, Talbot (Sunbeam) and Darracq (collectively known as STD) who had innovation ambitions. Then 1922 saw them announce intentions to introduce the Talbot-Darracq cab, French-built on an English body — a convenient arrangement as the Sunbeam-Talbot Darracq group had recently absorbed the du Cros Company but it failed to progress beyond drawing-board stage. Consequently, W & G opted for American importing, hopefully for better quality and price. We meet the salesman shortly.

Meanwhile, fare arguments waged on for another three years, pressure intensifying for reduction. Transport policy, originally controlled by local authorities, headed for nationalisation. Politicians sought 'nationalised' buses and underground railways under one roof, bitterly opposing competition from independent organisations like coach and local bus operators. They were also keen to restrict taxicab growth. So that taxicabs should rival buses' service, the two-seater cab was proposed. Consequently, unrest was rife, owner-drivers, particularly, fearing increased operational costs and reduced net earnings.

A second committee was appointed during summer 1925 by Baldwin government Home Secretary Sir William Joynson-Hicks. From 1924, effectively heading the Metropolitan Police and thereby the PCO, he sought major changes in London's transport system. The argument in favour of two-seater cabs lay in the inability of conventional taxis to run economically without charging at least 1s per mile, too expensive for most. It was believed that smaller cabs, cheaper to build and run, could profit at 9d. The cab trade, owners, drivers, etc., strongly opposed this, complaining of far too many taxis already. Many drivers were already down to working two–three hours daily.

An Owner-Drivers' league — some authorities term it 'cab drivers' Joint Trade Committee' or JTC — was formed to promulgate the view that two-seaters would force members back to driving for large organisations and both the Motor Cab Trade Protection Society and Transport and General Workers' Union joined the bandwagon opposing lower fares. They wanted cabs that were cheaper to purchase and run but still insisted on four- rather than two-seaters running on a higher basic tariff. Use of two-seaters would result in drivers' four-seater investment being lost. The committee called seventeen witnesses, including manufacturer and licensing authority representatives, as well as cab traders.

A leading two-seater light was R.W. Owen, director of Hammersmith's firm White, Holmes & Company, which had taken over the National Motor Cab Company (1922). From 1926, they were building prototype two-seater cabs based on their KRC (Kingston, Richardson, Crutchley, British design engineers) light motor car. He argued:

a) Trade was already poor, largely because high fares, as indicated, discouraged customers.
b) Cheaper fares would encourage new clients into taking taxis regularly. Two-seaters, cheaper to build and lighter, saving on oil, petrol, tyres and purchase price, could make greater percentage profits, enabling drivers to justify claiming 40 per cent commission, improving on their current 33 per cent.
c) Four-seaters were wasteful, seldom filled to capacity, estimates suggesting 10 per cent or less of hirings involved three-plus passengers. Waste resulted, engines and chassis having been designed to carry more than necessary.

Sadly, in practice, both trade and passengers had effectively committed themselves early in the twentieth century when four-seater chassis were built. Lorry and bus trades had deemed this intolerable economics but cab traders had been tolerant. The two-seater ban stood in London but a few were running provincially, built on chassis designed for small cars, typically Berliet, Clyno and Morris. There were also a few two-seater motorcycle sidecar taxis in Bradford, Brighton, Cambridge and Nottingham, easily undercutting four-seater rivals.

Against this, cab drivers were unimpressed with White, Holmes & Company's 'biased' views and felt it inappropriate to operate two-seaters in London. Already down to minimal work, more taxis would worsen an already intolerable position. Furthermore, with two fare rates, the principle of hiring the cab by rank-queue order would have to be scrapped – surely customers would expect rights to choose their price. The police maintained that the current 'law' was unwritten and unenforceable; customers could choose any cab. Drivers added that cheaper rates on two-seater cabs would endanger livelihoods of four-seater cab-drivers, the worst sufferers being recent owner-driver HP purchasers who were still paying. Additionally, they believed differential fare rates would, long term, force all fares down, disadvantaging both owner-drivers and fleet operators. H.J. Dunn, an Owner-Drivers' League leader, saw fit to distinguish between arguments against two-seaters and those against lower fares. He maintained that, if several owner-drivers wanted to run two-seaters, others, running four-seaters, under threat to their livelihood, would have to return to large-fleet companies, effectively restoring the pre-Great War position. To prevent this, he proposed an overall 50 per cent fare reduction, believing this would, at least, double trading turnover without increasing working hours. Thus effectively a cab would earn its keep for 90 per cent of its working life against the current 30 per cent.

Other drivers' representatives – The Motor Cab Trade Protection Society, The Motor Cab Owner-Drivers' Association and The Transport and General Workers' Union – suggested compromise, insisting on an initial charge for the first mile but a reduction for longer journeys. The committee insisted that convenience of the public be paramount, taking precedence over considerations of financial strain on drivers, operators and owners; therefore every effort should be made for cheaper fares. They apparently attached more importance to the interests of a small proportion of customers paying slightly more for a larger-than-necessary cab to that of drivers' livelihoods, a questionable attitude.

The committee had doubts regarding logistics of different cab types with varying fare structures. They did however, approve of two-seaters in principle, their report of August 1926 recommending:

a) Home Secretary should not exercise power to establish an Order prohibiting licensing of a vehicle compliant with Scotland Yard regulations on sole pretext that it carried fewer than four passengers.
b) Best restrict to one fare set.
c) Home Secretary should call a conference, attended by cab-trade representatives, aiming to agree and arrange fare reductions for all cabs.
d) If no agreement for a uniform fare for two passengers was finalised, two-seater fares should be 9d for the first mile and 3d for each third of a mile thereafter; hourly waiting time 4s.

Thus effectively, Jix (as Joynson Hicks was nicknamed; Mule might have been more appropriate!) told the JTC that they must accept his terms or face lower fares, leaving them little alternative but concession. Fresh Conditions of Fitness for new cabs displayed differences as follows:

a) Minimum ground clearance reduced to 8in;
b) track (wheel-to-wheel) width reduced to 48in;
c) smaller wheels and tyres needed;
d) size of passenger compartment reduced but driver's compartment unaffected; and
e) 9d flagfall fare and 9d per mile thereafter from 1 May 1927.

Several other associated bodies, not directly represented on the Committee, expressed views. E.S. Shrapnell-Smith (Commercial Motor Users' Association) feared that, with two-seaters clearly cheaper to run and hire, four-seaters would be excluded, leaving serious overcrowding when three-plus passengers arrived. He also suggested possible single-seaters, suitable for businessmen and other 'loners', being introduced without threatening serious competition to larger-capacity cabs. Paris had enjoyed this. Also, in a minority report, R.C. Morrison MP felt that the first and third of the above were likely to increase taxicab numbers. Consequent traffic congestion could only be avoided if the Home Secretary specified limits on *total* cab numbers before allowing licences on two-seaters, a suggestion already made unsuccessfully several times.

By Home Secretary order, two-seater licences were made available only from spring 1926. Rules were laid down for physical differences between the two- and four-seaters, tabulated in Appendix 13. The Committee also recommended a two-tier tariff but Joynson-Hicks overruled, two-seater (JIXI) fares being fixed at 9*d* per mile.

After all this, two-seaters only reached prototype stage, one example used by the PCO for testing. There were plans for White, Holmes & Company to build new cabs, hopefully in considerable numbers – press commentators mentioned around 500 – by autumn. This company was experienced as successor to the National Motor Company, which had run a pre-war Unic fleet. However, the General Strike ruined such ideas; only afterwards could they even contemplate proceeding. Selling at £300, £200 below Beardmore's four-seater, they had one model licensed in Scotland and several in the Yorkshire spa town of Harrogate, but despite London drivers making little complaint during testing, none reached London. Unable to meet requests for mass production, financially impossible following the industrial disruption, the small company left doors open for larger organisations.

Two other firms submitted Jixi designs. A Leyland Motors-backed company, Trojan of Kingston-upon-Thames, reputed for cars and vans with unconventional two-stroke engines, running on solid tyres, had built fifty saloon taxis for Tokyo in 1924 but switched to pneumatics, offering bodies in saloon or landaulet style. However, only two prototypes were built. The French firm Berliet, leading in car and truck manufacturing since about 1900, principally based their vehicles on a 10–20hp chassis, but their taxis used 6.5-litre engines, running at 40hp in their native city, Lyon, and other major French cities up to the First World War. Two-seaters were particularly popular in Paris. Scotland Yard passed them from March 1927 but, before any appeared, as expected in April, the Home Secretary changed his mind, rescinding the two-seater order. He added insult to injury by imposing a tariff still lower than that originally applicable. This effectively meant that, while not banning two-seaters, he insisted that they run to four-seater Conditions of Fitness and tariff. Another blow to the already suffering trade ruled out Berliet's plans to build 200.

Trade representatives were naturally furious and, claiming double-cross, announced withdrawal of their support for the lower tariff. Arguments were rife but it was eventually agreed that new rates be tried for an experimental period even if effects would be extremely harsh in an economic environment experiencing over 50 per cent inflation since the armistice. This had resulted in cab prices doubling against only one fare increase of barely 1s 6*d* in 1920. Many cab drivers and owners faced likely bankruptcy. JTC asked Jix to reconsider. He refused, leaving the trade to make the best of a bad job.

They agreed to a new fare schedule, 6*d* for the first two-thirds of a mile or 7½ minutes duration (whichever came first) and 3*d* for each subsequent one-third or 3¾ minutes with an extra 6*d* payable for each passenger over two plus 3*d* charged per piece of luggage carried externally. This amounted to 9*d* per mile, a 25 per cent reduction on previous rates. Two-seater firms were – not surprisingly – stunned and mystified and Mr Owen doubted that the Home Secretary would prevent Jixis from working after so much capital had been spent on them. No luck; two-seaters never appeared – neither the first nor last time private investments proved wasted on a politician's promise.

Joynson-Hicks received correspondence from nobody less than British Fascist leader Sir Oswald Mosley. Mosley maintained that, if demand and profits were to be maintained while costs were minimised, cheaper four-seaters would be necessary. So, in some respect, he was siding with the cab trade. Jix, relaxing his attitude, wrote to Police Commissioner Sir William Horwood to the effect that on present fare scales drivers would have difficulty in meeting punishing regular payments due on vehicles. Horwood replied, blaming the manufacturers for charging far too much for vehicles and insisting unjustifiably that Conditions of Fitness were causative. He admitted, however, that he would stand by the turning circle minimum or 'lock', so instructing the new PCO head, Supt. Claro.

Claro, in addition to supervising the PCO's move from Scotland Yard to Lambeth Road's new premises, participated in a committee, established by Joynson-Hicks in 1927, to consider the effects of the Conditions of Fitness on current cab costs and whether modification was justified. So far, cabs produced had a front-heavy and box-like appearance, looking progressively old-fashioned against private motor cars' lower, smoother and shinier appearance. Comparison was also made with more up-to-date Parisian taxis with front-wheel brakes. Fearing sudden stops and likely encouragement of ill-timed faster driving, these brakes were banned in London until 1929. Consequently, very few companies attempted to join manufacturing markets.

The committee's appointed chairman was Capt. Douglas Harding MP, then Home Office Parliamentary Secretary, three engineers, including one from the Transport Ministry, also joining. Their initial findings heavily criticised both general cab industry treatment and Jix's two-seater obsession. They concluded that problems were primarily caused by poor competition, making recommendations, primarily aimed at bringing taxis closer to parallel with private cars:

a) Minimum clearance reduced from 10in to 7in
b) Minimum turning circle increased from 25ft to 40ft
c) Four-wheel braking be permissible.
d) A dashboard panel fuel tank could be included – no longer forcibly placed below the driver's seat.
e) Advertisements be permitted inside vehicles but not externally.

Scotland Yard accepted all except the turning circle. Thus new lower cabs appeared in the years following, most notably Austin collaring about half the sales by 1930 and to a lesser extent, Morris, who ushered in a new manufacturing era in taxicab history. All major designers and trade builders were encouraged to breathe fresh air and improve on past models, many new designs appearing as the 1920s ended. The recommendations above were binding from the end of April 1928.

By winter 1926–27, Unic chassis production had ceased and thus Unic's ability to supply to Mann and Overtons. That gave United Motors' Ernest Mepstead an opportunity. So far, Unic had been making the 11cv (*cheval-vapeur*, current French horsepower tax-rating system) Type L (model designation) with side-valve engines just under 2 litres.

Around now, only four cab makes were marketable but this paints a deceptively bright picture. Beardmore's MK IIs were too expensive for most. So too were Unics, only in limited supply anyway, the company having stockpiled several chassis following production closure the previous year – worth a year's supply at best. Citroën, whose taxi-market entry is discussed shortly, had similar problems and Hayes taxicabs were virtually unavailable. As illustrated in Appendix 10s new licensed-cab numbers early in the decade, conditions were stifling.

With the market too small for serious manufacturers, Joynson-Hicks was heading for more trouble. Once new fares operated, drivers realised that rescinding of the two-seater order applied only to those intending to charge lower rates. Thus, working strictly legally, they could ply provided they charged four-seater rates. The trade considered this a 'breach of promise'; consequently, their Joint Committee felt justified in withdrawing its consent to fares reduction. Jix countered that he was privileged by Parliament to fix fare rates without needing external consent. Following considerable parliamentary argument with cab-sympathetic MP's, it was agreed to try new rates for an experimental period. They stood until 1933 when the basic rate was raised by 3*d* per mile.

That did not, however, attract big manufacturers. The committee contacted The Society of Motor Manufacturers and Traders for help. Circulars were sent out but only three candidates replied positively, only two, Morris and Humber, sending representatives. Humber proposed the new 14/40 but it cost a prohibitive £575. Their representative, Ted Grinham, was dubious, assuring the committee that anything under £600 was out, ruining the PCO's hopes of 'cheap' cabs. At that time, Morris were working on their new 'Oxford' car, selling at £240 and their representative, Miles Thomas, talked of more competitive variants at £335. Both representatives, however, stressed that principal obstacles to mass production of London cabs lay in ground-clearance requirements, turning circle and fuel-tank positioning.

However, the two-seater idea was still alive. October 1928 saw a new company formed, Two-Seater Taxicabs Ltd, hoping to market by the following year but nothing materialised. The early 1930s saw the idea crop up again when three-wheeler passenger cars enjoyed a modest boom. Several names, notably BSA, Morgan and Coventry Victor were building pleasant three-wheeled four-seaters. *Commercial Motor* magazine reported that one manufacturer had produced a three-wheeler saloon, apparently suitable for taxi use. Scotland Yard were approached but proved reluctant to grant London licence. The magazine's reaction suggested that, if such vehicles proved success-ful provincially, London licensing would surely follow. Sadly, provincial opinion proved unfavourable, many deeming these too similar to sidecars, rejected for safety reasons a decade earlier; they were therefore refused. However, a one-passenger three-wheeler had modest success in Berlin around 1931 but the full-size version dominated London unchallenged until minicabs appeared in 1961.

The early 1930s saw ideas appearing for cabs designed primarily for provincial use. The three-wheeler 'Tri-cab', actually a Coventry Victor Coupé, seemed worthwhile at £125 with an £8 insurance rating and fifty-per-gallon mileage at 25 miles an hour. Comfortably accommodating one passenger with two luggage pieces, the proposal was to charge 3d per mile. Sadly, restrictions proved too demanding for acceptance.

For London, a further idea was the Jixi-style KRC, mentioned earlier. Manufacturers proposed to contact theatre-ticket agencies, departmental stores, hotels, etc., using them as vehicle-hire agencies, giving fare coupons as perks. The intentions were to fit well-illuminated meters and 'FOR HIRE' signs, using ticket-printing and receipt-issuing meters. For drivers, turnout and courtesy were emphasised but the flat-rate system was rejected in favour of straight-commission basis – 40 per cent of takings plus allowances for extras like luggage as currently accepted. Bonuses were awarded for above-average performances regarding fuel economy and vehicle maintenance. Plans visualised having these available by winter 1929, increasing numbers weekly to about 400 by early summer. The freehold garage was in Sussex Place and the maintenance depot at Worlidge Street, Hammersmith, both equipped with modern driver and worker facilities.

Joynson-Hicks was promoted to the House of Lords, spending his remaining politi-cal career as Viscount Brentford. until his death in June 1932. The taxi-press obituary spoke of his harshness but that 'he felt sure he was right'. The two-four seater contro-versy cropped up again almost exactly then. The Raleigh Cycle Company announced their intention to build three-wheeler taxis, claiming petrol economy – 50mpg – for 6cwt vehicles. However, vehicles failed to progress beyond the PCO, to competitors' relief.

For completeness, I mention other cabs tried that decade, their competition forc-ing cab prices down. AML from Associated Motors Ltd of Maida Vale tried for about three years but never exhibited, with few manufactured. Mepward (introduced 1920) proved very unpopular, described by drivers as noisy and crude, at best slow and heavy to drive. Only a dozen were built by Mepstead and Hayward of Pentonville, London, the all-wooden body only putting extra strain on the probably already inadequate engine. Hayward reputedly disappeared from the business scene in dubious circum-stances but Ernest Mepstead continued, as explained later.

The Hayes (1925–28) was Canadian, built by Hayes Wheel Company (formed 1909) of Ontario with a British-built body powered by an American Continental 2.4-litre four-cylinder engine. The British company was William Watson & Co., Watson being a successful rally driver and friend of William Morris, later Lord Nuffield. Thus we introduce Morris Commercial as an early large-scale manufacturer entering the market after announcing design specification changes – details later.

Watson introduced the Hayes to Britain, *Motor Transport* magazine expressing welcoming views; its £425 easily undercut Beardmore's £625. Sadly, despite being described by many mushes as 'a really beautiful cab' it never rivalled the Citroëns, Beardmores or Unics. Efforts made in 1926 to form an owner-drivers' 'Hayes club' never materialised; it hardly lasted longer.

Returning to W & G, they purchased the American Yellow cab, John Hertz being synonymous with cab rental. He founded Yellow Cab Company of Chicago, later spending several months in Europe, investigating relevant conditions. Following intensive study of London's cab trade, he decided to introduce his cab into London and Paris. Consequently, a subsidiary company was established here – the Yellow Cab Manufacturing Company of England with an MP, Brigadier E.L. Spears, on its board. It is believed that his influence allayed fears that Hertz aimed to take over London's cab business, but the company never operated cabs themselves.

W. & G. delightedly replaced their outdated fleet of pre-war Panhards and Napiers. Assembly was completed in West London by Turpins. After public introduction in Olympia's Commercial Motor Exhibition of 1923, about a hundred Yellow cabs appeared in London that autumn, standing out with their canary colour, drivers wearing a grey uniform, peaked cap and leather leggings. In 1924, a chassis of shorter (by about 10 per cent) wheelbase was introduced for compliance with English regulations, a landaulet body replacing the American Racine. Sadly, combination with the American-style hood length gave an unpleasant front-heavy appearance. Drivers were described as 'butterboys' and were 'knowledge' trained by their parent company. All newly licensed drivers have been nicknamed 'butterboys' ever since.

There were fears that Yellow Cab 'manufacturers and operators' would flood markets here but their English subsidiary, The Yellow Cab Manufacturing Company of England Ltd, had no such ambition, treating cab-operating companies and individual mushers with equal respect. Turpins bought ten dozen Yellow Cab chassis during winter 1924, fitting them with American-style bodies but with a wheelbase 10in shorter. Acting as proprietor and agent, they sold several vehicles to mushes, contractually running small fleets. However, bigger fish were around and with Hertz diverging to truck and bus manufacturing, General Motors were tempted to take over the whole business from 1925 after which transatlantic cab delivery stopped. Hertz ran his company until 1929, leaving to start a new rental car company, Hertz Rent-a-Car, still running with their yellow logo.

The early-mid twenties saw the French company Citroën make its London debut. André Citroën, (founder, mechanical engineer) started production four years earlier, offering 1.5-litre vehicles from 1923, introduced by Stamford Brook car dealer Maxwell

Monson. Bodies were manufactured by Dyer and Holton of Brixton. Monson sold cabs on hire purchase to mushes, arranging for driver training on test cabs, 'wangles'. However, London General Cab Company proved his biggest customer. Needing to replace out-of-date Renaults and Unics, they found £625 for newer Unics excessive and turned to Citroën. By 1928, their fleet easily topped 200.

Citroën, unique among European manufacturers, used American-style mass-production techniques. He was determined to produce vehicles usable for many years for all-round economic benefit, earning him the nickname 'the Henry Ford of France'. Citroëns sold at £540 but an alternative HP arrangement of £50 deposit plus forty-five monthly £12 payments totalled near £600. Thus, for now, prices were middling between Beardmore and Hayes. Later, however, it was reduced to a more competitive £495 or, on HP, £75 plus £12 10s monthly for three years. This covered complete lighting sets, a year's insurance and taxi rental. Maxwell Monson gave extensive after-sales service, instruction to potential drivers and transport to the PCO for licensing formalities. Cabs were first exhibited at Olympia's 1923 Commercial Motor Show; they were swamped with orders.

These were pioneering in that electric headlamps were fitted as standard; for side-lamps, oil was still optional. Up to then, drivers were sceptical about electric headlamps, their disadvantage lying in time spent idle on ranks or traffic jam slow motion, unnecessarily draining dynamos for insufficient battery charging. The PCO also strongly opposed, it fearing dazzling. Many viewed that, as powerful headlamps were necessary for London driving, oil lamps were best rearwards with acetylene frontally. February 1924 saw the British Lighting and Ignition Company marketing lighting sets for £18 15s, including free delivery and fitting. With this installed, dynamos could charge batteries down to 8mph in top gear while batteries, producing 60 amps per hour, ensured running a considerable time at even lower speeds. Further savings could be earned by dimming lights on rank. Sets thus included 6 volt dynamos, batteries, cut-outs, circular switchboards fitted with ammeters and arranged for bright or dim lights as needed, two 6in double-purpose side-lamps, taximeter lamps and tail-lamps.

Updated four-wheel 1923 model variants were standardised from 1926, selling competitively at £325. However, problems already threatened. Supplies were inevitably limited; chassis were built in Paris but termination was approaching. To avoid McKenna duties, in late autumn Citroën started manufacturing its latest model – the steel 13/30 – at a Slough factory. In principle, they used the same engine as for private cars and Citroën-Kegresse half-track vehicles but chassis redesign and steering modification were needed to meet regulations. Original ideas were for seven-seaters for Paris use. A number of provincial operators were approached but the modified design proved unavailable and Citroën, for the present, disappeared.

Around this period, another firm, C.A. Vandervell of Acton, produced sets in which dynamos could produce constant outputs, irrespective of cab speed. They included two each of headlamps and side-lamps, tail lamp and interior roof lamp with a taximeter lamp fitted with blue glass, their distinctive 'trademark'. These sold for £18 18s, Mount Pleasant Cab Company purchasing 200. Cabs also had low-pressure balloon tyres, the whole body being placed markedly below predecessors' level. Most were operated by London General, others sold to owner-drivers.

Up to 1929, British cabs were distinctly disadvantaged against French rivals, French designers being exempted from strict PCO limits. British cabs thus attracted increasingly adverse press criticism. Designers were up against insurmountable problems when trying to build comfortable and capacious cabs within limits of 14ft length, 40in internal height (set to seat bowler-hatted gentlemen comfortably but making impressive-looking designs impossible) and 25ft turning circle (necessitating a wheelbase shorter than most light cars with half the cab's capacity). Further, the floor level was set at a maximum of 15in above street level so that passengers stepped up and down with minimal danger.

Beardmore's MK III Hyper, nicknamed 'Farthing Cab', followed in May 1929. (Some authorities suggest 1926.) Earlier, Beardmore had produced an expensive 12hp passenger car, but after disastrous sales the factory was closed to cut losses. However, chassis were to prove useful as cab bases meeting current body requirements.

Weighing 25cwt, smaller and lighter than its predecessor, it displayed elegance, a capacious interior, low centre of gravity and a competitive price (appropriate nickname), well below its predecessor's. Its main attraction was fuel economy ascribed to its new cast-iron, four-cylinder, side-valve unit with a newly patented Duplex manifold, a pipe arrangement with several outlets, ensuring that each cylinder received its fuel and air supplies in correct amounts and proportion. This necessitated dividing the induction pipe all the way down to the carburettor so that on induction cylinders could not rob one another of mixture. Previously, this had been a source of power loss and uneven petrol distribution, very wasteful and leaving carbon deposits requiring regular attention. The 1.95-litre engine was smaller than its predecessor but had improved power for 26-plus miles per gallon.

For the first time, brakes were four-wheel and of internal expanding drum type, fully compensated between front and rear. Commentators thought this alone would make the Hyper, 6in lower, more attractive than the comparatively old-looking Morris. The Hyper also offered a comfort advantage, Morris compartments still being open to the elements. The four-speed gearbox ensured smoother rides and lighter steering while clutch and pedals required reduced effort.

The Hyper's body was further streamlined in 1930, production continuing until phasing out between 1932 and winter 1933–34, being replaced by the MK IV 'Paramount'.

Luther and Allsworth, mentioned earlier around 1914, bought up Beardmore's taxi section and with it Lord Invernairn's share (about half). The Paisley factory henceforth confined production to high-speed diesel engines for truck and marine industries. Thus, in 1932, production ceased in Scotland, later work completed in Grove Park, Colindale, North West London. Luther had acquired a concession in Austro-Daimler.

Paramount used an engine and gearbox from former Maidstone car dealers Rootes Brothers, their chief engineer, Jack Irving, acting as consultant. Available from 1934, it was gradually improved over two or three years, notably with a capacious luggage rack beside the driver in a partially enclosed compartment affording modest protection from the elements. With relevant laws still archaic, from 1930 he was allowed a complete front windscreen but his left-hand side remained completely exposed; he was only allowed a right-hand door window from 1938.

In turn, the MK IV was replaced over winter 1935–36 by the MK V 'Ace'. Though retaining many previous features, it had a radical design. Paisley's factory's days were already numbered and with its closure, chassis manufacture ceased. Rootes offered Beardmore an alternative, the 2.9m wheelbase chassis applicable to Hillman 14 saloons. The novelty was Rootes' 'evenkeel' transverse leaf, independent front suspension but as the PCO had disallowed this design since well before the Great War, a beam-type axle and leaf springs, as used in Commer's 15cwt van was required. The Commer engine was used before but the crash gearbox was replaced by a four-speed synchromesh, used by Rootes' larger passenger motor cars. The overall length, 4.3m, exceeded maximum PCO-stipulated length but they relented. Thus a bigger passenger door could be fitted. The back axle was moved behind the rear seat, hopefully for more comfortable riding.

Longer wheelbase and lower body improved room for both driver and passengers. There was a new front, flared forward wings, a dropped glass window on the driver's door and a screen separating him from the luggage compartment. Many displeased drivers argued that all positives were frontal, nicknaming it 'greengrocer's barrow'. Nonetheless, competitively priced at £435, it attracted larger fleet owners.

The MK VI 'Paramount Ace', the last of the pre-war series, followed in late autumn 1937, having a ¾ landaulet body (here landaulet is defined as an automobile body with open driver's seat, enclosed rear section and collapsible roof), driver's window and all four gears modified. However, Beardmore's prices were higher than Austin's, a single landaulet costing £480 and a ¾ landaulet £485; sales suffered accordingly. Beardmore's cab production ceased at the outbreak of the Second World War in favour of war supplies.

However, 1929 saw a new idea from South Africa. Cape Town designer W. Gowan produced 'Cape' body cabs, with oval sides and rear windows but without side-facing doors; passengers entered and departed via transverse sliding doors lying across the chassis frame immediately behind the luggage area. This eliminated chances of opening doors to hit pavement obstructions, lamp posts, or passing pedestrians. Prototypes were two-seaters but Gowan assured those interested that they could be modified to four. The driver was isolated on a frontal bucket seat but the absence of an offside door or screen was disadvantageous, leaving him exposed to windy conditions.

Nonetheless, *Commercial Motor* magazine commented on passengers' complete privacy, useful in countries with high racial tension. Ideas appealed to Morris Commercial who proposed to build two-seater versions on standard G-type chassis. The PCO was dubious, fearing sliding doors would crush fingers. Only one prototype was built; Scotland Yard allowed London testing but it was never fully licensed.

However, 1930 saw licensing granted for four-seater variants, over 100 being built. These were greeted with sarcasm from *Steering Wheel* magazine, unworried about fingers but more concerned that doors could be opened without risk to outsiders. Describing the cabs as 'unconventional', they felt that eliminating such dangers was 'ruining the fun'. Nonetheless, several body builders, notably Arthur Mulliner and the New Avon Body Company, happily persisted with Cape designing until winter 1936–37. In August 1931 the PCO approved vehicles in which Mann and Overtons had Cape bodies fitted to heavy 12 chassis, granting licence permission for a dozen. Autumn that year saw a further variant include two cricket seats, inclined forward to avoid the sliding door; bodies were built by Strachans (pronounced Strawns) of Acton. In 1933 a modified version of the two-seater was licensed, some twenty Austins being fitted with these doors. Two years later approval was given for four-seater versions built on Morris G2 chassis.

Three months after Citroën's July 1929 arrival, the Austin Heavy twelve/four appeared. Elkington Carriage Company of Chiswick built both landaulet and four-light saloon versions. Austin were now Britain's second largest car manufacturers. Two cars, the legendary Austin Seven and the Austin Twenty dominated markets and a scaled-down variant of the Twenty became the basis for the 12/4. These sold, respectively, at £375 and £395 with options to pay £50 deposit and £11 monthly over three years. Prices sounded favourable but were effectively higher as incomes were low at this time, not to mention financial disasters following the Wall Street Crash. Nonetheless, this was successful provincially, notably in Manchester. Provincial cities were governed by legislation less strict than London's; therefore the 12/4 was acceptable in standard form. The relevant legislation was 1847's Town Police Clauses Act, applicable to Hackney cab licensing. The 'enabling regulations' gave local police commissioners option *without compulsion* to license local cabs. Nowadays, discretion rests with local authorities, given rights to choose which vehicles are licensed but the Act is binding in respect of licensing rules and driver conduct. However, the turning circle, braking system and V-shaped windscreen failed to satisfy London specifications.

Updating of London's Conditions of Fitness offered new prospects. Regarding Unics, William Overton appreciated that the immediate post-war model needed replacing; import duties had now overpriced it anyway. He arranged to meet an old friend, now Austin's senior engineer, Mr Harfield, who satisfied him that chassis and steering could be modified to meet London's 25ft turning circle limit and that brake rods could replace the cables used currently.

Could Herbert Austin be convinced? In previous years, Austin had produced town carriages and the like – vehicles usable as taxis – and undoubtedly Herbert Austin had been approached already regarding taxi design, firmly declining. Inevitably, Overton viewed the possible meeting, in spring 1930, with considerable trepidation.

Legend has it that Overton arrived in Longbridge, requesting an audience but was told that Austin wouldn't meet him. That might have been 'curtains', but Overton belonged to the 'Never take "No" for an answer!' school, sitting outside until 5 p.m.; (did he arm himself with a copy of *Gone With the Wind* or, perhaps more appropriately, *War and Peace?*). Austin eventually emerged to greet Overton with 'Are you still here?', getting the reply 'Yes, and will be all day tomorrow unless you see me now!' Assured that Overton wanted to place an order for 500 chassis satisfying Conditions of Fitness, Austin relented, appreciating that publicity in London would be beneficial in struggling with his bigger rival, Morris. The meeting cemented a relationship lasting for many decades.

Proposed alterations included a different front axle with rod-operated brakes, contrasting cables used by provincial models. The steering column was to be more erect, the nearside front door disappearing. Austin agreed to supply modified chassis and following PCO approval of the 12/4 chassis in autumn 1929, Mann and Overtons put the tall conventional cab, 'High Lot', on sale in 1930. Several names were involved in body manufacturing including the Chelsea Carriage Company, Dyer and Holton, and Strachan and Jones, the last two proving most popular. Cabs were sold from Mann and Overtons' Battersea Bridge Road premises from early June. The introduction of new ball-change four-speed gearboxes improved 'user-friendliness'.

Its arrival caused minimal publicity but Austin dominated for many decades thereafter taking more than three-quarters of the market and benefitting from flexibility of supplying chassis only on which a variety of coach-built bodies could be fitted; (Beardmore built complete cabs). By Christmas 1931, its competitive price, the reliability and power of the 12/4 engine and excellent service backing ensured top place in London's cab market league. Total sales outnumbered those of rivals Beardmore and Morris by nearly three to one, approaching 1,200 by 1935. One Austin taxi, built that year, underwent, in 1953, the ultimate endurance test, taking an adventurous driver, Michael Marriott, across the Sahara's crusty 'roads', boulders, dunes and quicksands. The problems suffered by the radiator, condenser and engine in intense heat and sandstorms make exciting reading.

Back on London's 1930 streets, the first example, appearing in the spring, was owned by A.W. Barker, well-respected chairman of London Cab Trade's Mocatra Athletic Club. Variants following included the Austin TT, 'upright grand piano'. More than 2,000 cabs of both types sold between 1930 and 1934.

Another idea floated was a six-seater 'car-coach', powered by a six-cylinder engine. Possibly the cab trade could thereby compete with private-hire firms and small motor-coach companies. Such firms were running seven-seater cars, which, according to the press (*Motor Transport* magazine) were 'outside the scope of the thirty m.p.h. limit' but also did not require a fitness certificate. A well-known example was the Fordalette seven-seater, a *de luxe* model, finished in royal blue cellulose with blue leather upholstery. Standard features also included luggage rails with parcel nets, sliding windows behind the driver's seat, roof lights, ash trays, arm rests and rear-view mirrors for passenger use – £335.

With a similar mentality, the Twin-Coach Company introduced a seventeen-seater 'taxi-coach'. Divided into three distinct departments, each with its own door, two carried six passengers each (three facing three), the frontal third carrying five (three facing two, the two facing forward) with the centre seat for the driver. Each seat had its own electro-pneumatic slot machine for fare payment.

Returning to 1934, design changes saw the 'form' axle replacing the 'crown wheel and pinion' type. That enabled propeller-shaft repositioning and a consequent drop in floor height of 6–7in. The result was appropriately named 'Low Loader', or the Austin LL. Licensed in early November, it became the most familiar interwar cab.

Eight body types were initially built by the New Avon Body Company of Warwick, then painted and trimmed by Strachans at Brixton, central pillars having distinctive rearward inclination. Roof luggage rack rails were plain and straight, the rear standing slightly proud at the base. Lighting, however, was restricted to one interior bulb and there were no rear seat arm rests. The PCO suspected the roof's strength, deeming the driver position too 'exposed'. However, they allowed licences for half a dozen; all appeared during winter 1934–35. In May 1935, an improved version included a driver's door and a sliding window between his and the passengers' compartment for better communication. Several types of Low Loader served throughout the war, many remaining in service to the mid 1950s. Standard extras included fire extinguisher, horn, number plates, licence holder, taxi sign, Trico visual windscreen wipers and speedometer. The interior trim included leather (antique or plain) upholstery with blue exterior cellulose finishing.

Henceforth, many bodies were built by Jones Brothers of Westbourne Grove. Approved from spring 1935, additional distinctive characteristics included:

a) rear panelling tailed out into a curve or swept tail, 'fishtail' for easy accessibility to the welled spare wheel;
b) accentuated curling end to the roof rack;
c) near oval-shaped door window frame;
d) tucked-in rear 'charabanc' (horse-drawn or motor vehicle with several forward-facing rows) appearance;
e) tubular pillars;
f) Dunlopillo upholstery;
g) half-moon shape of the petrol filler recess, deeper than in rival cabs; and
h) boot lid hinged at its bottom.

These sold at £400 – a £5 premium on those from Vincent and Strachan. Nearly 6,000 Austin cabs were sold in London between spring 1930 and Christmas 1938; sales figures, in Appendix 14, illustrate Austin's rise to the top.

That year also saw Mann and Overtons become a public company; henceforth dropping the pluralising 's'. J.T. Overton's son, Robert, became a part-time board member. The flotation brought in considerable funds. Thenceforth, as Low Loader sales increased, the company could offer financial assistance to prospective purchasers, notably owner-drivers competing with more dominant fleets. They had to put up about one third of the £395 price, beyond the pockets of many. Robert Overton became a full-time board member from 1938, taking charge of this financial branch, 'Mechanical Investments Ltd' when Mann and Overton's premises moved to Wandsworth Bridge Road, Fulham, remaining there until 1983. New buildings housed comprehensive machine shops, which, combined with improvisation and mechanical skills, proved invaluable in providing repairs and maintenance to keep taxis running during the following hostilities.

Austin's last landaulet coachwork cab of the interwar period was the Flash Lot, or 'Flash Job'. At drawing-board stage during summer 1934, thirteen significant defects needed correction. Despite promises for 'quick' solutions, Mann and Overton delayed final presentation for two years. This was a streamlined cab, described as 'swaged' (decorative) and built on the 12 chassis with a full-length driver's door. This introduced 'futuristics' like a parallel-lined radiator grille, counterbalanced windows instead of winders, high-mounted headlamps supported at one end or 'cantilevered' from the radiator structure, or 'fairing', and flare wings. However, traditionalists dominated several areas, with wheels and mechanical layout unchanged; bodywork supported current landaulet styling despite the new door. This was produced to the outbreak of the Second World War, but in 1938 sales were poor, scarcely exceeding 200, largely because 3-to-4-year-old big fleets were clearly going to be around for the foreseeable future and looming war spelt economic recession.

However, a few were delivered up to early 1940; about 400 chassis were sent to the army who fitted them with light truck bodies, primarily for driving instruction. About three-quarters survived and they were returned to Mann and Overton, who dismantled them, stocking parts as spares. Vincents of Reading built early bodies but then Jones Brothers and Goode and Cooper took over. Sadly production was curtailed following declaration of war.

The early 1930s produced another novelty, London General's Chinese Austin. This was a hybrid – Austin 12 chassis on which were mounted discarded Citroën bodies. Nearly 200 were so constructed but fitting was poor and purchasers – mainly owner-drivers – mystified as to whether they were Austin or Citroën, gave them this nickname (from the idea of a Chinese puzzle). Possibly combining Austin and Citroën and calling them 'Austrian' (nearer home) might have been more appropriate. Citroëns had brought out their C4F taxi in 1930, replaced in 1931–32 by the more impressively finished C4G, last in that series but gradually dropped out during the second half of the decade; the few survivors were firstly used for new owner-driver training, later for war duty. Post-war, few were fit for public use.

Detailing Austin's prospective trade dominance, nearly all had landaulet bodies, constructed so that in hot weather the rear portion could be opened for fresh air.

Two types were available, the vast majority being single landaulets, passenger compartments being restricted to two main windows (with a rear small circular window, a London General cab feature), but there were rare examples of three-quarter landaulet style (i.e. including two extra quarter-light type windows) initially popular but gradually fading out by 1940.

First on view was the Morris 'International' model (named for Kenning's international cab company), using the same commercially powered engine as their lighter trucks. It had an English steel panel body, winding triplex glass windows and shock absorbers. New extras included passenger-driver microphone communication, door-operable roof lights and rear blinds fitted to quarter windows. Luggage space was additionally available on roof racks. However, Scotland Yard regulations demanded no front or side screen for the driver. They also stuck to rear brakes only, disadvantageous compared with Beardmore and Austin who took advantage of permission for four-wheel brakes.

Cabs were initially sold at a modest, all-inclusive £395 through new distributors, The International Taxicab Company of Sheffield. Manager George Kenning, well known in the motor trade, was a Morris motor dealer and proprietor of Leeds' International Cab Company. Later, Morris Commercial cabs were distributed by the Liverpool-based William Watson & Company. Early Morris models were variants of the poorly sold Empire Oxford car. Design faults included weaknesses in rear axle casings, which frequently cracked.

Kenning proposed that the Empire, appropriately modified, might succeed as a taxi. Faults were corrected on subsequent designs. Thus the first 800-plus were converted from unsold Empire Oxfords in Birmingham's Soho suburb, where Morris Commercial had a giant factory. Axles were narrowed, meeting the PCO's track-limit requirement. The van chassis was shortened and the 30cwt truck engine was used: 2.5-litre sidevalve with an overhead worm-drive rear axle, set ensuring 10in minimum ground clearance. Early models were marketed with three-quarter brown landaulet bodies from Morris Bodies' Cowley factory. Cabs were sold from January 1929 at £377 (£465 on HP) but the price soon rose to £395. Headlights, initially absent, were soon added. Similarly, rear brakes with two shoes were replaced by four-wheel brakes when new Conditions of Fitness were enforced. Total output increased to around 1,700.

Morris had visions of Commonwealth market demand. But again problems arose, competition-wise. North American rival makes, built in Canadian factories, avoided McKenna Duties.

In June 1929, Morris added a new model, the Commercial hire car with four doors and a two-piece windscreen replacing predecessors' three-quarter screen. Booked for long life to around 1950, further modifications were introduced in 1930 – in the G1 International – including a full windscreen, headlights, bumpers and four-wheel brakes as standard fittings thereafter. There were 840, mainly in London.

Looking antiquated by the early 1930s, it was replaced over winter 1931–32 by the smaller G2, 'Junior', sold from Adderley Park (Wolseley's old plant) in suburban

Birmingham. Based on G-type chassis, this had a smaller 14hp Hotchkiss-type engine borrowed from the Morris Oxford car or light van and lower lines than the International's; hence the name. This engine was needed because the G-type engine was only available in the variant of just under 18hp (now used for large trucks) but oversized for cab use. The body, however, was of new G-type design with pressed steel panels mounted on an ash frame.

Later in 1932, London distributors Morris Commercial Cabs Ltd, William Watson & Co. Ltd, moved premises from Eccleston Place, Victoria, to Grosvenor Road, Chelsea. The floor area, over 20,000sq.ft, accommodated over 100 cabs with three petrol pumps, offices being a floor above. The decades following saw ownership change hands several times.

In August 1934, G2S (Junior 6) became one of few six-cylinder vehicles in trade use. Press comment spoke of 'being built like a tank'; it appeared good value at £385, direction indicators and windscreen wipers included. Drivers also welcomed excellent roadholding, steering and passenger comfort.

A commercial version, with no overhead valves, was manufactured as the 'Senior'. In 1937, its streamlined version, Super-Six, the G2SW was built with the added luxuries of full-length doors, driver's drop window and speedometer, selling from 1938. Morris taxicab production ended when war broke out although there were futuristic designs.

A number of coach-building firms, London and provincial, developed trade interest, notably:

a) Chelsea Carriage Company;
b) Neighbouring Christopher Dodson;
c) Ricketts of Euston with their distinctive wooden window pillar and protruded rear, forming an approximately square-shaped boot with enclosed recess for the spare wheel, curl-like ends to the luggage rail and rear mudguards spread outwards; toolbox under the driver's seat; Low Loader bodies were considered to be an improvement on basic originals;
d) Goode and Cooper, Brixton;
e) Vincent of Reading with their Low Loader *de Luxe* body.

Nearly all their cabs were landaulets; the rear portion could be opened in hot weather.

Austin ended foreign cab superiority but still faced rivalry. Unic, whose sales during the 1920s had fallen dramatically, primarily because of excessive import duty, retaliated with a revised model, forming a new company, Unic Motors (1928) Ltd, based in Cricklewood, West London. Initially concentrating on importing French lorry chassis, in July 1930 they produced their new KF1. This was both designed and assembled in London although engines were initially French-built (subsequently, United Motors, under licence for Unic Automobiles Ltd, took over). The landaulet body interior was more capacious than most others and there was electric passenger-driver communication.

Sadly, heavy and expensive, it failed on reliability compared with predecessors, and became very unpopular. Its appearance was clumsy, reminiscent of American gangster-type vehicles. Manufacture was consequently terminated after three years although, of nearly 100 originals, a handful survived to 1951. However, over 1930–32, Unic, now considered antiquated, faded out.

Citroën fared better, producing their own cab at their Brixton factory in 1929. Chief engineer Mr P. Geldard had designed their own channel-steel frame and landaulet body with wheelbase chassis longer than its ageing 1920s predecessor. Cabs were licensed to seat four comfortably with the driver's seat upholstered. They were deemed 'luxury' cabs with comfort-orientated suspension on quarter-elliptic front springs and rear double quarter-elliptics. There were two fold-down stall seats facing a well-cushioned rear seat and well-trimmed dark blue or green leather interior. Exterior body panels were handcrafted in aluminium with black moulding, but customers could choose line colour and painting.

With this model earning some success, London General was encouraged to modify its existing Citroën fleet, taking maximum advantage of relaxation in design specification limitations. They used 1923 model chassis to carry their own bodies, known as the 'Coup de Ville'. The old-fashioned appearance was updated by the removal of roof racks; wheels of reduced diameter were fitted with a fixed hood installed. The fabric cab interior was impressively upholstered with safety glass added. Mechanical equipment and interior fittings were overhauled, introducing an electric dictaphone. The resultant 'General' cab was mainly used by the company, following their acquisition of Red Motor Cab Company. The company's Brook Green, Hammersmith service centre offered efficient maintenance service, having ready spare parts and service facilities. In the fiercely competitive 1926 market, Citroën reduced their price to £495, well below Unic's. But that was excuse rather than reason – political forces were relevant following 1924's legislation.

Thus the trade saw brand-new designs running parallel to antiquated models like pre-war Napiers, Panhards and two-cylinder Renaults, which had laboured on against constant criticism for at least a decade. The press deplored it; The Daily Mail complained that the public had to pay identical rates for old two-cylinder cabs, completing a journey in fifteen minutes, as for new four-cylinder cabs, taking ten. Other London papers denounced old taxis, speaking of decay, engines threatening to surrender their ghosts at any moment, wheezing their way through the gears with a fierce clutch, jerking the passenger from his uneasy seat on to decrepit upholstery, and weary springs. Further comments spoke of recognition difficulty – many were adorned with a new bonnet and coat of paint. Madame Tussaud's Chamber of Horrors was even mentioned. In Paris, older cabs charged lower fares, new cab owners proudly displaying sizeable notices: 'Nouveau taxi à quatre cylindres'.

One engineer, Mr A.W. Miller, refused to be daunted by the attempted exclusion of antiquated vehicles. He completely modernised an old Renault taxi into an acceptable touring car.

One way suggested to eliminate old-stagers was to institute stricter tests. Currently, apart from fitness regulations, empty vehicles only had to make 20mph on the flat or 6mph up a gradient, with drivers being allowed time for cab tuning before testing. Members of Parliament made periodic requests for stringency but now authoritarian attitudes surprisingly turned humanitarian, showing reluctance to be firm, arguing that, with many older cabs owner-driven, there was risk of livelihood loss. Hence the Home Secretary and Minister of Transport insisted that actual age or antiquated appearance should not be considered discriminatory factors. So everyone, including hansoms and growlers, calmly continued … at least until August 1933, when the Assistant Commissioner of Police, then controlling cab trading, announced that cabs with fifteen-plus years' service, would be gradually withdrawn unless owners could demonstrate fit condition; and even then, no promises. No time schedule was specified but a cab's working life was thereafter progressively reduced to a decade. Furthermore, Dunlop, principal taxicab tyre suppliers, had been making tyres of a specific size for Unics, Citroëns and older generations of Beardmores. With numbers decreasing, tyres would be phased out in favour of smaller-gauge equivalents (balloon style). However, they supplied conversion arrangements enabling older cabs to take new tyres, continuing from 1933 until aged ten.

In practice, plans were frustrated by the Second World War's outbreak, being renewed when the last pre-war cab withdrew in 1955. Although the ten-year limit was never enforced, a new test was introduced making older cab maintenance une-conomical. Thus, once the 1930s new design rush had subsided, consolidation and gradual improvement were emphasised rather than innovation. As older cabs rapidly disappeared, only three major firms were in serious production, varieties dramatically reducing. Ford made a mere token gesture in 1936 with an experimental cab – a specially designed limousine body being mounted on a standard 22hp V8 chassis – but the 40ft turning circle ruled it out. (Updated Metropolitan Police Regulations for Construction and Licensing of London Motor Cabs are in Appendix 7).

Perhaps for this reason, and growth of rival forms of transportation, London's cab population never exceeded the 10,000-plus of the pre-Great War era. The interwar years saw the figure at around 8,000. However, drivers far outnumbered cabs, many 'doubling' – day and night.

Regarding major differences between day and night driving, day drivers, as we shall see, are much safer but must face traffic jams – reliable in urgent cases like pregnant women suddenly going into labour – and stiffer competition from rival forms of transport, buses and the underground, although both run limited night services. Demand patterns also differ. Early morning sees fares as desert oases, most drivers preferring to start on local ranks. With queuing and demand at major railway stations at best unpredictable, they might get half a dozen short rides before rush 'hour' ends after 10 a.m. Thus their day's work gradually warms up. Problems often arise in late afternoon with well-to-do ladies, off to hairdressers or beauty parlours, or tourists, looking for museums, art galleries and similar attractions. Such people are rarely hurried while the drivers *are*, obliged to return to hand over vehicles. They must politely refuse late fares or have adequate excuses ready if they are overdue.

Against that, night drivers tend to pick up several early quick fares but must face impossible demands and criminals. Notably some foreigners regard cabbies as the local *factota* who will, for example, have drugs readily available. Night drivers are often directed to secluded back streets and then robbed of their day's takings. Assaults, even murders are common. Others are expected to act as agony aunts and listen to lengthy outpourings of passengers' problems – marital, social, financial. Against that, drivers have been lavishly entertained to meals, drinks and even holidays although they need to beware of dubious sexual invitations.

Current legislation prescribes that drivers may refuse fares if clients are obviously drunk, misbehaving, acting in a threatening manners or demanding journeys exceeding 12 miles. Drivers must not refuse on the grounds of race, creed, colour or sexual orientation.

Returning to tipping, the 1935 Hackney Carriages' Act made it strictly illegal. Drivers were debarred from either demanding or accepting money exceeding the meter display. In practice, there was no police interference unless the drivers demanded extras, then deemed deliberately overcharging. Opinions varied. Some drivers expected anything from 10 to 25 per cent as 'standard'; others felt it degrading to count on tips. There were views that tipping could be abolished but only by increasing basic fares considerably – a measure the Home Office ruled out.

As indicated, big fleets had gone, the only serious survivor being London General Cab Company. During 1931, for example, they boasted a 550-strong fleet, 320 Citroëns, the remainder their own. To secure night-driver service, they offered a free bus service (twenty-seater home-built Chevrolets) between 1 a.m. and 4 a.m. covering half a dozen routes from Brixton HQ. Drivers were keen, earning more for themselves and the company. Later, the company offered further perks including group insurance, free legal aid and advice, extras always welcome in an uncertain trade. Supply exceeded demand, there being few, if any, working-class hirers. Ranks were often full of frustrated drivers waiting hours for fares if they got any at all. Even at railway stations, long waits abounded. Waterloo, for example, had its famous Rats' Hole, accommodating 100 cabs, all awaiting Dover's Boat Train with varying patience.

Thus the mid 1930s was a frustrating time with taxi glut but manpower shortage. Prospective new drivers spent seven days a week studying the knowledge. A popular meeting place was Marcantonio's restaurant, neighbouring the PCO in Lambeth. In the drivers' 'club', trained ears could tap considerable information. Knowledgeable drivers were expected to keep abreast of the latest changes in street names, new roads and buildings, potential traffic problems at times of festivals, marches, visits of foreign dignitaries and the like. They also learnt about police restrictions, notably possible plans to limit cab numbers.

Still on traffic jams, I explode one well-publicised myth. Very often, if a particular area has heavy traffic, a driver will prefer the 'long way round' admittedly increasing the cost to passengers in terms of distance but saving time. Many believe that taxi drivers abuse this, deliberately taking a longer route to increase the total charge. This is fallacious; it does not benefit drivers to make extra money like that – false economy. Throughout taxi history, fare scales have always been front-end loaded so that drivers making many short journeys will, long-term, do far better than rivals making fewer, longer trips. Once drivers have picked up fares, their aim is to complete journeys as soon as possible (*time-wise* rather than *distance-wise*) and then pick up the next fare. However, the longest journey recorded involved a Finnish couple hiring a cab from their Nokia home, taking the driver south through Western Europe down to Spain before returning – two weeks' driving earned £9,000.

Even qualified drivers were at the mercy of the gods. They may have had the advantage of being their own boss, typically using a taxi supplied by a garage for two-thirds of takings but had no guarantees on numbers and/or size of fares. Furthermore, if they suffered vehicle breakdowns, be they by accident (their own or another driver's fault) or faulty vehicle, they had to hope that their garage could supply a spare or, if not, another could help. Thus gambling elements were considerable. Nonetheless, the profession attracted several students – typically medical – who, by dividing their time sensibly between driving and study, could earn towards their keep without total dependence.

Comparisons are made between cabbies and prostitutes – remarkable similarities. Both work with strangers picked up off the street; both at odd hours of the day when demand dictates and both are constantly in legal trouble. The difference, of course, is that, while it's well known that customers often hire taxis to engage in sex, cabbies are only rarely involved. No joke – police have firm control over taxi drivers' business, even to the degree of potential interference in private lives. Wives are known to threaten husbands with PCO action if they run off to gamble the day's takings away or indulge in extramarital favours. Of course, drivers also have problems, being unable to guarantee even approximate times for return home from work. At best, they leave wives very annoyed if not suspicious.

The Hackney Carriages' Act is one of many outdated pieces of legislation giving police considerable powers; they can revoke licences if they suspect inappropriate behaviour. Full details applicable to the Second World War are in Appendix 15. New drivers receive a small handbook 'The Abstract of Laws', briefly summarising requirements. Equestrian-orientated laws remained in force despite the animal's absence! Thus motor drivers had to be prepared for vehicles to 'drop dead', be ready to spray the 'corpses' with carbolic acid or similar disinfectant and be bound by rules governing everything from fodder to excrement!

Laws are problematic generally – notably those applicable to rank standing. Expressed in legal language, they leave even qualified lawyers, never mind drivers, with difficulty understanding them. All branches are full with ambiguities with vast scope for difference of opinion, even among experts. Long-term experience advises avoidance of arguments with police. Drivers have learnt to treat them with outward respect, if only because, when evidence conflicts, magistrates, irrespective of the truth, tend to favour the police. This was particularly relevant before the days of compulsory speedometers. Drivers must, therefore, suppress contemptuous feelings. That, of course, requires remarkable self-restraint on occasions, as police seem to enjoy catching drivers parking – even if only because 'offenders' have to visit washrooms. There are therefore well-known stories of drivers relieving themselves 'discreetly' against their vehicle, only to be 'done' for indecent exposure. 'Heads, I win …'.

That, of course, ignores health risks and here law struck again. In 1936, a Public Health Act came into force, under which drivers were forbidden from carrying corpses or passengers suffering from infectious diseases. How was he supposed to know if the passenger said nothing? And one common infectious disease around in the 1930s and '40s was venereal, hardly a topic for discussion with cabbies. However, an offence would not be punishable if drivers rectified matters by paying a modest sum to authorities for cab disinfection – particularly important if a passenger had died during the ride.

Further laws governed taxi sharing. The Public Service London Passenger Transport Act of 1933 permitted a one-off share but regular arrangements over given routes were prohibited. The idea was to protect the interests of rival forms of transport like buses and coaches but what happens in a case where two people shared a taxi once, became good friends, thenceforth continuing the arrangement – how is that illegal when they are, if anything, saving money and helping relieve traffic congestion? In Israel, typically, shared taxis, *sherouts*, are the norm! Morocco also allows sharing, notably for long journeys to suburban areas. One law tried to cover taking children to school, specifying that one person must pay the fare as opposed to a proportion each. There are a number of similar conundrums and police themselves have been guilty of law breaking in overcrowding taxis. They say that 'the law is an ass'. That poor, defenceless animal has never been so insulted.

Regarding other laws, few realise that, for cabbies, speed limits apply from both ends! Drivers must not exceed the 30mph speed limit, throughout most of London apart from arterial roads and dual carriageways where limits, always signposted, can rise to 40, 50, the national speed limit of 60 or, on motorways, 70mph. But at the other extreme, they must not loiter, hoping to pick up fares; they must move with the flow. Police tended to be strict prior to the Second World War, when plenty of officers were available; post-war saw some relaxation.

Sensible so far but once the 6-mile limit is considered, common sense has, as Margaret Mitchell put it, gone with the wind. The limit was introduced in deference to horses, hooves tending to become worn after longer journeys. Once the motor car took over, this rationale disappeared but the limit stood, relevant legality being, at best, vague. It was unclear whether a driver was allowed to charge extra if he exceeded the limit. In theory, magistrates could use discretion regarding suspected overcharging. In practice, drivers were convicted and fined (further relevant laws in Appendix 3).

Drivers were also expected to 'play the game' regarding 'common sense honesty', primarily regarding lost property. Gloves, umbrellas and scarves are the commonest possessions 'forgotten', but frequently handbags and briefcases, often with large sums of money and/or important documents like passports, expensive jewellery, even mink coats are left. Drivers are duty-bound to hand them to police within twenty-four hours. Authorities are not obliged to offer more than a £10 reward even if insurance claims involved run to far more. However, the Commissioner of Police may use discretion, awarding more if appropriate. It seems sensible that drivers instruct passengers to double check that they have not left anything, quickly scanning vehicles between journeys – this does not appear to happen in practice.

The year 1938 saw Ernest Mepstead drop out, selling his Fulham garage to Mann and Overton. The purchasers announced that their coachbuilders had large stocks of materials available. War preparations had escalated prices, notably to prospective purchasers outside military services; thus the company could still impose 'additional expense charges' on customers. The last completely peaceful month, August 1939, saw them deliver over thirty new and eight reconditioned cabs. The previous January saw the sales company, Beardmore Taxicabs Ltd, go into liquidation ahead of its prospective merge with Nuffield's organisation.

Also in 1938 came the first major threat to the licensed cab trade – the 'Streamliner'. The private-hire vehicle was fitted with a taximeter but charged lower rates. Operating in London's suburbia, it took advantage of the allowance of suburban taxi drivers' licences, which had been instigated from the previous year, and infuriated private hire operators, protesting against area invasion. Several groups were formed, some even employing licensed cab drivers for standard wages. The Joint Trade Committee approached Home Secretary Sir Samuel Hoare who commissioned the Hindley report, published in January 1939. This recommended licensing private hire. In practice, it never materialised because fuel rationing, necessary during hostilities, effectively eliminated streamliners. The report also discussed possible instigation of a period, below a decade, for compulsory cab replacement, achievable by manufacturing cheaper vehicles. However, problems surfaced in balancing one consideration – cabs doing far more work than cheaper private-car counterparts – with another – passengers wanting up-to-date vehicles.

Hostilities saw cab manufacture virtually ceasing, reducing London's fleet. The early months saw near normality. Beardmore were even manufacturing and selling new cabs but with these being based on Hillman chassis, such activity ceased when supplies ran out. Similarly for Mann and Overton – they had several cabs ready but as hostilities intensified, materials became increasingly scarce, order completion inevitably becoming more difficult. Prices increased and by spring 1941, government restrictions practically ended manufacturing. Thenceforth, they concentrated efforts on their machine shop, making and repairing spares. They did, however, run their fleet of sparsely available cabs.

The 1940s Blitz, with bombing raids expected daily, saw over 400 cabs requisitioned for defence. Painted London Fire Brigade grey, they were fitted with machine guns for anti-paratroop patrol operations. Two thousand more were used by the Auxiliary Fire Service (AFS), trailers were bolted to the chassis for loading with ladders, axes and stirrup pumps. Luggage compartments conveniently accommodated fire hoses. Some owners drove themselves, towing trailer pumps, earning £3 weekly for driving and another £1 17s 6d for lending their cabs. Austin Low Loaders were common, recognisable with blackout markings and covered-up headlights.

The Home Guard also took several cabs for military transport service and training (fortunately proving unnecessary) was even given for possible invasion. Use could be made of the drivers' excellent geographical knowledge and more manoeuvrable cabs could usually arrive on troubled scenes well before large, heavily loaded fire engines. Such cabs carried up to five men, usually older drivers unsuitable for military service, easily distinguished by their London Fire Brigade uniforms and steel helmets.

Similarly for hospitals, older drivers were recruited to drive ambulances, 'Great War experience' proving invaluable. However, blackouts took their toll, with countless fatal accidents involving both drivers and pedestrians. Further complications were caused by road closures enforced by bomb damage. Bilking increased dramatically, nothing being easier than disappearing into the dark. Little notice was taken of authoritarian comments about 'conscience'. Police even refused to allow illuminating meter flags; only buses were allowed indicator board lights. Only comedians had field days – a well-publicised navigation tip was: 'If you drive down The Mall and hit a cyclist with your offside wing, assume you are too far to the right and vice versa – easy!'

Thus the total pre-war cab force, nearly 6,700 (including seven growlers and one hansom – horses still there; the hansom driver made the last hire-ply application from September 1946, keeping his licence to April 1947) was reduced considerably. Heavy bombing caused losses exceeding the Great War's and by 1945's armistice, the population had dropped below 3,000, leaving many drivers unable to find cabs. Despite desperate efforts by Mann and Overton to keep damaged cabs active, many were ruled out, lacking spares. Even lucky drivers faced petrol rationing and a consequential one-third reduction in earnings.

Premises were similarly affected. Beardmore's Colindale works were turned over for war necessities. Their Great Portland Street showrooms were bombed into demolition, offices being re-established down the road at Luther's Austro-Daimler Concessionaire building. Beardmore, however, maintained their interest, negotiations taking place between Luther and Lord Nuffield aimed at replacing William Watson as London agent for Morris Commercial cabs. There were plans for new vehicle production at Wolseley's factory in Birmingham's Ward End suburb. Charles Van Eugen was recruited as designer, planning a box-sectioned, cross-braced chassis. The engine, designed by Nuffield's Marine/Commercial Division, was a derivative of the XP series 1.8-litre engine used in the Morris 10 and MG Midget. This had a dry sump with an oil tank mounted under the radiator. Coach-landaulet style bodies were supplied by Paddington's Jones Brothers; 1940 models were deep blue.

Of two prototypes, the first was presented to the PCO for approval in mid June of that year but met with initial reluctance, the PCO clearly wishing to 'have their cake and eat it' wanting cabs to closely resemble contemporary private saloon cars while still displaying clear distinction. In mid July, Beardmore's representative, Mr Vaughan, presented the second. They ran it throughout hostilities, covering over 100,000 miles (using other cabs' rations) being driven by a young licensed cab driver medically exempt from war service. This eventually became the 'Oxford' in 1946, detailed later. Mass production was postponed indefinitely. Despite the cab being clearly below required standards, approval was granted but plans were then abandoned.

Hostilities prompted the government to institute an immediate daily limit of two gallons per cab but in October, this was relaxed to three. Drivers were encouraged to use nearly 200 telephone-equipped ranks. Provinces were hit harder, restricted to twenty gallons monthly. However, following protests by W. Seaton, representing the Streamline Taxicabs Owners' Association, to the minister responsible, Sir Geoffrey Lloyd, a more generous allowance was gradually introduced for London parity by winter 1940–41. Sadly, late autumn 1943 saw further problems when MP John Mack requested Parliament to reduce numbers of permissible taxis, hopefully saving more fuel. Following nearly a 100 police prosecutions of drivers who had refused customers, another MP suggested that journey lengths be limited. In respect of numbers, the Home Secretary emphasised that they were heavily down already with a consequent shortage of taxis. However, a Control of Fuel Order of March 1944 imposed a 5-mile journey limit unless travellers were police or other servicemen.

As the war progressed, increasing numbers of younger drivers were called up, giving a silver lining in that fewer drivers sought cabs. Women could not be recruited for lack of geographical knowledge. The war's end in May 1945 saw scarcely half the drivers demobilised considered medically fit to resume normal employment. Nonetheless, despite labour and parts shortages, there were well over 5,000 taxis serviceable and although most were 10-plus years old (the PCO having relaxed the ten-year rule), many could continue for another decade.

5

The post-war period: 1945-61

Armistice found the trade in a poor, depressed state with no new cabs available for several years. Survivors – fewer than half the originals (the fleet probably reduced to between 3,000 and 4,000) – were, at best, battle-torn. They would only benefit from minimal maintenance in an environment where labour and spares were, at best, in short supply. Of cabs returned from London's Auxiliary Fire Service, more than half were unfit to resume normal duties. However, many of their parts could be 'salvaged from the wreckage' for other vehicles; beneficiaries were used well into the 1950s, some serving as taxis, others converted into vans or sold privately.

The PCO decided that, at least for the present, the Conditions of Fitness should stand. Thus Nuffield engineers, led by Charles Griffin, managed to get the first post-war cab, the Oxford, approved during autumn 1946. With a new composite body – pressed steel panels placed over an ash frame with a fixed head – production commenced in 1947 around Birmingham, at Drews Lane until 1949 but mostly at Morris-Commercial's Adderley Park plant thereafter. Cost was critical. Inevitably, war caused considerable inflation but, worse still, the government imposed a one-third (33⅓ per cent) purchase-tax levy on new cabs. Overall effects increased the new Oxford's price close to four figures, more than double its predecessor's, the G2SW. The trade could thus ill-afford to replace all cabs lost.

Additionally, increased petrol prices necessitated higher fares for a public left with little to spend. In consequence, cabs 15-plus years old had to be maintained in an industry booked for a long, hard struggle.

The first taxi produced – the MK I, London's first radio cab; Cambridge and Bournemouth had pioneered them a year earlier – came in February 1947, during the notoriously cold winter. The prime difference between pre- and post-war cabs was the change from coach-built landaulets – thenceforth, with the folding hood, to be passed into history – to fixed-head limousines of pressed steel or aluminium.

Between 1947 and 1955, about 1,800 Oxfords were built, based on a 1940 pro-totype that had 'proved itself' with 100,000 miles' wartime service. But such new taxi development was hampered for several reasons. Firstly, craftsmen needed for coach-built bodies based on ash frames proved unavailable post-war. There were design faults, primarily attributable to rushed, poor-quality development. The 1.8-litre, four-cylinder overhead valve engine had been linked with a three-bearing crankshaft, failing frequently, at best operating raggedly. The autovac fuel system was also unreliable. Secondly, the available steel was substandard. Thirdly, Purchase Tax, doubled to 66⅔ per cent, made the price, £997 8s 4d, prohibitive. Early models had no window to the driver's left but a fully enclosed version was introduced in 1948. The dark interior of the four-light body may have met pre-war standards, but two years later saw a private-hire variant with a nearside front door and a six-light body in line with contemporary Austins. In 1949, the MK II and then the 1950 MK III showed improvements on several counts.

Pre-war distributors were William Watson & Co. but ageing Mr Watson recom-mended that Beardmore, who had no post-war cab themselves, take over to sell about 1,800 vehicles. However, in the rival camp, Austin offered Mann and Overton a modi-fied variant of their 12hp chassis. Mann and Overton had no new cabs to sell, 12/4 chassis having run out of production. They did, however, acquire a number of pre-war cabs, used by the AFS, in near-new condition. Their numbers, however, would hardly begin to meet demand. Fortunately, the head of Austin, (Leonard Lord, appointed by Herbert Austin from 1938) assured Robert Overton that Austin had full commitment to cab trading. Austin, knighted and awarded a peerage, died in 1941.

The variant was already ten years old but was combined with a 14hp, 1.8-litre side-valve engine, effectively a 12hp unit with extra boring, and a steering wheel adapted for the 25ft turning-circle. The first such chassis was delivered in autumn 1945, the magazine *Steering Wheel* publishing detailed specifications in December. Austin placed identification letters, typically BBS or BSQ on each model, their new taxi series bearing the code FX. Mann and Overton started tests on the chassis with a body from an old cab and the engine, (the light 12/4 of 1.5-litre capacity), gearbox and other compo-nents from the old Austin 12 car adapted in their own workshops. They found several shortcomings, the engine's 40bhp being insufficient for the 28cwt cab to keep up with contemporary traffic.

That ruled out the prospective FX1; it only reached drawing-board stage. However, Austin persisted. Their sales designer, J.W.R. Penrose, sent drawings for a new chas-sis – the FX2 – to the PCO and approval was granted early in March 1947. Robert Overton, convinced modernist, was particularly keen on pressed steel replacing old-fashioned ash frames. Coach-built pre-war cabs were considered too expensive, both to manufacture and maintain. While Austin could provide the chassis, they felt that they had neither production space nor labour – specialists demanding £15 per week – to build steel bodies. On the advice of Austin's Joe Edwards, the Overton brothers approached the Ministry of Works for advice on prospective body-building companies. They were introduced to Ernest Jones and Jack Orr and referred to Bobby Jones, founder and administrator of Carbodies Ltd.

Thus 1945 sees this important company joining our story. Briefly, Jones, in car-body manufacturing since 1919 under the umbrella of timber merchants Gooderhams of Coventry, had worked with his son Ernest and workshop foreman Jack Orr. Other important designing names joining later were draughtsman Jake Donaldson, Don Cobb and Bill Lucas. Robert Overton joined in 1934. Austin had already used Carbodies' skills with Kirksite (an alloy of low melting point) tools during the war in manufacture of Three-Way Vans. Carbodies had often accepted small jobs uneconomical for bigger companies.

On Bobby Jones' retirement in 1954, having sold Carbodies, dealership was passed to Beardmores in Hendon. Their sustained efforts resulted in Morris Oxfords being passed fit from late autumn 1946, going into mass production the following year so that Beardmores could sell them to a decimated trade. Now suddenly, Mann and Overton, market leaders for so long, found themselves dethroned, desperately need-ing a new start for survival.

An agreement was signed under which Austin would supply chassis to Carbodies. Carbodies would then build the bodies, mount, paint and trim them and arrange for delivery of complete cabs to Mann and Overton's London depot. Provincial sales were conducted by Austin themselves through their own depot in Redditch, Worcestershire. In addition to the FX2 taxi, a hire-car version, FL1, was planned. Jake Donaldson and Eric Bailey of Carbodies completed the design, first exhibited at Earl's Court's Motor Show.

Mann and Overton (50 per cent) joined Austin and Carbodies (25 per cent each) to fund tooling, costing £250,000, and body manufacture. Financially, holding the major share proved crucial for Mann and Overton's future.

Early FX2 drawings were delivered to Carbodies' chief draughtsman, Don Cobb, near Christmas, 1946, Jack Orr directing prototype building. Several years' London work was planned before selling to York but problems surfaced. Cash flow was slow, Mann and Overton being dependent on revenue from reselling pre-war cabs. Consequently, contrary to plans, the first prototype was designed and manufactured in 'coach-build' style, with aluminium panels.

On Mayday 1947 (appropriately?) Ernest Jones sent body drawings to the PCO ahead of the Offices' inspectors' arrival at Carbodies on 20 May. Joining the inspec-tors' meeting were Robert Overton and Herbert Nicholls of Mann and Overton with Carbodies' Jack Orr and Ernest Jones. Mr H. Gould, the inspectors' chief examining officer, reported to the Commissioner of Police giving an outline of general style. No explicit rules for taxi design were enforced but he indicated a problem in that many cab-trade members – notably night drivers – favoured three-quarter limousine style affording greater passenger privacy. One solution was to fit panels partially covering their window. But this apparently spoiled the modern appearance, turning it into an old-fashioned, almost hearse-like vehicle. They thus proceeded with the three-window saloon style, allowing darkened glass for passenger back windows and forgoing internal rear-view mirrors.

Other problems included the excessive size of 'hire' signs. Also the PCO could not decide on which shade of yellow was appropriate for front windows. After Ernest Jones's trials with companies like Pilkington and several refusals from London, three weeks elapsed before a binding decision was made.

Final shade approval arrived in June 1947 but further problems arose during October when chassis and body approval were confirmed. Austin's plans for private cars involved using larger engines than those planned for cabs and, as it was uneconomical to produce separate engines for relatively modest taxi numbers, Mann and Overton had to accept the offer. A 2.2-litre engine, used successfully on the Austin 16 saloon of 1945–49 (and fitted to the later A70 Hampshire and Hereford saloons – no 'Hertford' model was produced) was therefore fitted early in 1948. This produced 52bhp at 3,800rpm, later increased to 56bhp. Thus, inevitably, preliminary tests revealed slightly increased fuel consumption. The hire sign was altered and with minor changes, the new cab became Austin's FX3. Final approval for the passenger compartment's rubber mat arrived in mid November and for tinted windows, in May 1948.

The FX3 – marketed as Austin Metropolitan Taxicab – was introduced in June 1948, from Mann and Overton's Wandsworth Bridge Road premises with a body longer and lower than pre-war predecessors'. While the kerbside luggage platform remained, the landaulet top was removed. Front bulbous wings flared wide, sweeping down to the front shield or 'apron' to which was attached a steel bumper. Other modern features included domed headlamps, a raked windscreen and a rounded bonnet. The bonnet opening retained its 'vintage' style, being designed in one piece, opening upwards. The more traditional side-opening was fitted later. Additional standard equipment included a locker on the left-hand running board and a tool-box under the driver's seat. The boot accommodated modest extra luggage and the spare wheel. The driver's compartment was completely enclosed with a glass sliding partition between him and the luggage platform for easy taximeter access. The windscreen was adjustable to the horizontal position, helpful in fog. The driver's door had a spring-mechanised drop glass, all others having spring-loaded glass. The passenger compartment maximised comfort and ease of service with a tinted rear window, against sunlight and snoopers, a rear bench-type seat and two other folding seats, hand-trimmed with buffalo ('buffed') leather hide.

The floor was matted, easily raised for chassis access. Door-panel ashtrays could be emptied externally. Twin interior lamps were operable by driver and passengers. A ventilator was positioned above the rear luggage platform partition. Although not initially standard, provision was made for internal heating, warm-air outlets being placed beneath the rear passenger compartment seats and near the driver's feet. A hydraulic jacking system enabled the vehicle's front or rear to be raised for maintenance.

This cost £936 1s 8d including purchase tax (hopefully the £2 premium over the rival Oxford would be outweighed by the value of the new features) but became more expensive, just over £1,270 including more than £450 PT (double the previous level) by 1952. Purchase tax doubling on most motor vehicles was introduced for military funding – far-east battles, notably Korea and Malaya, and the Cold War was (most inappropriately) warming up as threats from Communist Bloc countries intensified. The spring budget of 1950 was expected to raise over £800 million.

As expected, early sales disappointed. Both fleet owners and mushes sensibly considered the investment at best dubious with expenses doubling while fares remained unchanged. Then an increase of one-third was permitted, flagfall raised to 1s 3d. However, benefits were short-lived and effectively nullified by a further increase in cab cost of about £100, and that of petrol to 21.25p per gallon, not to mention restriction of the hire purchase period to eighteen months. With the situation becoming intolerable, Robert Overton, with two transport unions' representatives, lobbied the government for removal of purchase tax on cabs. Luck was in, with the government having changed from Labour to Conservative and new incumbent R.A. Butler being sympathetic towards the trade. In addition to tax abolition, he insisted on legislation banning any future such tax on all PCO-approved vehicles. Purchases now increased markedly; pre-war vehicles rapidly withdrew.

Earlier, summer 1948 saw sufficient funding forthcoming from Mann and Overton, enabling Carbodies to arrange tooling for full-steel-body production. 'Full' is slightly misleading in that wood was retained surrounding the iron, wheel-encircling ring or 'cant' rails, windscreen header and arches, giving structural strength to the lower part of one of the supports or 'pillars' and the cab a satisfying 'coach-built' feel once doors were closed.

As indicated earlier, there were two main FX3 variants. The 'taxi' was a three-door Hackney carriage with an open luggage compartment. The 'hire car' (FL1) introduced in 1950, had four doors with a bench-type front seat. A year later, rubber floor mats were introduced with two forward-facing seats replacing the taxi's rear-facing tip-ups; a frontal full-width bench accommodated a fifth passenger beside the driver. An umbrella-type handbrake replaced the tunnel-mounted lever but the floored gear change was retained, despite the rest of the industry's column-style uptake. Costing around £930, this was popular provincially. A diesel variant was also offered but overall, sales were only a quarter of the FX3's. The financial position worked against it. When purchase tax was taken off FX3s, there arose the question of approval for a four-door version. Despite no legal bar, the PCO was reluctant to approve.

Consequently the FL1 could not, in the eyes of Exchequer authorities, be considered either a taxi or commercial vehicle. Thus, still incurring purchase tax, it fetched about £972. At this time, there was a serious home-market car shortage, but the hire-car operators could buy pre-war Rolls-Royces, Daimlers and American cars assembled in Britain far more cheaply, even allowing for heavier running costs. Later on, as the home market improved and rival spares became increasingly rare and expensive, FL1s became more viable market contenders. They had success as passenger ambulances for day-care outpatients well ahead of the Ford transit minibus. (Note, however, that several provincial authorities approved four-door FX3s and, with added weather protection and an extra seat, they earned some popularity.)

In a further variant, 'scuttle', the chassis had front wings as well as bonnet and windscreen pillars to which further body additions were attachable. Two London fleet garages took a working prototype each: Central Autos of Chelsea the original coachbuilt cab, while W.H. (Henry) Cook of West London (mentioned earlier, 1860s), the other, steel-bodied. Operating the largest fleet of Austin cabs in London from their main Baker Street area garage, they provided full facilities and driver benefits, including insurance and sick pay.

October's Commercial Motor Transport Exhibition had the FX3 as an important exhibit. This and seven more cabs joined the fleet from December 1948. It was offered at basic cost in usual black cellulose, other colours being available at a premium. Although legally cabs could be non-black, few took the option, most buyers – fleet owners – preferring to save, choosing the cheapest 'standard' item. The FL1 was exhibited at Earl's Court's Motor Show later that year but heavy purchase tax ensured slow sales. The FX3's on-the-road price, £940, was double that of the old Austin 12/4. Everybody was struggling to recover after six years' inflationary strife. Worse still, the big Austin engine's fuel consumption reduced mileage per gallon from 25 to 18 although rectification was attempted with a smaller carburettor. A variant was licensed for America but tried unsuccessfully in New York. Drivers rejected manual gear-change.

Thus the early 1950s proved a poor period for London's cab trade. Comparing to pre-war, fuel prices had increased by 83 per cent to 3s 3¾d (16.5p decimal) with the cost of living more than doubling. Over 1950–51, fares rose by 66⅔ per cent, 9d to 1s 3d per mile, hopefully to restore some balance to operators' and drivers' financial position but public reaction was predictably negative, leaving the trade still depressed. Figures for 1950 show licensed cabs numbering slightly under 8,000. Wartime cabs were gradually scrapped – Low Loaders, around since the early 1930s, clocking over 2 million miles – owner-drivers and companies could ill-afford to buy new; many had to stop trading; only about 130 new cabs were licensed in 1952. That year saw Austin and Nuffield merge as the British Motor Corporation, (BMC); it was realised that the market could not accommodate two taxis. Following Nuffield's retirement soon afterwards, Leonard Lord was deputised; hopefully to lead Austin to partnership dominance.

With the FX3 having the newer design, the similarly priced Oxford needed phasing out over the next two years with spares available for at least a decade. Nevertheless, problems still appeared. The FX3 had embarrassingly high fuel consumption, hitting fleet proprietors. Worse still, drivers, dissatisfied with their modest share of fares, struck, being rewarded with an increase in their meter fare share from a quarter to three-eighths.

Beardmore were told that Oxford production would end in 1953; they would be denied rights to continue. They could thus choose between servicing existing Oxfords until spares ran out or turn immediately to a new design. Preferring the second option, they returned to making their own MK series at The Hyde in Hendon. Next was the MK VII. Beardmore had the Rubery Owen Oxford chassis available so, after initiation, involving the Ford Consul, works manager J. Bates planned a cab with new running gear. A meeting between him, Francis Luther and the PCO's Superintendent Gould heard Gould express concern at the possibility of jamming in the steering-column gear-change linkage – similar problems occurred in Ford cars – but welcoming innovative change, he encouraged Bates and Luther to produce a prototype. Beardmore aimed to produce the lightest, most economical and versatile cab marketable. It thus needed a high-quality crafted body, using the finest materials for maximum longevity.

They reluctantly admitted inability to afford tooling costs necessary for an entirely steel body; facilities did not match the required types, viz. those at Carbodies, anyway. Also Hendon was too small for economic production scale. Thus Luther's wish for traditionalism was satisfied in the choice of a coach-built body built by next-door neighbours Windover. Rather than steel they used more expensive, but more readily available, aluminium for lighter weight and lower fuel consumption. The cab was submitted for approval early in summer 1954; the PCO found several design faults but Bates rectified them successfully by mid autumn. The first production model was due the next February.

However, Beardmore, facing problems with aluminium roofing, were already contemplating changes, plastic replacements being submitted for approval. June 1955 saw body modification with a different back end, a 'notch-back' style boot and shallower windscreen. The new back was included on a different-numbered chassis but roofing had to wait another three years.

This effectively left a two-horse race, Austin having improved their market share of twenty years previously to 80 per cent against Beardmore's 20 per cent. Beardmore faced further problems following the takeover of Windover (just on centenary) by Henlys motor chain. Body manufacture was thus discontinued and Beardmore turned to Weymann of Metro-Cammell Weymann for further supplies. In the current climate, Beardmore had to sell cabs at minimal profit to maintain competition with the FX3.

Nevertheless, prospects were still poor. As indicated, spring 1952's purchase-tax doubling contributed to the cab population dropping dramatically to under 5,500 by 1953. Despite deputations by cab-sympathetic MPs, the government would not relent. Robert Overton decided that, alluding to Edward VIII's immortal words to Welsh miners, 'something must be done'. He aimed for monetary relief by joining several leading cab-trade organisaitons, notably London Motor Cab Proprietors' Association and the Transport and General Workers' Union, to approach the Treasury, requesting that vehicles complying with London-ruling fitness conditions be exempt from purchase tax, then 33⅓ per cent. Following long, hard-fought negotiations, the Runciman Committee recommended lifting purchase tax and hire-purchase restrictions. The 1953 budget accepted these recommendations, as well as a complete abolition of PT on police-approved vehicles, reducing the FX3's price from £1,100 to £834.

Recovery was accentuated with the small diesel engine, the two effects combining to ignite sales take-off. Diesels had been used on heavy commercial vehicles for twenty-odd years and even pre-war, one cab driver, writing in *Commercial Motor*, proposed 'oil-driven' taxis. Diesel oil – a refinery product, 'DERV' (diesel-engined road vehicle) – carried minimal tax, selling at half petrol's price. Further advantages included 36mpg against petrol's 12–18mpg and engines that were less likely to stall in heavy traffic. Thus the extra purchase cost of £120 would be more than repaid in 50 per cent running-expense saving. Sadly, there was no home-manufactured oil engine under 3-litres capacity, i.e. one appropriate for London taxis. However, in 1953, the Hackney Transport and Engineering Company adapted the German diesel 1.8-litre engine (Borgward Hansa) for FX3s, fitting being completed by Dives Ltd of Stockwell. The result was, as expected, far higher mileage per gallon, albeit at the expense of power, cabs being markedly slowed down. Later that year, Standard Motors joined, bringing out a 2-litre, four-cylinder diesel unit – a Ferguson tractor variant nicknamed 'Fergie'.

Birch Brothers of Kentish Town, taxi operator and transport engineering company, offered a conversion scheme, charging £325 plus labour per new engine. Engineering company Perkins offered a similar service for a P4C diesel engine for £280. Birch were present on 20 August 1952, when one of their vehicles was passed by the Metropolis commissioner, fitted with a 2.1-litre diesel engine, manufactured by the Standard Motor Company, for use in 'Fergies' tractors. In 1954, they developed a prototype cab (called SJJ 111) with Standard running gear in a body manufactured by Park Royal Vehicles – the first four-door vehicle licensed in London. The seating arrangement was unconventional, three passengers at the back, the fourth beside the driver, facing rearwards. Luggage was stored in a rear compartment, accessed by a full-sized nearside door. However, only one prototype was made, licensed by the PCO just before Christmas 1955 and put to successful six-month testing in early 1956. Standard, concentrating on their new Vanguard, proceeded no further.

Ferguson's engine, used initially but seriously lacking in power, was unwelcome everywhere. The city's longest-serving and largest cab fleet was the London General Cab Company. Geoff Trotter, 1952 fleet manager, now managing director, remarked that neither Mann and Overton nor Austin were keen on engines being replaced by Fergusons. Following negotiations between Robert Overton and George Harriman of BMC, Austin responded in 1953 by announcing manufacture of their own light diesel engine. As indicated, this was more expensive than the petrol engine (£942 against £847) but cheaper running costs made it more competitive with the Morris Oxford and Beardmore. Consequently, within a year, London agents were selling nine times as many diesels as others. In 1958, Perkins brought out their '99' 2-litre diesel for installation in Winchester and Beardmore cabs.

By mid 1954, when Carbodies were taken over by giant conglomerate BSA, Austin had produced a diesel variant of the 2.2-litre petrol unit. On gaining approval, a few were fitted out for a six-month trial. Tests were successful, showing improved mileage, 30 per gallon from the cheap fuel, extra expense being comfortably outweighed by fuel-cost saving. The only complaints forthcoming related to excessive oil consumption and several cracked valve seats. Thus it was proudly displayed as the FX3D at that year's Commercial Motor Exhibition. However, Trotter was still unhappy, referring to difficulties regarding split plugs and blocks with core plugs blowing out. He also considered the doors over-sized, overweight and opening the wrong way.

Take, for example. an American serviceman, who, arriving at this destination, was in such a hurry to leave that he opened the door before the vehicle stopped. Damage was caused; he was fined by local magistrates. However, the need was felt for a design revision to avoid such incidents. The cab was refitted, rear doors having forward-facing hinges. Up to then, according to the Conditions of Fitness, rear doors had to be hinged on rear pillars, the PCO insisting that forward-hinging favoured bilkers. However, for improved safety, they relented. Thus this cab was re-admitted with no consequent trouble; but so far, it was alone. An Overton cousin, now their new manager, decided to wait for further authoritative reaction before building more cabs so designed. Eventually, he decided to stick with the old one, seeing little point in spending money on something not legally necessary. Despite the court case, Trotter felt that rearward-opening doors were still unsatisfactory.

He was also unhappy about the bonnet design and – more serious – 'reverse running'. Unless cycle timing was perfect, the engine could fire before the top of its stroke, sending it into reverse with smoke clouds belching out everywhere, terrifying the driver. Problems were eventually cured, Austin fitting a freewheel preventative device and although, even then, it was not ideal, 90 per cent of new FX3s sold in 1955 were diesels, purchasers proving happy to pay the extra. By that year, one-third of London's taxis were diesel powered. With petrol costing 4s 1½d (20.4p) per gallon, diesel buyers saved about 10 per cent.

In 1954 FX3s also enjoyed considerable bodywork and fitting updates. Steel replaced wood for wheel arches and supporting posts and semaphore indicators or 'trafficators', problematic in service and maintenance, gave way to roof-mounted Lucas Limpet flashers. Tail lights were also redesigned for compliance with anticipated legal changes. Details were submitted to the PCO in May as one cab, selected from Levy of King's Cross's fleet, was fitted accordingly; strangely it already differed from others for another reason – doors.

Meanwhile, foreign buyers caught on and exports, about 700, to countries as widespread as Spain (about 250), Eire, Sweden, Denmark, Iran and New Zealand increased sales to five figures. Furthermore, several petrol-engine owners arranged for conversion to Austin diesel power as did others with Fergusons or Perkins. Their wisdom was proven by the 1956 Suez crisis, which caused severe petrol rationing.

As mentioned earlier, radio-controlled cabs started shortly post-war. In 1953 a group of owner-drivers clubbed together, establishing a company, Radiocabs (London), buying up a station and paying £25 each for two-way sets with a weekly user charge of £1 8s (£1.40). This arrangement is normal today but then traffic congestion played havoc with those trying to organise trips, time-wise, and after six years, they gave up. However, other companies were more successful and 600 cabs operating during the 1950s were joined by 200 more by 1971 — particularly helpful when working with emergency services.

Once they ran out of Wolseley Oxfords, Beardmore brought out the MK VII in September 1954, exhibiting at The Motor Show. This was their first post-war design but the last with three doors. A fourth was added in 1965. Presentation to the PCO and approval took place either side of Christmas before cabs were offered to drivers for testing in January 1955, coming into service the following month. Appearance-wise, it looked old-fashioned but the most dramatic change was in body construction — aluminium — and fibre-glass wings. Early examples also had fibre-glass roofs but here, following peeling and paintwork cracking problems, steel was preferred. Using Ford-Consul running gear, it markedly improved on predecessors, being a pioneer in using hydraulically actuated brakes.

Production ceased in 1957, managing director Francis Allsworth starting work on its replacement, the MK VIII, with a chassis earmarked for prototype-construction early in 1960. The beam front axle and cart springs remained but the wheelbase was extended by 2in. A year later saw plans submitted to the PCO, with the Totton, Southampton firm of Hampshire Car Bodies set to build the prototype body from Glass Reinforced Plastic (GRP). Mid March 1961 saw Mr Perrett, Chief Inspecting Officer of the PCO, visit the new model. He found Conditions of Fitness satisfied but was disappointed on several counts. Wheel arches were of unacceptably acute shape and the grille was too flat. The roofline, 3in above that of its predecessors', was too bulky. Nonetheless Beardmore, undeterred, approached the London General Cab Company for finance. Board representatives turned up at Weymann in Addlestone but, also disappointed, and feeling a need for more compactness, refused. However, it became the basis for the futuristic Metro-Cammell-Weymann — London Cab Company's Metrocab. October, 1958, saw general sales manager Ted Vaughan contact the PCO, informing them that winter 1959 would see Beardmore close the Colindale factory and move cab manufacture and assembly from Hendon to Weymann's factory in Addlestone. Graham Terrace Motors, a Beardmore associate, fulfilled servicing.

Also in 1958, the Perkins 1.6-litre diesel engine variant was introduced. Initial drawbacks, notably excessive noise and axle-beam-mounted semi-elliptic front springing, proved off-putting to many test drivers, notably mushes. However, soundproofing and other modifications, introduced over the next few years, rectified most of the trouble and, as with Austin, greater running economy earned modestly improved sales. The coach-built body, by neighbouring Windovers of Hendon Ltd, had aluminium panelling. Subsequently, Weymann of Addlestone, Surrey, produced finished cabs until 1965, when production moved to Metro-Cammell-Weymann in Birmingham's suburb, Washwood Heath.

All cabs were now fitted with four doors and four-speed gearboxes. Engines of both types were available, the 1.7-litre Ford (petrol) or Perkins 4.108 (diesel). Sales were disappointingly sluggish; only anti-Mann and Overton buyers remaining loyal. That year saw Mr Boote, works manager of Metro-Cammell-Weymann, submit preliminary drawings to the PCO of a new prototype – 'Metro-Beardmore', using Rootes equipment, including the 1.6 Minx petrol engine. They also planned to offer a diesel alternative, using Perkins' 4.99 but this was in short supply. They thus planned their own diesel engine, an 'increased-capacity' variant of the 1.6-litre petrol engine, actually 1.725 litres.

However, time was short and when Perkins introduced the 4.108 engine, Rootes decided enough was enough. The London General Cab Company sent board members to examine the prospective Metro-Beardmore but they rejected it as oversized and overweight. Beardmore's last MK VII was delivered early in 1967. Maintenance for existing cabs was offered from St John's Wood's Threeway Garage but soon the party was over. Invitations were sent to regular customers to pay £100 to have their cabs filled with available spare parts. Once these ran out, the PCO started trouble by refusing to allow drivers to use imitation or 'pattern' parts, fearing substandard quality. That left owners with little option but to sell their cabs, driving Austins instead. This precipitated the FX4's monopoly, reigning for a decade or more. Beardmore's trading officially ceased in 1969 but still solvent, they remained registered for about three decades more.

On announcement of Beardmore's effective demise, Rubery Owen ceased chassis manufacture. Winchester now reconsidered. The original body had proved a poor installation on their original chassis so this was an excellent opportunity to redesign the GRP, arranging a new chassis. Again Wincanton Engineering were building and they produced an up-to-date design based on several elements from modern rivals. The back window was from Austin's FX4 while the tail lights came from Hillman's Hunter Estate. The interior sought economy with a plain grey double-skin finish. For design and manufacture of new chassis, Winchester turned to Southampton's firm of Keewest Engineering. The Ford Transit axles and the 1.7-litre Transit V4 petrol (Perkins 4.108 diesel) engine were retained. This was the Winchester MK IV, which displayed reasonable fuel economy but had arrived too late for significance.

Having envisaged an approximately decade-long life for FX3s, a rising junior manager, David Southwell, had begun talks with Jack Hellberg and Austin's design department regarding prospective replacement. Hellberg had moved from Nuffield on the sale of Carbodies, becoming commercial manager. He was requested during February 1955 to collaborate with Austin. Commencing negotiations in early 1956, they were blissfully unaware of incepting the longest-running and most widely recognised British vehicle to date. Loved or loathed, it became part of London's street 'furniture' as Austin's second postwar model – FX4 – the world-famous London 'Black cab'. York Way Motors operated a prototype from July 1958 but September saw its official introduction at the Commercial Motor Show. Sales started after general type approval was granted in late November.

It had started 'life' in Austin's Longbridge drawing office as ADO6 (ADO stood Austin Drawing Office, not much 'ado' about nothing here). A team of engineers and one of draughtsmen, led respectively by Albert Moore and Charles Benlow, started planning the chassis while Eric Bailey led his department on body design. Although no specification demanded that London cabs required separate chassis, it seemed economical to update the old FX3 frame with modern running gear from BMC's spare-parts stores. Tooling changes, costing £250,000, would take a year.

Early drawings and design stages saw major discussions centred around, amongst other things, a fourth door. The PCO would sanction it provided luggage space was not significantly restricted. Thus the FX4 had a nearside front door enclosing the (previously open) luggage compartment and accommodated three passengers on rear seats. Consequently, with two jump seats, capacity was up to five although Scotland Yard restricted it to four in London. Thus partitioning to the driver's immediate left was omitted for improved elbow room. Also – innovation – his seat was adjustable vertically. Secondly, there was a safety problem regarding the bonnet. If it was upward hinging, it could be blown open at speed, dangerously blinding the driver; hinging it to the chassis front was therefore preferred. A third controversy focused on the fixed windscreen. With likelihood of dense fog, common in London prior to clean-air legislation, an opening option was recommended. However, modern manufacturing trends favoured the fixed version and it was held. Fourthly, rear-seat headrests, deemed unhygienic, were dropped.

Adoption of independent front-wheel suspension had enabled engine repositioning, allowing greater space for driver and passengers. Frontal styling occupied the full width with a large radiator grille so that with running boards omitted the impression gave markedly greater width than the FX3's (actually 1 in excess!). Several innovations were apparent, notably American-designed Borg-Warner three-speed transmission for automatic gear change, independent-coil front suspension and a door to the luggage platform, all three making London taxi debuts. Borg-Warners became standard by September 1958. Sadly, the FX3's hydraulic jacks proved unacceptable on the new design.

(To be accurate, automatic transmission had been tried on the FX3 with the Borg-Warner DG150M unit – DG stood for Detroit Gear – and an automatic FX3 was submitted to the PCO in March 1957. Approval was granted for twenty cab conversions; eighteen materialised. They found general approval, complaints being restricted to oil leaking and mileage dropping by 3 or 4 miles per gallon. However, Austin never mass-produced automatic FX3s.)

Once mock-up design was approved, manufacturing the first prototype took eighteen months. London cab-trade representatives were invited to view it, giving unpleasant reactions. The principal criticism, in foul language, was directed against the overall bulk and weight although it was actually only 6in longer and very slightly wider than the FX3. The new length of 15ft was the maximum permitted by the PCO. Initial press reaction was exaggerated; they described it as 'considerably lower' (difference actually under 2in) and more streamlined than its predecessor, style traditional rather than advanced. A further, more serious complaint centred on the rear doors, which, like the FX3, were hinged at their rear edge in traditional style – deemed the 'suicide' doors. If a passing car travelling in the same direction were to hit it, passengers' legs would be sandwiched against the bodywork, whereas a forward-hinged door would simply be pushed away with far less injury risk. It thus seemed obvious to insist on front-hinged doors, enabling the driver to lean back, opening the passenger door without leaving his seat. Sadly, many thought this would favour bilkers.

The FX4 lasted about eighteen years, but there were several changes and modifications, detailed later. Early sales were all automatic diesels – 'FX4D', engine size just under 2.2 litres, supplied by BMC – their K series. Manual and petrol options became available, respectively from 1961 and 1962. The 2.2-litre petrol engine was favoured by owner-drivers who, commonly undertaking longer journeys, welcomed higher speeds, typically up to 75mph. Fleet-operated drivers spent more time crawling around crowded town centres. From 1971, a larger 2.5-litre British Leyland engine was preferred.

Production continued until October 1982 but eventually old diesel engines were discarded, failing to meet incoming European exhaust emission standards. Forced outside Europe's Free Trade Area, they went to India.

Once again, although petrol engines were cheaper, quieter and vibrated less, their higher running costs resulted in poorer sales. In fact, the Noise Abatement Society protested against diesels in 1968; other critics described them as 'proprietors' darlings' and 'cabbies' devils'. Many cab drivers disliked them – noisy, cumbersome and uncomfortable. One writer suggested that drivers be consulted at drawing-board stage, deploring early secrecy between Mann and Overton and the PCO.

The automatic gearbox was clearly futuristic but initially proved unpopular. Neither Austin nor Borg-Warner anticipated selling difficulties. Older cabbies particularly argued that 'automatic' was a very unnatural driving method. Encouraged to leave the cab in DRIVE at traffic lights, they undesirably had to keep the footbrake depressed. Extra cost and poorer fuel consumption also discouraged many prospective purchasers. Rectification was attempted by reducing top-gear engagement speed to 15mph. DG was unusual – top-gear engagement enabled by-passing of the torque converter, effectively using a direct drive through a single-plate clutch. That implied forgoing a major advantage of the torque converter – ability to dampen out twisting, or technically 'torsional', vibrations. This was critical as diesel engines were particularly vibration prone, resulting in excessive stress on the gearbox train, even causing break-up of the direct clutch's damper springs.

Thus, with poor and costly introduction to automatics, early production was slow; fifty per week were optimistically envisaged but barely 150 appeared after the first year. Early production exposed serious tooling inadequacies. Neither complex roof curves nor bonnets could be satisfactorily pressed. Production had to be postponed amid profuse apologies from David Southwell, writing to the PCO, explaining the delay. (He became joint managing director from 1966, Will Overton retiring after fifty-eight years' service as did his brother-in-law Herbert Nicholls after fifty. Robert Overton thenceforth became chairman.)

Consequently, many FX3s, licensed for ten years according to recognised London cab practice, needed extension for a longer working life. Such extensions were only granted on proprietors' special requests. The last FX3 retired in 1968.

The FX4 was now a decade old and August 1968 saw the Consumer Council pointing out that, if the taxi carried one passenger, (s)he effectively occupied 44sq.ft of road space against 6 with a bus. Therefore proposing that smaller cabs were more appropriate, they called for more compact vehicles with the positive characteristics of current models. However, they accepted that the FX4 should be retained for certain work and the difficulty of operating two cab types. One would drive the other off the road as in 1926. The council also suggested introduction of taxi-sharing, along the lines of Israeli *sherouts*, taxi wardens being placed at big railway stations etc. organising passengers wanting similar directions.

Accordingly, a 1970 Central School of Art and Design student, 24-year-old John Redmond, produced a blueprint for a six-passenger taxi-cum-minibus of 13ft length. It would work as a normal taxi during off-peak hours but during morning and evening rush hours, as a variable-direction minibus. The first hailing passenger would choose the direction; the area would then be displayed on a panel above the windscreen after which others, similarly-bound, could join. This was electrically powered by two electric motors running on lithium-nickel fluoride batteries.

Another possible alternative was proposed in June 1971 by the staff of *Autocar* magazine. Their more conventional idea was based on the Bedford CF van chassis, the van powered by a Vauxhall Victor 2000 engine under a short bonnet. This accommodated four passengers in a vehicle of only 12ft 6in length, significantly advantageous over the FX4's 15ft. While complying uniformly with Scotland Yard requirements, the proposed vehicle appeared markedly different to the taxi. However, when Vauxhall Motors were approached, they declined, feeling that the considerable development work and retooling were unjustified, considering volumes of expected sales – problematic on all new taxis.

Even on delivery, problems still abounded, sophisticated machines being more likely to fail. No amount of manufacturers' workshop testing could comprehensibly anticipate street troubles. It only needed a modest front suspension bounce for the bonnet to jump off its safety catch. The best-known example saw a cabbie near Heathrow, whose bonnet flew back, crushing his FOR HIRE sign and blinding him for an accident. The original door design, theoretically excellent, proved hopelessly difficult to manufacture and finish. Interior door handles, originally from Austin Westminsters, proved very brittle.

Also on the 'brittle' list were front door cables, used by drivers to pull doors closed. The obvious solution was a thicker cable but none was readily available if only because large orders would be needed for economy. Clearing old stock was also time-consuming. While the fourth door provided much improved weather protection, shortcomings in this area appeared. The PCO refused to allow soundproofing, fearing increased fire risk. The diesel engine's excessive noise proved tiring for drivers, not to mention increased difficulty in talking to passengers through small circular partition windows. Tall drivers found compartments cramped. The circular partition was changed to a centrally placed vertical rectangle in 1960 but other problems took a decade to solve. Austin decided that present tooling was largely inappropriate. The FX4 was costing Carbodies money, Austin having to provide £100 subsidy per cab.

The new decade, however, saw changing fortunes. In 1960 Austin retooled the boot lid exterior and roof as a four-piece assembly. They split the cost, over £180,000, into thirds, Carbodies and Mann and Overton contributing the other two. By early summer 1961 Mann and Overton needed more money for retooling of the door arrangement to the 'clinch' type and the following year saw the old FX3 external door handles replaced by others of greater size, sturdiness and leverage. There were requests to introduce manual synchromesh gearboxes. September saw the PCO grant type approval for the four-speed Austin Gypsy gearbox for FX4s as an option to automatics. The following year saw all chassis fittings required for a manual gearbox becoming available so that the 2.2-litre, A70 petrol engine of FX3 days could also be used as an option with diesel. Consequently, of over 8,700 licensed vehicles in 1970, fewer than 1,000 were automatics. (Automatics were dropped from 1964). Provincial drivers who appreciated the extra speed, as well as hire-car and hearse operators, for which the chassis was thought particularly suitable, were most interested in the petrol option.

New models had a fourth door for a more complete appearance in line with current Austins, which had first appeared seven years earlier. Several other minor improvements, notably roof-mounted flashing indicators, appeared. This was manufactured in modest numbers until summer 1967 but sales hardly compared with Austin's and it seemed senseless to continue production. Beardmores commissioned a new design for an MK VIII variant but with re-tooling costs prohibitive, this did not progress beyond building a small-scale model. However, this design also found its way to Metro-Cammell-Weymann of Birmingham. Other work pressures precluded devoting full resources to rivalling the FX4. They started work on a 1:4 scale model but held it until 1968 when a pause in bus production gave the necessary breathing space.

There were other further possible rivals to the FX4. In 1960, The Owner Drivers' Society (who, for many years, ran Westminster Insurance Society for their members) took up manufacturing. After a questionnaire consultation with members, they offered a new cab design, 'Winchester'. Forming the Winchester Automobiles (West End) Ltd company to build it, they appointed leading light Ken Drummond as managing director.

Selling at a few pounds under the FX4's £1,171, the Winchester emerged during winter 1962–63, the first cab whose body was manufactured in GRP (glass-reinforced plastic). The first model, MK1, had a lightweight fibre-glass body, free of rust and corrosion, the bane of pressed-steel cabs. The illuminated recessed step was helpful to the elderly and infirm. Many were converted to run on liquid petroleum gas. The upright radiator grille was a distinctive 'taxi-style' feature. The obvious advantage was low maintenance but major faults attracted poor public and press awareness. Drivers complained of low power and excessive noise, despite fitted silencers. The unduly high chassis placement, necessitating a door step for convenient passenger entry, caused inconvenience to the driver's seating (very low and could not be lifted without painful steering-wheel interference) and left the internal running board 'on view' when doors were open. Also operating pendant-style pedals caused severe backache.

Manufacturers were the West Drayton, Middlesex company James Whitson. At best, production was slow at one vehicle weekly so Winchester could not compete effectively or buy parts in economic quantities. No two vehicles were identical, as expected from efficient production lines. Winchester were also unable to match Austin in respect of servicing provision. Most cabbies, particularly mushes, therefore opted for Austins.

The MK II variant, introduced in September 1964, attempted to correct these faults without adversely affecting running costs. With a similar body to its predecessor, it used a petrol engine. In turn, it was succeeded by the MK III from September 1966 on a new chassis, manufactured by Keewest. Predecessors had used rear axles and brakes from old Jaguars but these had been phased out, leaving the Ford V4 Transit engine, four-speed gearbox with rear axle and brakes on stage. New 14in wheels set the new vehicle slightly lower to the ground. The body was updated in 1968 in MK IV form, discussed later.

While failing to rival Austin there were still nearly 140 Winchesters around by Christmas 1970. However, Winchester Automobiles Company closed in 1972 following disappointing sales; with no further cab production liquidation soon followed. Two hundred were manufactured, most run by owner-drivers but some by W.H. Cook of Hammersmith. The dealership was largely run by Lots Motors Ltd of Chelsea. Only fifty were actually sold against very heavy competition, which soon arrived. Thus the proportion of London's cabs in mid decade was 98 per cent Austin FX4s, the handful of Winchesters and Beardmores making up the remainder, as the figures in Appendix 16 illustrate.

Also that year, John Birch designed a new cab – his MK 2. Standard Triumph's designer, an Italian, Giovanni Michelotti, had masterminded the Standard Atlas van, on which new cab styling would be based. The unit-constructed body had the engine and front suspension unreliably bolted to it. Furthermore, power was inadequate and there was frontal overweight imbalance. The front track was of insufficient width, instability resulting, leaving the van with little prospect. However, regarding cab conversion, there were several positive features. The 29ft turning circle could easily be reduced to meet the Conditions of Fitness. The new manufactured chassis could be bolted to the Atlas front sub-frame comfortably. Also Standard four-speed gearboxes worked well with Perkins' diesel 4.99hp engines for adequate power. Park Royal Bodies were thus commissioned for body modification, reshaping the roofline and re-orientating the rear window, creating extra space for the boot.

Assuming everything went as planned, Birch hoped to undercut Austin's FX4 by at least £200. The crucial last fence was, of course, PCO approval. Spring 1961 saw the PCO voice objections to Sir Austin Strutt of the Home Office. The chassis design displayed a narrow front track causing potential instability; furthermore, kingpins mounting directly on the transverse leaf spring were dangerous; spring breakage could seriously disrupt the steering. They therefore declined.

In 1968 the FX4 received its only major facelift. Earlier plans for replacement (ADO39) were abandoned. Rear wings were redesigned to accommodate tail lights from the MK II variant of the BMC 1100/1300 vehicle. Roof-mounted turn-indicators were henceforth unnecessary. However, separate front indicators were needed and were mounted on the appropriate wings below headlamp level. Drivers welcomed this updating, being even more pleased with noise reduction (long awaited), and 4in of extra legroom, achieved by angling the partition for a more tilted driving position. Sadly, this interfered with the rear-door aperture so that standard wheelchairs could not be admitted (not then considered serious; the FX4 had not been so designed, legislation not requiring it). Three years later, winter 1971–72 saw the 2.2-litre engine replaced by a 2.5-litre variant, raising top speed from 60 to 70mph, useful for motorway driving, notably to airports. However, this begat a new problem – drum-brake efficiency – discussed later.

That year, Metro-Cammell-Weymann entered the taxi field. Managing Director, and leading industrialist Tony Sansome sent design drawings to the PCO in late summer under the heading 'Project HO 10180'. The PCO accepted, expressing reservations only regarding wheels and humped floor. A scale model was commissioned from the Huntingdon firm of Specialist Mouldings (earlier linked with Beardmore). The London General Cab Company were invited to Washwood Heath to inspect a full-scale model. Sadly, Sansome's request for large-scale production and purchase was rejected. The board dismissed it as an oversized 'box on wheels'. However, they did not rule out revisions, offering consultation on future purchase should improvements prove adequate.

That same board then inspected another new model built by the Sandy, Bedfordshire company of Haring Conti Associates and mid October saw Messrs Whomersley and Cupwell of MCW visit the London General's Brixton premises for discussions. London General's chairman, Sir Neil Cooper-Keys, joined Messrs Trotter and de Ciantis, making up the negotiating sextet. The London General Board deemed the new cab hardly more than an over-expanded Austin FX4, leaving three options possible:

a) front engine with front-wheel drive;
b) rear engine with rear-wheel drive; and
c) integral body-chassis arrangement (i.e. sharing the stress equally): 'monocoque' construction.

London General felt that MCW needed to modernise, primarily for reduced weight and improved performance. However, MCW deemed modern ideas impractical, given limited time and funds. Compromise was needed and they eventually agreed that MCW would develop a conventional, reduced-size prototype.

Early 1969 saw Messrs Trotter and de Ciantis join PCO Chief Inspection Officer Mr Collins to see a mock prototype. Satisfied, Collins encouraged London General to invite MCW to produce a running prototype. Metro-Cammell's railway engineering team, directed by Frank Bonneres, produced designs of a box-style frame with an X-shaped brace for extra strength and rigidity. The Motor Industry Research Association were approached to assess quality, choosing one of three offered. A 1.75-litre Perkins 4.108 diesel engine was incorporated with a 30cwt Ford Transit all-synchromesh gearbox, a steering box with a new crash link and front and rear axles, the front axle having a beam narrower than on predecessors. The GRP body was designed in up-to-date style by Haring Conti Associates and built by Southampton firm Henlycraft. The large curved windscreen improved visibility. The overall length was a foot or more shorter than the FX4's, leaving tall drivers slightly reduced seating space but the weight was down by 56lb. Other new features included universal telescopic shock absorbers, servo-brakes and alternator.

A major problem – the steering ball joint – saw the PCO stand firm. The Conditions of Fitness demanded that such joints be fitted with bolts pointing downwards into the steering arm to which they were attached – 'non-pendant'. The PCO insisted that, unless this was respected, the low turning circle would result in excessive loading on pendant ball joints, accelerating wear for potentially dangerous consequences. MCW, however, argued that pendant style had been used in lorries and buses with minimal problems. Inevitably progress was delayed, with intervention by the Transport Road Research Laboratory finally persuading the PCO to relent.

Work started on the 'Metrocab' during autumn that year; just before Christmas, the chassis prototype was successfully presented to the PCO for approval. However, on presentation of the whole cab, the 'rough and ready' prototype, normally considered adequate, was rejected. Now the PCO demanded near 'production perfection', complaining of nearly sixty faults, notably around the front axle. Mr Everitt, inspecting, refused to accept modification, correspondence from Ford adding weight to his decision. He promised further cooperation but only if his advice was heeded.

Winter 1970 saw the revised version introduced at London General's petrol station in Southwark Street, but three more attempts by MCW were needed before type approval was granted that summer. Even now, this was deemed only 'provisional', further modifications being required before full production could start. Thus an experimental Metrocab appeared from then on, under the auspices of the London General Cab Company who ran the prototype for several years.

The new cab, given blue livery to match London Generals' pre-war variant, appeared more aesthetically pleasing than Beardmore's original prototype with its slab-sided body and large 'overgrown' fibreglass bonnet. A front-wheel drive set-up, 'monocoque' construction was proposed. With PCO regulations very strict, neither was adopted but the ideas were not that stupid. Metropolitan Cammell and Carriage & Wagon successfully produced nearly 200 London Transport trolley buses with no chassis. The cab's body and engine performed well in early years, low fuel consumption being particularly impressive.

The second prototype, a variant with similar bodywork, appeared in 1971. The collapsible steering column and servo-assisted brakes were standard fittings for the first time. Although the initial project was shelved within two years – among other problems, which included spare parts and the appearance of an improved FX4, and negotiations with Carbodies encountering union trouble – the Metrocab reappeared, as discussed later.

That 'new improved' FX4 was the brainchild of two famous inventors. Alec Issigonis, of BMC 'Mini' fame, was joined by David Bache of Rover, basing their design on the Austin-Morris JU260 van, currently weighing 15cwt and due for replacement. In the event, their LM11 proved a failure and Carbodies designed a variant, accepted as improvement. Mann and Overton, however, disagreed, deeming it unnecessary. The project never started.

As Christmas 1971 approached, Austin-Morris introduced the 250EA one-ton van, replacing the outdated Morris LD. The 2.2-litre engine (currently used in the FX4) was replaced by the more powerful 2.52-litre, 25V variant. This was then incorporated into the FX4, giving improved acceleration and a final ratio for top speed exceeding 70mph. A new alternator worked with a negatively earthed electrical system backed by a 12-volt battery.

Beardmore continued cab servicing until closure in July 1969. However, well over 100 MK VIIs were still operating by Christmas 1970, repair and maintenance adopted by Maida Vale's Clifton Garage. That, in turn, soon closed, ending Beardmore's cab association after just over fifty years. There was keen trade and press clamouring for a new cab, mirroring private-car advances. However, financial strain, affecting BSA and BLMC's Austin-Morris division restricted such progress. There was talk of a new LN11 but that was a non-starter, leaving nothing new but the disappointing Winchester.

In 1968, Birch Brothers built a Standard shooting-brake-style experimental cab but it never appeared. Trying again a decade later, 'Birch' taxis were designed very much in caravan and bus style by Alfred Hill of Park Royal Bodies. Breaking with tradition, the estate-style model had one passenger sitting beside the driver but facing rearwards while three more sat normally on the rear seat, placed forward from its customary position over the rear axle, affording more room. Frontal styling was typical of current Standard cars with rear luggage space allowing drivers extra room for personal belongings. One model was built for a six-month experimental run, actually continuing for four years. With Birch's trade well respected, some interest was shown but no further cabs so-styled appeared.

Further FX4 fault rectification was also needed. Carbodies' Chief Engineer, Peter James, suggested rear-end adaptation to accommodate new tail-light units so that the universally disliked clinging or 'limpet' indicators were removed. Beneath the bonnet, the two large 6-volt batteries were moved from their current position, resting against the bulkhead, one placed above each wheel arch. That eliminated problems of rainwater collecting beneath, rotting the metal over three to four years and giving the driver's right foot an impromptu drenching. His compartment had the same dimensions as the FX3 but new drivers had been brought up (operative word!) under the welfare state and being, on average, taller than predecessors, required greater leg room.

A long struggle saw Austin and Carbodies twisting Mann and Overton's arm (pulling their leg surely more appropriate) to allow for the whole partition to be angled backwards, enabling fitting of a tilting seat for four extra inches. The sliding sideways partition, used in the FX4's hire-car variant, was installed and repositioned but lack of foresight precluded wheelchair access. This was then considered unimportant, few wheelchair-bound people using taxis; twenty years passed before the truth emerged. Upholstery colour was changed to black. Vinyl had replaced leather for the trim from 1967. Finally, soundproofing was approved.

A modified automatic gearbox became available in 1968 along with radical interior design changes. Seat coverings had brown plastic, replacing hand-buffed leather. A year later, black vinyl was introduced with the passenger-driver division moved back a few inches, giving drivers slightly more room. Externally, the roof-mounted 'bunny ears' direction indicators were replaced by round flashers positioned between headlamps. At the rear, redesigned tail-lamp clusters from the BMC 1100/1300, incorporating amber flashers, were introduced. The tinted rear window ('privacy glass') gave way to clear glass, earning tourist approval but the opposite reaction from snoggers, who also resented the new driver's rear-view mirror, added as a 'safety' feature. Other alterations included removal of narrow radiator grilles, which had supported the centrally placed Austin badge, replaced by fractionally larger grilles with a revised-style badge offset to the nearside. The FOR HIRE indicator was replaced by 'TAXI' for universal recognition.

Additional improvements were, however, still needed. Body modification from 1970 included the distinctive roof-mounted traffic indicator being replaced by a more conventional arrangement. Driver communication was by sliding partition and cricket seats were of simpler construction. A new modified variant was displayed at 1971's London Motor Show, boasting a 2.5-litre engine, compliant with forthcoming noise and emission regulations and ensuring near saloon-car power. Furthermore, an increased rear-axle ratio permitted increased safe cruising speed. Optional extras included fog lamps, an electric clock and decorative embellishers. Non-black colours cost £25 extra. The most luxurious examples, offered by Bristol Street Motors, sold at £2,600. Police started showing interest in FX4s as observation and tailing vehicles, 'Q' cars, detailed shortly.

By now anti-theft devices, including four-door locks, had become standard, as were quarter-lights and an updated dashboard, on which passing light and horn controls were adjacent to the steering column. New problems concerned drum brakes, currently 1958 versions. With modern traffic flow demanding greater power and efficiency, two options appeared: switch to disc brakes or update by fitting larger drums with 'servo' assistance. Disc brakes had been tried on Austin Westminsters but fouled the suspension arm, restricting the turning circle. This necessitated fresh designs of either braking system or front suspension. A design for full servo braking was produced with attaching or 'pendant' pedals. Permission for alterations was obviously needed from Austin of Longbridge. Already losing interest in current FX4s, they acquiesced. However, finances were needed but Mann and Overton, while accepting need for improvement, refused, being in poor financial health following rampant mid-1970s inflation. Cab prices had rocketed from £1,500 (1971) to around £7,000 (1978), fares hopelessly lagging behind, leaving them in a wretched condition – certainly with no spare money for products not even ordered. The approach is detailed shortly.

The FX4's hire-car variant, the FL2, boasted a higher-speed crown-wheel assembly with the 'For Hire' sign omitted. The interior differed, the driver's compartment fitted with two separate seats rather than the FL1's bench. The extra passenger seat could be folded up against the full-width driver-passenger division, allowing extra luggage space. In the passenger compartment, two folding forward-facing jump seats complemented the heavily cushioned rear bench seat. There was also the option, popular with hospitals, of rear-facing taxi-style seats.

For FX4s themselves, further problems surfaced in 1973, manufacturers becoming duty-bound by EEC regulations, enacted from 1974. New requirements included a collapsible steering column, a safer facia and burst-proof door locks. Additionally, vehicles required crash testing. An appropriately modified cab with separate chassis was submitted for MIRA (Motor Industry Research Association) testing, being driven into a concrete block at 30mph. The company's worries proved unfounded. Later that year, the 2.2-litre petrol engine was withdrawn after satisfaction of new exhaust-emission legislation, operative from January 1974, proved too costly.

Thus, the FX4 and FL2 were thence only available with diesel engines.

Now there were plans for an FX4 replacement after thirteen years' production. There had been thoughts from 1965 when Mann and Overton had consulted traders, notably Ronald Samuels, for prospective improvements. Samuels listed as priority considerations:

a) smaller size
b) more economical running
c) simplified servicing arrangement
d) built-in taximeter from inception
e) separate chassis
f) sliding doors
g) forward control

The new model, the FX5, is discussed shortly.

The 1960s saw comparatively low inflation but, at any level, this had, historically, always been the cabbies' greatest nightmare. Fares could not be increased to mirror money devaluation without representatives going, cap in hand, to the Home Office, only to find no sympathy. The government's first consideration was always the customer and it is heartbreaking for someone, already working sixty-plus hours weekly, to be pushed harder still. The point that, unlike lorry and coach drivers, who had to take specified hours of rest for safety reasons, no limit for cabbies existed, merely rubbed salt into the wound. Taxi drivers have no benefits like golden handshakes, pensions and licence resale value and many less well-off drivers, unable to maintain required payments, had to return their vehicles after a few months.

Around 1962, rental arrangements were introduced, proprietors accepting that Home Office negotiations were hopeless. With running costs increasingly uncontrollable, they encouraged drivers to take up weekly rentals, under which they bought their own petrol and worked as long as they wished to earn as much as possible by 'going on the flat'. Drivers paid £14–16 per week (slightly more for brand-new taxis) to proprietors, who took on vehicle maintenance and upkeep. Thus they felt 'ownership' of their taxis without having to pay and could earn all excesses over the hiring charge. They also enjoyed extra security, being promised another vehicle should taxis be unroadworthy through accident or other reason.

The setup worked well for drivers but proprietors faced problems in securing enough staff. Insufficient numbers were willing to do the two-year knowledge stint on a moped; large garage proprietors had to open 'knowledge' study schools. Students paid modest fees on the understanding that they would be contracted to work for that particular garage for at least one year after qualifying. In practice, the obligation was met but then drivers moved to other garages offering cheaper rentals and/or higher commission terms.

Eventually, in 1969, the Home Office woke up, allowing considerable taxi fare increases but purchase costs increased in parallel. Proprietors raised rent up to around £25, leaving thousands of journeymen finding it more economical to buy cabs, typically for a down payment of £300–400 followed by £7 per week. They had to allow about £22 per week for repayments, fuel, insurance, meter rental, road tax and 'depreciation' for annual overhaul. The figures were similar to those for renting but, once repayments were completed, drivers enjoyed ownership. The disadvantage was that too many accidents and/or breakdowns would result in heavy repair bills and idle periods, second-hand spares proving too troublesome and expensive to be worthwhile.

Nevertheless, the advantage proved its worth and within days, new taxi waiting lists exploded; prospective buyers, formerly waiting a few weeks, now faced nearly two years. Many stunned proprietors retaliated by selling many of their vehicles to impatient drivers, thereby reducing fleet sizes. They also expanded activities to hiring out self-drive cars and offering wider repair and overhaul services to new owner-drivers.

With increasing popularity of London cabs in major provincial cities, Mann and Overton were offered distribution rights. In 1968 Austin amalgamated into British Leyland, dominating London's market with 95 per cent of active taxis; a handful of Beardmores and Winchesters making up the numbers. The management emphasised London's importance, focusing all efforts on that area. Provincial sales were therefore left to a few selected Austin dealers, primarily concentrating on outlets in Manchester, Birmingham and Glasgow. Overall figures topped 13,000 by autumn 1971. However, exports were nowhere near the FX3's. BMC decided that exporting without sufficient back-up (spares and services) was likely to discredit the company's reputation. It was uneconomical to maintain spares in foreign cities for vehicles whose annual production was under 1,500.

Thus the story of the 1970s differed from the previous decade. There was new blood on the board, with Andrew Overton, who worked on sales from April 1970, Michael Ray (cab driver's son working with Mann and Overton) and Carl Harvey, running parts operations nationally, all joining from 1974. Austin-Morris's division of British Leyland faced frightening financial problems and welcomed George Turnbull, from Standard-Triumph, to try rectification. He appreciated the necessity of closing loss-running plants, including Adderley Park, which had already confined activities to building FX4 chassis. Turnbull offered it to Carbodies, Bill Lucas accepting on condition that employees were transferred en bloc to Coventry without redundancies. That left Carbodies as sole FX4 manufacturer.

However, the new board members were wary of improvements, deeming them unnecessary modifications; Bill Lucas favoured working under new management. He thus approached Dennis Poore, owner of Manganese Bronze Holdings (manufacturers and suppliers of precision parts for the automotive, telecommunications and aviation industries) to give him forceful encouragement to buy Mann and Overton. Poore was a former motor-racing and motorcycling ace and – coincidentally, if readers recognise my name as a bridge-writer – a well-known rubber-bridge player. Although keen on cab-trading, he was not currently interested.

Fortunately, he soon changed his mind. BSA, which had encompassed the lion's share of the motorcycle industry with Triumph, Sunbeam and Ariel and since 1954, Carbodies under its umbrella, was running into trouble. Since the retirement of manager Jack Sangster it had found Japanese competition overwhelming. The government stepped in and approached Poore for help, clarifying that, without it, they would feel obliged to nationalise the remainder of BSA. Poore would thence face government-backed competition – not for him. Thus 1973 saw Manganese Bronze take over BSA and, with it, Carbodies.

For Carbodies and Mann and Overton, this was worrying news; they feared the new owners might close Carbodies, relegating the FX4 to history. This could have multiple adverse effects, even on the industry's legal environment. However, with Poore being a regular cab customer to his City offices, these worries proved unfounded. He was honoured to have this position; production continued.

From Britain's 1973 EEC entry, relevant vehicle regulations, explained earlier, had to be respected. Firstly, new safety regulations required protective steering, anti-burst door locks and crash-testing. Assessors would then try to guess whether (dummy) passengers would survive. Austin-Morris, already deeply financially troubled, now had to modify the chassis engineering. A crash link had to be placed in the steering column and the current steering wheel needed replacing by a rubberised centre variant. A protracted search eventually produced a German innovative door lock, modifiable and combinable with a push-button operated handle. The mechanism could be incorporated by moving interior handles to a central position on the door. A new instrument panel was added and the rear seat cushion modified. Emission restrictions were due the following year.

Mann and Overton offered a new cab for testing the new chassis and were successful, MIRA being keen to give a positive impression. Production could now continue with new energy. Spring 1974 saw the FX4's manufacturing figure exceed 25,000. Nonetheless, brake problems still abounded, the 1958 drums needing updating, if only to match the more powerful new engines.

Several ideas were tried. Ventilated front drums proved inadequate. Disc brakes (Austin had plentiful spares) were possible but required expensive front suspension re-engineering. MGB style discs fitted to suspension uprights would restrict the turning circle; circumnavigation would require excessively expensive front-suspension modification.

So drums were necessary and Carbodies engineer Peter James designed an arrangement by which full servo braking could be achieved by attaching pendant pedals. Sadly, neither Austin nor Mann and Overton could offer the necessary funds. With the clock ticking, Mann and Overton suggested a cheaper compromise, servos on the front brakes only. Motor engineers advised against this but production proceeded.

Incredibly, the PCO (probably hesitant about annoying Mann and Overton with the FX4 the only marketable cab) passed it, sales starting in 1976. The engineers were vindicated, cabs proving dangerously inconsistent. At low speeds, drivers couldn't taper the cab to a gentle stop – brakes 'snatched', stalling abruptly. Anyway, drums wore out within 5,000 miles, linings being even worse at 2,000. Trade press and independent expert reports were scathing but Mann and Overton stood their ground, insisting that drivers must accept the best of a bad lot.

The FX4 may have survived but the new rules had its victims. Austin's 2.2-litre petrol engine, failing to meet standards, was scrapped, Winchesters were abandoned without even testing. Doors, chassis and fibreglass were clearly booked for rejection; production had already ceased in 1972.

The new decade introduced another factor. Earlier, comparison of diesel with petrol had centred on price. Henceforth, however, exhaust fumes and atmospheric cleanliness were critical. Several owner-drivers tried to reduce running costs, using liquefied petroleum gas (LPG or simply propane). This proved advantageous with no exhaust fumes and carbon deposits just ½ per cent of gas used against petrol's 6 per cent. W.H. Cook and Sons of Hammersmith offered conversion facilities, fitting a special tank into the boot, moving the spare wheel to the luggage compartment. Converters were the Lipton Liquid Propane Carburettor Company, principally forklift truck manufacturers, but pioneering conversion during the1956 Suez Crisis. They fitted a gas cylinder into the boot, attaching a regulator to reduce gas pressure to atmospheric level and added an adaptor to the carburettor. Despite addition of 100lb to cab weight, £150 to its price and reduction in mileage per gallon to eighteen, propane proved a great economy, costing 16p per gallon (not taxed as road fuel) against 32p (petrol) or 30p (DERV). Conversion thus paid for itself in about eight months. Also engine bonuses included reduced wear and tear, at least on moving parts, and quieter running.

April 1970 saw three examples emerge; by March 1972, Cooks had converted 200 cabs. However, in 1971, the government announced purchase duty on LPG. Managing Director,Vernon Cook wrote Parliament a strong protest letter stating his case, speaking of the 'end of all hope for cleaner cities'. He claimed that the advantage of cheaper fuel would be lost, emphasising relative carbon emission. Relevant new legislation was enforced from New Year's Day 1974 and should have reinforced his case but, in practice, had precisely the reverse effect, ending all hope. The FX4 and FL2 were then the only cabs using this engine; as it did not meet new legal requirements, British Leyland Motor Company had to decide on modification or scrapping. Modest sales directed them to the scrap heap.

Attempting to solve the fuel problem, several experimental taxis were tried. (Joseph) Lucas Industries built an electric cab during autumn 1975 and another in 1977. Mitsubishi displayed their MMT forward-control cab on a van chassis at 1980s Motor Show. This won a coachwork section prize but got no further. One major problem with battery-driven vehicles centres around arranging garage-charging facilities.

The government, fearing inflationary effects, imposed dividend restraint, leaving companies unable to satisfy shareholders. Thus, inevitably, near doubling of profits in 1976 from £500,000 to £900,000 left the company vulnerable to takeover. Various prospectors came forward, successful candidates being Lloyds and Scottish, jointly owned by The Royal Bank of Scotland and Lloyds Bank, who staged massive purchases – described in some circles as a 'dawn raid' – of Mann and Overton's stocks in 1978, arranging to take over the entire share capital. The group were trade-experienced, having financed cabs around Glasgow through Scottish Discount, a subsidiary company. In 1978 Robert Overton passed 70 and retired from the chair, being replaced by Industrial and Commercial director Bill Renilson. Overton's family thus lost direct control but Mann and Overton, hardly distressed, would be compensated by improved financial security of larger firm ownership and – arguably more important – enjoy cohesion with new owners keen to help cabbies financially.

On takeover, opportunities for Carbodies to enjoy increased operational control disappeared. The FX4 was still in full production, being the only cab on the assembly line and thus the major income earner. However, most spare-parts production had been run down; thus it was important to make hay while the sun shone. London's cab trade had benefited from two recent financial boosts, easing of hire-purchase restrictions and minimum deposit reduction. Thus drivers could buy new cabs more easily. Mann and Overton, with long experience of financing cab purchases of both owner-drivers and fleets, now deemed it prudent to introduce something new – leasing – to benefit mushes (more economic details in Appendix 17).

However, arguments with Carbodies over extras and manufacturing progress, raging since the early 1960s, continued unabated. Carbodies needed to raise funds to replace the FX4's substandard body pressings. Drivers' complaints to Mann and Overton in respect of:

a) leaking rainwater
b) poor draught-proofing
c) rapid rusting
d) difficulty in topping up of oil because of the rocker-cover arrangement
e) ineffective fresh-air vent arrangement

were still abundant.

There had been some improvement in b) and c) with new shaping but drivers were still dissatisfied. Apparently, however, these complaints were not passed to Carbodies until Bill Lucas had discussions with the PCO.

Meanwhile, new trims (midnight blue and dark brown) were added to colour options of white and carmine red and following protracted discussions with the PCO, drivers were allowed personal radios, all delightedly accepted. But there were altercations regarding two-speed wipers and weekly sales levels. Outdated or not, Mann and Overton had their way, Carbodies fuming helplessly.

(The London Vintage Taxi Association was formed in 1978, dedicated to preservation and enjoyment of taxis of all ages. With Americans always having great sentiment for London taxis, there is a North American section. Both publish regular bulletins.)

Leyland now experienced considerable upheaval. They had discussed with Mann and Overton and Carbodies the possibility of building the FX5, mentioned earlier. But Leyland had too many other worries to concentrate on innovations, having already decided to move sales activity from general dealers to appointed specialists. These included companies like John Paton of Glasgow (owners of Manchester's Cross Street Garage), Carbodies Sales and Services in Coventry and Mann and Overton so that they assumed responsibility throughout the country in an industry with excellent growth potential. Paton sold it to Dennis Poore.

Bill Lucas, however, did not see sales policy as first priority. Mann and Overton worried over Carbodies' poor profitability over the period from BSA's takeover to the early 1960s and having seen their astronomical quote for initial body production, had started looking elsewhere. Winchester indicated a fibre-glass body was possible and there were consultations with sports-car manufacturers like Jensen and Keeble. Joe Edwards of BMC displayed his expertise in body manufacturing, recommending pressed steel, reckoning that GRP had not yet proved suitable for long-term use.

Rapidly losing patience with Mann and Overton's reluctance to finance FX4 improvements, Lucas took on FX5 development himself, Dennis Poore's board giving initial approval. Lucas instructed chief engineer Jake Donaldson, already assigned to deal with British Leyland, to make initial design drawings, Peter James assisting. Sadly, Donaldson, already unwell, died within months, after over four decades of service.

There were serious initial concerns, primarily over door-lock problems. Lucas's fears were vindicated in 1982, with separate FX4 incidents seeing one child killed and a second seriously injured in a fall. A shocked taxi trade, so far proud of its safety record, was promptly contacted by the PCO, insisting that a window sticker be placed indicating that doors were opened simply by pulling the handle down and that handles be encased in clear transparent plastic shields. In 1983 Carbodies complied by installing automatic locks, which ensured that doors were securely closed, not only when the taxi was moving but also when stationary by footbrake application. Initial teething problems were solved in subsequent improvements; thus bilkers and impatient passengers could be held.

Initial FX5 expenses, if designed afresh, were likely to be forbidding, so adapting an existing model seemed preferable. Lucas's first thoughts centred on the Range Rover with its large roof panel. A three-year feasibility study proved the body shell too bulky and inappropriately proportioned for cab suitability – plan rejected. Lucas tried a new design based on the Rover 3500 marketed from 1976. Its running gear would be mounted on a chassis of extruded steel tubes with a MacPherson front suspension for the rear axle. Overall development was slow – four years alone for the seat supporting frame or 'buck'.

But by now Manganese Bronze Holdings had effectively taken over BSA, thereby becoming Carbodies' financiers. Keen on the FX5, they gave full encouragement. A life-size model was built, representative viewers being impressed with specifications and modern appearance. However, Carbodies were short of capacity to organise engineering and body manufacture, their tool room and tool-making facilities having run down.

Consequently, work needed external sub-contracting, raising cost problems. A 2.5-litre Land Rover Unit was suggested but insurmountable difficulties arose. The whole power setup was unsuitable – high revving, low torque – taxis needing exactly the opposite. Valve train and combustion chamber designs were also unsatisfactory. Never having been tested under heavy London traffic conditions it was ruled out. Peugeot, however, were keen on involvement, proposing that their 2.5-litre unit be tried. Unhappily, Bill Lucas's health began to fail; prior to FX5 completion, he retired in February 1979; however, he enjoyed a long retirement to his death in August 2008. He was replaced by former British Leyland Cowley plant director, Grant Lockhart.

Satirical cartoon showing the king being carried in a sedan chair. (Library of Congress)

Horse-drawn cabs in Piccadilly Circus, c. 1900. (Library of Congress)

Cabman driving tourists in a carriage in the morning. (Shutterstock; © pryzmat)

Horse-drawn English-style cab in Hyde Park. (Liana Bitoli)

Row of Victorian London black cabs. (Shutterstock; © David Burrows)

Hyde Park Corner, c. 1900.   (Library of Congress)

Piccadilly Circus in 1968, including advertising signs, traffic, tourists and Eros. (Wikicommons; Roger Wollstadt)

Black cabs and red double-decker buses, 1996. (Wikicommons; InSapphoWeTrust)

Black cab. (Wikicommons; James Barrett)

Black cab. (Bugdog)

A London taxi passes by a telephone booth, a double-decker bus in the background. (Shutterstock; © SK Kim)

Silhouette of pub signboard . (Shutterstock; © Tomo Jesenicnik)

Black cab in London.
(Jeremy Jones)

Taxi at Parliament square.
(Ross Parker)

Big Ben, the Houses of Parliament and Westminster Bridge, London. (Shutterstock; © Luciano Mortula)

Tower Bridge close-up with vintage taxi in London. (Shutterstock; © Songquan Deng)

Close-up of a typical black cab in London. (Shutterstock; © mikecphoto)

The first attempt presented cylinder-head problems, persisting on the second. There were also excessive vibrations; on one occasion, the propshaft tore loose, crashing through the floor. Obviously Peugeot would take ages to find solutions, if indeed any existed. That left three further options: Perkins' 3 litre, Ford's 2.3 litre and the Land Rover unit. Lockhart favoured the Perkins, which performed well but was too powerful. At the other extreme, the Ford was underpowered and time-wise they could not commit themselves to a 2.5-litre version. For several years, chassis construction at Longbridge had been sub-contracted to Coventry's Carbodies' factory and unsurprisingly, in 1982, Carbodies effectively took over control of cab development engineering. This effectively ended the three-way deal between them, Mann and Overton and Austin, severing the Austin link after more than fifty years. At this time, production in England of the well-known Austin 2.5 diesel engine unfortunately ceased, leaving Lockhart little option but to buy the Land Rover 2.2 litre, despite opposing advice. This proved an unwelcome engine to drivers although associated advantages of power-steering and full servo-assisted brakes made driving easier. Also Rover's five-speed manual gearbox was markedly lighter than the old Austin's. A cab trial was conducted and it proved competent, smooth and reliable in normal driving conditions; conversion could hopefully be completed in about three months.

By the late 1970s, automatic vehicles were becoming accepted normality. So far, no automatic gearbox had been combined with Land Rover's diesel engine. The Austin manual gearbox was fading out, necessitating replacement. Rover had a five-speed unit for their 3.5-litre model but this also had never been fitted to such an engine. Other ideas were proposed but reluctantly Lockhart decided to scrap the FX5, deeming the chassis too heavy. Little or no attempt at rectification with modern materials had been made; also body-tooling costs were prohibitive.

Forced to consider alternatives, he re-examined Bill Lucas's original Range-Rover base idea. This was the basis of the new (City Rover) CR6. Rover used a five-speed manual unit for their 3.5-litre model, also yet untried. The plan most acceptable to Land-Rover engineers involved combining it with Borg-Warner's model 40, as used on FX4s since their Hertfordshire plant's 1980 closure.

CR6 development was initially held until engineering revision for the Land-Rover-powered FX4. Unless that was completed satisfactorily, no further finance was available. Practical problems abounded. Attainable speeds of 80-plus mph implied the need for modernised braking. Fortunately, the necessary full servo system had already been designed in 1978, avoiding extra cost. However, the disc brake possibility was ruled out so that modification would only be a stopgap before CR6 completion. Also, at the time, Range Rovers were two-door, necessitating conversion. Artwork completed, a scale model was built and after Carbodies' approval, the four doors with internal hinges were displayed impressively. The 2.25-litre Land Rover diesel engine was used with the chassis, originally designed for Peugeot, appropriately adapted. For clear visual distinction between the new cabs and established Range Rovers, the nose was reconstituted to include headlights and interior units from Morris Italians. Considerable efforts were made to satisfy the entire export market with left-hand drive versions being prepared as well as variants for America and hot-climate countries.

A quarter-scale model appeared in June 1980. Initial enthusiasm and expectation were great but problems soon surfaced, most important being wheelchair accessibility. The Department of Transport had already begun preparations for the forthcoming Year of the Disabled, holding meetings for the disabled themselves, transport providers and local vehicle manufacturers. Carbodies did produce a one-off wheelchair-accessible cab for a customer and were approached, in August 1981, by the Ministry of Transport to build new taxis with regular wheelchair accommodation. There was some hostility from within the company but by the following December, a modified prototype was produced with a split driver-passenger partition enabling the luggage-platform side to be slid forwards, accommodating a rear-facing wheelchair passenger.

Later, just before Christmas, the new cab was unveiled at Marsham Street. Several celebrities, notably racing driver Stirling Moss and Health Secretary Norman Fowler, attended. The press presentation speech was made by another promising Conservative, then junior Health Minister, Kenneth Clarke. Cab trade representatives viewed the newcomer with mixed feelings. The modern appearance of the airy light champagne-beige vehicle with a huge windscreen certainly impressed but driving space – the Achilles heel of both FX3 and FX4 – remained cramped. Nevertheless, overall prospects were promising with the chassis, suspension and relatively simple concept reasonably inexpensive.

By 1981, FX4 engines and manual gearboxes were supplied by Austin-Morris, the FX4 obviously carrying the Austin name. But new problems loomed regarding European legislation, numbering the FX4's days unless Carbodies could rescue it. They thus applied for and acquired what were termed 'intellectual rights' from British Leyland and obtained National Type Approval under their own name. Thenceforth, cabs were known as 'Carbodies FX4'.

With earlier candidates ruled out, Land Rover's diesel engine was chosen. Carbodies had already developed a good relationship with Rover during CR6 cooperation. A successful trial was made on the FX4, conducted by the Birmingham company Horace Faulkener. CR6 tests were running in Newcastle-under-Lyme and Peterborough, but time was short, Carbodies feeling that three months was the maximum needed to implement the necessary modifications. A new engineering director, Barry Widdowson, was appointed to organise design processing but even working overtime proved unsatisfactory.

Decisions were needed regarding transmission. A modified FX4 variant was christened FX4R (Rover); British Leyland supplied parts initially but this became the first product exclusively manufactured by Carbodies. Large sales were anticipated, primarily to provincial purchasers where manual was preferred to automatic. Thus the Rover variant of the Jaguar five-speed SD1 was chosen. The engine was the 2.25-litre Land Rover diesel, with a petrol variant available. There was an automatic alternative –

Borg-Warner's 65. Here the change lever was mounted on the floor, contrasting the manual steering-column selector. There was also a one-off, extended or 'stretch' variant, built by coachbuilders Tickfords. Originally coachbuilders (Salmons Ltd), the company had started in 1920. Tickfords was a brand name, a convertible vehicle or 'drophead' raised or lowered by winding a removable handle. An extra 9in section was added to the basic FX4R with an extra pillar between the doors, giving more all-round leg-room, accommodating an additional passenger in front.

The initiator was Bill Wallace, an American doctor, keen on British interests. However, wanting this for American limousines, he needed left-hand drive and engine compliance with local exhaust and safety restrictions. He was lucky on three counts in that Carbodies had already started negotiations with American company D.F. Landers, primarily vehicle manufacturers, with a view to producing FX4 variants suitable for America. The Pinto 2.3-litre Ford petrol engine was appropriately designed. Furthermore, after a fourteen-year break, Carbodies had recommenced production of left-hand drive vehicles so that C3 three-speed automatic gearboxes were ready. For completion, power steering and power brakes were also being introduced.

After several modifications, the finished product displayed an interior trimmed with grey Connolly leather, red and grey Wilton carpets and wool-cloth headlining with burr walnut cappings and facia. Additional features included a cocktail cabinet with Waterford crystal decanter and glasses. A fixed window was set in the roof, with a sliding sun-blind. Side and rear windows had privacy curtains. Air conditioning, needed in Dr Wallace's native southern states, was fitted in both front and rear with windows electrically operated. Maximum speed was about 75mph but performance was optimum cruising at some 20mph lower, 55mph conveniently being the maximum speed limit on American state roads.

Power steering was debuted in a London cab. Mann and Overton, expected to provide finance, were unsurprisingly reluctant. However, realising that current steering boxes were outdated, they accepted the need to modernise. Full servo brakes, developed earlier, were, at long last, to appear with master cylinders, originally located below the floor, placed under the bonnet. However, restricted time and money precluded disc brakes.

Introduced in autumn 1982, it cost between just under £9,000 (manual without power steering) and just over £10,000 (automatic High Line Special (HLS) with power steering). Automatics were slightly delayed, the PCO awaiting a braking problem rectification. There was initial enthusiasm, notably for the quietly smooth-running engine. However, this quickly turned to anger and dismay as further irritations occurred – it worked poorly with the FX4, quickly acquiring a reputation for unreliability.

The engine was poorly designed, combustion chambers alarmingly releasing excessive black smoke, with fuel consumption poor at 20mpg. Combination with the automatic box gave minimal torque, resulting in miserable acceleration which some considered dangerous. Rockers were not centrally pivoted resulting in unnecessarily heavy load on valve supports, which consequently suffered excessive wear. The injector pump drive transmission gear, pressed against the shaft, was liable to slip, ruining the injector timing, further exacerbated by timing-chain weakness and liability to stretch with excessive use. Furthermore, much of the engine's power was needed to operate steering, reducing its already disappointing efficiency. Drivers approached Mann and Overton in large numbers demanding better tuning for improved fuel economy. The company conducted various tests, withdrawing badly behaved engines.

Additionally, the inadequate radiator caused chronic overheating, notably in warm weather. Manual variants exhibited serious clutch problems, largely due to the poor choice of first motion shaft bearing in installation of the five-speed gearbox. Vibrations caused its operating arm to rupture over the mounting bolt, and the plastic hydraulics pipe was liable to blow itself off under pressure. The wrong clutch components had been combined and the flywheel's male end or 'spigot' bearing tended to disintegrate, ruining the gearbox.

Unsurprisingly, Land Rover engineers were appalled at their engines' performance in taxi use. Their bosses refused to hear of proposed alterations or modifications and anger thus intensified as problems were accentuated with sales of several cabs to Gulf Arab states: Dubai, Qatar and Kuwait. Faced with a hostile desert climate, servicing intervals became progressively shorter, to customers' irritation. Camels seemed far more reliable and orders ceased.

Following this dissatisfaction, a new variant was tried from 1985, the FX4Q. This largely comprised reclaimed and reconditioned parts – the old Austin engine, imported from India, chassis, suspensions and rear axle – from previous FX4 variants, the remainder with new parts – FX4R-style servo brakes, Borg-Warner 40 automatic gearbox with floor-mounted selector but no power steering. Chassis on the production line were fitted with new bodies and trims. Department of Transport legislation then ruling that models should be given the initial 'Q', depicting no specification regarding manufacture year. Thus cabs were sold via Carbodies Sales and Service to trade buyers through an East End subsidiary of E.A. Crouch, (well-known fleet proprietors) called Rebuilt Taxis Ltd. At £8,300, it undercut automatic FX4Rs by some £1,500. Actual specifications were akin to those that old FX4s should have had fifteen years previously.

Mann and Overton were gravely displeased with this development – angry with Carbodies if only because every 'Q' sale meant one less 'R' sale. Furthermore, 'Q' introduction amounted to Carbodies' admitting 'R' shortcomings. Mann and Overton preferred to feel that any problems were grossly exaggerated – if indeed they existed – and were aggrieved at having to deal with complaining owners of brand-new cabs. There was further friction when, as Christmas 1985 approached, the LTI Carbodies' subsidiary Carbodies Sales and Service Ltd, contrary to their hierarchy's wishes, produced a wheelchair-accessible variant. Body engineer Roger Ponticelli modified the access, turning the doors around to hinge on B-posts and arranged for the driver passenger partition to slide back and forth, accommodating wheelchair entry/exit. The variant was offered, for £1,700 plus VAT extra, from spring 1986.

In 1984, Barry Widdowson approached the experienced Sussex engine design research establishment Ricardo Engineering. They recommended the Japanese Nissan TC series 2.5 litre. But this raised a new transmission problem and although Nissan were delighted to receive a prestigious order, the TC series was already being deleted and they decided to use the 2.5-litre Land Rover engine (which worked with the current transmission) while awaiting the next series, TD. Carbodies were obviously keen to steer clear of FX4R failures and only had the manual option, no automatic gearbox existing to work with TC series engines. By 1987, Carbodies had tired of Land-Rover engine problems, being pleased to see TDs ready early in 1988. The new range included sizes of 2.3, 2.5 and 2.7 litres, LTI choosing the 2.7. This arrived as a complete power train with options of four-speed automatic or five-speed manual gearboxes. Despite its obvious quality, it proved painfully unpatriotic to install an expensive Japanese engine in what was otherwise a totally British institution – the London taxicab. However, decide they did and the chassis was re-engineered accordingly.

Even now, there were installation problems, the new fuel pump proving troublesome. Its mounting, very low on the block, necessitated raising the engine at the front and inclining it left at a modest angle. New engine mountings had to be ordered from Metalastik but they proved unsatisfactory – unpleasant vibrations occurred during engine tickover. Internal plastic draught excluders were added to the doorsills and insulation was included under the dashboard. Rocker-type switches replaced the now obsolete Lucas toggles and electric screen-washers were included to put cabs on a par with private cars, at least regarding these facilities. New gearboxes had to be purchased from Australia (their Model 40) following closure of Letchworth, Hertfordshire's Borg-Warner plant.

Thus the new variant, FX4S, introduced at Carnwath Road during autumn, was built over 1985–87. It cost slightly more than its predecessor, just over £11,200 for a basic manual. Torque showed marked improvement, albeit at the expense of a few extra decibels and overall improved performance resulted in better sales. FX4R owners were also offered the new FX4S engine for £2,400.

Nonetheless, problems still surfaced, at least initially. A faulty set of timing belts caused serious internal engine damage on snapping. The radiator, unchanged, was substandard, some drivers feeling obliged to purchase extra electric fans.

Later, as the Year of the Disabled progressed, a mock interior of the future CR6 (as indicated earlier) was manufactured for display at Kensington Town Hall, disabled occupants being impressed with the best facilities to date. Following their initial attack on wheelchair problems in 1980, the Department of Transport established a research group to examine the mobility needs of the wheelchair-bound, approaching the Road Research Laboratory at Crowthorne, Berkshire, who, in turn, established a Road Transport Study Group based at Newcastle University.

The CR6 had also been sent to British Leyland's test track at Gaydon, Oxfordshire and its progress pleased Carbodies' managers. Plans were published, talking of an inception date during winter 1983–84, trade and press representatives being invited to a test drive. These 'guinea pigs' were most dissatisfied. Apart from the perennial problem of cramped driving space, the new model was significantly heavier than the FX4, rolled poorly on 14in wheels and felt more cumbersome.

From July 1982, the CR6 was tried provincially – Peterborough, Stoke-on-Trent, Newcastle-upon-Tyne – before exposure to the more testing London environment. Local drivers' reports were positive towards the wheelchair facility but, notably in Peterborough, there were problems with inadequate headroom. Back-strain beckoned for taller passengers travelling with bowed heads; the roof therefore had to be raised. In Newcastle, wider doors were requested. A research team report recommended an overall bigger size, notably with increased roof height and door width.

To accommodate all this, Carbodies decided on a 4in chassis expansion, putting another £2 million on the bill. The government, displaying sympathy for the disabled, were willing to donate £1.3 million of this through the auspices of the Departments of Transport and Trade and Industry, the remainder coming from the Greater London Council who were pushing their campaign for equal opportunities for the disabled, visualising the CR6 as the 'taxi of the future'.

It took eighteen months to establish Conditions of Fitness (European standard) compliance. Once licence was granted, Carbodies assigned their own name to it; previously the Society of Motor Manufacturers and Traders had deemed Carbodies purely 'body maker' despite their manufacturing the whole vehicle since 1971. From spring 1982 they were deemed official manufacturers.

A second and later a third CR6 variant included a longer wheelbase and higher roof pressing, which certainly solved the above problems but at the expense of making already bulky cabs still bigger. A further problem surfaced regarding steering mechanism – insufficient ground clearance. Carbodies now ran into financial difficulties as FX4R's marketing dwindled. It suffered more pronounced depreciation than its Austin-engined rivals in an economic environment of record-breaking interest rates. Mushes and fleet owners could do little but hang on to their older models, leaving Carbodies with minimal sales income and no spare cash for new development. By now the CR6 price, originally 10 per cent above the FX4's, had risen to more than 20 per cent above it. Mann and Overton had already been obliged to produce nearly £2 million and were due to pay a further similar sum. Additional project costs were estimated at some £4.5 million; clearly about £1.4 million was needed additionally to finance factory extensions. New Year 1984 saw Carbodies announce a production delay for at least twelve months; all came to nothing.

Carbodies' progressively worsening finances sent warning signs to Mann and Overton who now feared looming bankruptcy. Andrew Overton thus felt obliged to find another manufacturer. Backed by finance from their owners, Lloyds and Scottish

Plc, he gave instructions for new cab designing, again under the FX5 name. The Panther cars design engineer Robert Jankel was approached for the new chassis. The new cab would be powered by a 2.3-litre Ford diesel engine. Work started, but once the chassis was built Overton realised that his fears were unfounded. With the promotion of Barry Widdowson to managing director from 1985, Carbodies' fortunes had dramatically improved and the project was suspended.

In 1984 Lloyds and Scottish was taken over by Lloyds Bowmaker. The new owners elected to sell Mann and Overton. Grant Lockhart repeated Bill Lucas's arm-twisting of Dennis Poore. Feeling increasingly pressurised, Poore raised a London Stock Exchange rights issue to buy the company. That materialised in 1985 and the new company, London Taxi International (LTI), under the umbrella of Manganese Bronze Holdings Ltd, was divided into three parts: LTI Carbodies for manufacturing, LTI Mann and Overton as London, provincial and overseas' dealers and Mann and Overton – shortly to become London Taxi Finance – as financiers. This continued in operation until 2005 and enabled the company to manufacture whole vehicles, provide experienced and respected in-house financial services and concentrate on what would be their sole product – the London taxi. Poore put his son-in-law, Jamie Borwick, on Mann and Overton's board. Marrying the boss's daughter had struck gold again! Sadly, Poore, approaching eighty, died suddenly shortly afterwards, Borwick replacing him at the head of Manganese Bronze.

In 1988, Overton moved to Coventry to take over sales and market expansion, and progressing to become a respected sales director, became managing director. Other management changes included the move of General Manager Peter Rigden to Parts Department administration.

The early 1980s also saw Carbodies start to advertise in European markets, the element of power steering coming to the fore. For London, Mann and Overton dismissed the idea as ridiculous but it was vital abroad. They therefore reluctantly offered it as an option, but the PCO refused to sanction it for several weeks as the box could not be prevented from leaking fluid. Despite the consequent loss of 15 per cent of engine power, it became so popular that it was accepted as standard within a year, diesel engines being retuned where necessary. A petrol variant was also offered, many being exported to Australia with the option of LPG conversion.

Domestically, by 1982 Mann and Overton had outgrown their Wandsworth Bridge Road premises. Market research indicated that most customers lived north or east of the London area, giving little reason for a south-west location. They first looked towards London's East End; secondly to Brixton's Acre Lane, 2 miles from the London Cab Company. Committed to selling by November 1983, they eventually took a third option – backed by Lloyds and Scottish – magnificent purpose-built premises on the Thames' north bank at Carnwath Road, Fulham. The £3 million cost proved worthwhile for ideal workshops, up-to-date spray booths and ramps with excellent customer accommodation.

Hardly had they arrived when there was a further change of ownership: 1984 had seen the demise of Lloyds and Scottish as an entity, wholly taken over by Lloyds Bank. The new owners decided against continuing to run a commercial/industrial division. Now, as 'Lloyds Bowmaker', they decided to divide Mann and Overton's dealership into finance and retail components, offering the latter for sale.

The mid 1980s had also seen investigation regarding possibly revising the FX4's interior. This involved a bakelite steering wheel, as appropriate to old Austin 2.5-litre cars, and the absence of power steering. Styrofoam was introduced and there were revisions on dashboard instruments and interior door handles. But a major problem was the radiator, insufficient for the new engine in heavy traffic. Tests proved the need for increased size, costing an extra £30. However, conservative to the last, the engineering director stuck to the *status quo,* many owners feeling obliged to fit auxiliary fans. The year 1984 also saw Carbodies break into the American market.

This period also saw LTI facing EEC regulatory requirements, under which doors hinged on the rear pillar were banned. Under the 'alpha' project, not only were doors to be re-hinged to B-posts but the windscreen was to be enlarged in a shell of modified shape. The project was greeted with dubious feelings; traders were apparently looking for a completely redesigned vehicle, which LTI, determined to be manufacturers of London's best taxicab, could ill-afford. The best they could do was step-by-step FX4 updating. Thus the alpha project was scrapped. Managing director Ed Osmond recommended modifying the FX4S. He brought in a former colleague from Coventry University, Jevon Thorpe. The new design, featuring the new dashboard and five-seater interior in a light shade of grey, had earlier been presented to Dennis Poore, sufficiently impressed to permit production. The initial version had the disadvantage of lacking a built-in wheelchair facility but a later variant, for nearly £1,000 extra, accommodated wheelchairs. Thenceforth, the FX4S-Plus outsold Metrocabs.

It was introduced at September 1987's annual London Taxi Driver of the Year Show in Battersea Park, which had evolved from modest beginnings fourteen years earlier and had become an important one-day trade event. Again there was a new interior in distinctive vinyl grey with the option of velour fabric seats. The newly moulded dashboard used the Austin Mini-Metro style of instrument panel with push-button switches, a face-level ventilation system and a courtesy light, coming on automatically if any door was opened. There was a further option of an electric front window. Thus everything to bring cabs up to modern saloon-car standard had been included. To improve ride smoothness, laminated plastic springs and telescopic rear shock absorbers were added. A new range of colours was specified and trims, already available in midnight blue, carmine red, white and black, were now available in others like city grey, Sherwood green and burgundy. Also rear-hinged doors could be modified to swing open to 180 degrees and the base of the rear seat had hinges fitted so that the seat could be raised vertically for greater floor space. This option cost rather less than that on the W predecessor at just under £1,000.

Wheelchair accommodation proved a critical step-forward in Carbodies' history. Clearly a selling necessity henceforth, the new 'beta' project was incepted. April 1986 saw the introduction of the conversion option to FX4W (wheelchair). For £1,700, an FX4 would have its nearside rear door hinged to the B-post with facility for sliding forward into the luggage area, enabling easy wheelchair-bound passengers' accommodation. From 1988, another conversion included an affixed dog-leg partition with a lifting back seat and the floor sloped at the rear for easier wheelchair mobility. The doors would be hinged on the C-Posts on throw-back hinges, implying the need to be secured against the rear wing when ramps were used. The modification of rear-hinged doors, mentioned as an option in the FX4S Plus, became standard on Fairways and available from February 1989.

However, it was appreciated that, for mass production, further door-design improvement was needed for full 90-degree opening for unimpeded wheelchair access. By early summer 1988, a new swan-neck shaped hinge was designed with the cooperation of MIRA, who also assisted regarding material choice. The next six months saw realisation that the safest wheelchair alignment was facing rearwards and held down by a belt attached to the partition. December saw completion of the new model, appropriately code-named 'Beta'.

In 1984 MCW chairman Tony Sansome, appointed a production manager, Geoff Chater, who had joined Carbodies from Jaguar five years earlier. Former Rootes design engineer Bob Parsons headed the design team. They worked together in the West Birmingham suburb of Oldbury. Parsons aimed for a box-type rust-proof chassis with the FX4's front suspension attached. Modification of the steering arrangement (wheelbase being longer than the FX4's) was required to satisfy PCO restrictions. He solved the problem by switching the left-hand drive variant of the power-steering box to the right. The GKN (Guest, Keen and Nettlefold) rear axle was established in a rigid arrangement, hanging on steel semi-elliptical multi-leaf springs. FX4 brakes were retained.

However, there were engine problems as advertised in its poor FX4S performance. Chater therefore replaced it with the new Ford FSD – direct injection diesel. Sample drawings, based on artwork published in the magazine were presented to Tony Sansome but, describing it as hideous, he instructed the two creators to produce something more stylish. The second attempt displayed the largest windscreen yet seen on a London cab with doors hinging forward on their B-post. It could accommodate five people with wheelchair access; the disabled passenger could face rearwards when positioned on the nearside front of the passenger compartment – the safest arrangement in MIRA's opinion.

The proposed body would be of glass-fibre bonded to a steel cage. MCW, unable to manufacture GRP bodies, turned to Reliant, an experienced company. The first white-finished prototype was tested before presentation for PCO approval. Here brakes proved the stumbling block, the PCO taking exception to handbrake cable operation, despite its being nothing new. They wanted a rod set-up and Parsons spent considerable time persuading them to change their minds.

Thus serious production had not commenced until 1986. This good-looking vehicle had a number of advantages over the FX4, including driver safety features like power steering with a collapsible column, disc brakes and wheelchair access (still considered futuristic for the FX4). In addition, the fibreglass body gave weight advantage with reduced running and maintenance costs. The large glass area obviously improved driver visibility. The side footboard or 'running board', omitted on the FX4, reappeared here. The most important improvement was in all-round space available. Even tall drivers had ample headroom. The dashboard's instrument panel (originally from the Austin Montego) had large push-button control switches, mounted centrally. The seating capacity was increased, accommodating up to seven passengers.

Early December 1986 saw the Metrocab launched in a dramatic ceremony at Wembley's Conference Centre. MCW's managing director, Peter Steadman, assured attendants that an investment of £5 million was earmarked for the cab without any government help. (That was in contrast to CR6, which relied substantially on the tax- and London rate-payer). David Mitchell, then Minister of Transport, was present and was expected to be impressed; his short address emphasised benefits to the disabled.

Nearly twenty years' work had included extensive testing by the London General Cab Company. The re-emergence had been announced in *Cab Driver*, shortly before Christmas 1983. John Paton explained that new cabs would be built in cooperation with British Leyland dealers Taggarts, who predominated distribution markets, at least in Scotland and Northern England. They planned for the new variant to keep its GRP body with detachable aluminium-manufactured wings. Two engines were considered – the 2.5-litre Land Rover and the 2.3-litre Peugeot with transmission via a four-speed manual gearbox or ZF four-speed automatic. All modern gadgets were included.

It received a surprisingly warm welcome from the nominally ultra-conservative cab trade with the notable exception of Carbodies' Grant Lockhart, who was displeased with the rival's appearance. There was also a possible third participant in the race, the RG7. Ross Graham Ltd were to build a cab in South Wales; the government was pleased to see prospective activity in this area following the near demise of local mining. The cab was either to be on Winchester MK IV lines, or else based on a Ford Transit or Leyland Sherpa chassis. Sadly, it never started.

Early clouds gathered for Metrocabs as teething troubles surfaced and sales proved sluggish. Initially, there were transmission problems. The prototypes carried a Borg-Warner 65 three-speed automatic gearbox but they did not have the Model 40, manufactured in Australia and used for the FX4S Plus, available for MCW. Ford could offer four-speed automatic transmission, but so far this had only been used in conjunction with engines suitable for low-speed airport service vehicles; modifications were needed. Three months' testing in Birmingham-based plants proved successful and MCW thought they were on target. However, launching the modified cab proved a dangerous minefield.

Metro Sales and Service had orders of 200-plus within the first quarter but the delay caused by the necessary gearbox tests was more than many customers could swallow, embarrassingly large numbers pulling out. What deliveries remained started in spring 1987 and sales steadily gathered pace, albeit to suspicious traders. The FX4 was, at least, 'the devil they knew'. The purchaser of the first model was a Mrs Sheila Anker, wife of a London Vintage Taxi Association member. It was the privilege of *Steering Wheel* assistant editor Steve Tillyer to present the first five-seater cab to the PCO for passing. The vehicle was awarded a number 1 plate but subsequent five-seater models had letter E as prefix.

Other problems centred around the gearbox and establishing the causes took time. Eventually, engineers discovered that the torque converter was flexing under heavy loads. Consequently, the short input shaft would wear very quickly, leaving the gearbox irreparably damaged. Even in cases where cabs were repaired within two days, dissatisfaction soon grew, reputation dropping rapidly. Additionally, nearly 100 faults were reported, few parts escaping criticism. Metrocab designer Bob Parsons took the hammering, and, despite his efforts, financial assistance from MCW was inevitably minimal. They were already in trouble, Laird, their parent company, already seeking possible purchasers. Matters were worsened by MCW proving very slow in meeting warranty claims; that generated little confidence.

February 1989 saw the new model released as the 'Fairway', a name favoured by Bobby Jones, keen to revive a Carbodies' name of the 1930s, golf being many cabbies' favourite pastime. Three trim options were offered – bronze, silver and gold with wood-like door capping on top of the range. It proved the most reliable vehicle sold to date and London's best-selling cab. One criticism referred to poor visibility but the windscreen was quickly given modest enlargement.

However, nobody took anything for granted and the Fairway's instant popularity was considered only a step towards LTI improving its prosperity by becoming a leading independent manufacturer in provincial and international markets. The well-established antipathy towards London taxis in provincial areas, where local legislation displayed different requirements, still had to be overcome. Overseas, where taxis were predominantly saloon cars, Mercedes, Peugeot and various Japanese makes dominated, with Britain firmly in the wings. However, two factors worked in LTI's (also Metrocab's) favour – driver safety and the Fairway being the first to offer wheelchair accessibility as standard. Attacks on cab and hire-car drivers had been steadily increasing here and abroad – German drivers carried firearms for self-defence. No official statistics were published but attacks on drivers of cabs that had solid partitions were significantly fewer than otherwise.

A left-hand drive Fairway variant was also manufactured and new energy was put into exporting, largely abandoned since Middle Eastern and other foreign crises had sidelined it. Taxis and limousines were sold to satisfy varying demand. Typically, in Japan, only limousines could be accepted, their rules requiring universal running on LPG –

Fairways used petrol. Fitted with leather seats, carpets and air conditioning, they proved popular with business executives who could use them as mobile offices – important as Tokyo's rush 'hour' can last up to three times as long and fitted telephones, fax and telex machines enabled bosses to keep in constant contact with employees and associates. They were also used for weddings, offering the advantage that brides could spread dresses without creasing. Orientally, the only country using Fairways as taxis was Singapore, purchasing over 100. Their famous Raffles Hotel also bought limousines for private use.

Later on, however, the possibility of Fairways using LPG surfaced. LTI dealers KPM (UK) Plc (Keith Marder, Peter da Costa, Michael Troullis, formed around 1975) offered a gas conversion, conceived by the Ecological Engine Company, the new variant named 'Ecocab'. The engine was an Eco 120, 0.8-litre four-cylinder, originally from the MG TF and converted for LPG by a company called Janspeed. Thus, for just under £3,000, drivers could run cabs on much cheaper fuel. This certainly appeared a long-term economic winner but low power and serious overheating proved problematic. An alternative, more successful, offer came from David Day's London Cab Company, who, from 1994 owards, could fit a 2.3-litre Ford DOHC petrol engine, adapted to run on LPG in LTI cabs, notably Metrocabs.

European purchasers included Denmark, Switzerland, Spain and Portugal with a handful sold to the governments of Turkey, Falkland Islands and Caicos Islands but the biggest buyer was Germany, keen on safety factors following 100-plus murders in their main agents' (Mercedes-Benz) Essen area. They and Spain were also particularly keen on wheelchair accessibility. The Fairway's supply to Spain exceeded original Spanish government orders and the authorities encouraged purchases of extras by offering every purchasing taxi driver a 2 million peseta cash bonus (then about £8,500). LTI honoured their own prerequisites for selling abroad – service, easy spares availability, etc.

Conveniently, financial markets had opened up, many brokers taking an interest in taxi trading. It was thus considered prudent to utilise one of them; consequently the distribution process was subdivided for the first time. Following a search in the late 1980s for a suitable second dealership, Mann and Overton shared with the merged KPM and UK taxi services. Peter da Costa, a former London cab driver, had built up a strong business with an excellent reputation for customer care – ideal as LTI were very keen that potential customers be offered maximum choice when purchasing new taxis. The other two had served apprenticeships in other motor-trade capacities. They had felt that mushes had generally been given second-class treatment against fleet-owned cab drivers and correctly envisaged increasing numbers of cab drivers buying their own cabs in future. They had started their business around Bethnal Green, aiming to become the outstanding cab garage in London. In 1976 they moved, perhaps appropriately, to a location under the railway arches in Dunbridge Street. UK Taxi Services was formed around 1978 to meet the financial needs of taxi drivers who wanted to buy their own vehicles. The two companies merged in 1988 to become KPM-UK Plc.

Three factors contributed to the final decision on the second dealership, taken in October 1989 – the track record of first-class service, their convenient location in London's East End, mirroring Mann and Overton's position in the West, and their complete service base, including a body shop with taximeter hire and on-site maintenance – features lacking in Carnwath Road.

Leading company figures were now Roy McMaster, recruited by LTI in the late 1980s, and Peter Rigden. They decided to relocate to an area more closely linked to London's taxi trade than their current SW address. In 1996 new premises were taken in Holloway Road, Islington, within striking distance of the City and East End. There was a further reason, economic, behind the move. With provincial taxi business growing rapidly – notably with local authorities taking an increasing interest in catering for disabled needs – basic changes were made regarding parts distribution. To date, Mann and Overton had been the principal suppliers throughout the UK and major city distributors Paton and Cross Street Garage had received supplies direct from London. Henceforth, a new contract was drawn up with Unipart DCM, under which they would stock all parts, providing a nationwide delivery service. Thus the volume of vehicles and parts needed at Carnwath Road was reduced appreciably, leaving a smaller site sufficient. The London taxi population was also in a healthy state of growth over this period, 1986 seeing 19,000 taxi drivers in charge of 14,000 vehicles. Over the next decade, respective figures had increased to 22,000 and 17,000.

Britain entered the new 1990s thriving economically. Metrocab, particularly, had cornered nearly a quarter of the market. But skies were already darkening. Many authorities blamed an incompetent government for the nation's plunge into recession, the Gulf War, starting early in 1991, worsening matters. Fear of hijacking discouraged American tourists from flying into London's airports, a principal source of taxicab drivers' income immediately dropping dramatically. Interest rates rose steeply and with drivers still expected to pay on mortgages and other outlays, financial difficulties spread throughout the trade. Stability returned in time but long-term effects took their toll over a much lengthier period.

Already, in early autumn 1988, *The Financial Times* had published news that Laird, planning to sell MCW, were still seeking purchasers. The following mid-January edition of *Taxi* discussed the story, throwing petrol on the fire, indicating that bus-trade losses combined with a bid to take over Leyland buses, which had been turned down, had led Laird to try to sell the manufacturing (taxi, train and buses) subsidiary. However, the taxi side, having so far proved profitable, would be sold as a separate entity. Their decision was announced just before Christmas.

One thing led to another. The MCW board announced four dismissals; firstly director Peter Steadman; later three of his co-directors. Gossip was rife that MCW was on the way out. But the next week's edition of *Taxi* published an interview with Metrocab Sales and Service spokesman Ernest Keats, also editor of *Cab Driver*. He had written to all Metrocab share owners to the effect that Laird had received no fewer than a dozen purchase offers. Rumours that the company was in serious trouble had obviously been spread by those who wanted to return to an LTI monopoly. Keats carefully avoided naming culprits but LTI had recently withdrawn advertisements from his paper.

Regarding the monopoly position, Austin had seen Winchester disappear as rivals but now the Metrocab was the new competitor for the FX4 and successors. Early on, for reasons already indicated, threats were relatively weak but it was clearly foolish to ignore them. Like Winchester, the Metrocab had a GRP body, impervious to rust and corrosion from salted icy roads. Thus they were very popular in cold Scottish cities, proving long-lasting. Using Ford running gear, they incorporated a tubular steel internal structure to provide optimum protection against the effect of accidents.

GRP manufacturers were Reliant, new owners of Metrocab, officially taking over from early summer 1989. They had built a variety of composite plastic products for nearly thirty years, including Metrocab bodies. The owners were beneficiaries of the 1980s property boom Carl Turpin and Christopher Johnson, who had diversified to the Reliant Group. The Kettlebrook factory, in Tamworth, Staffordshire, was modern-ised to cater for Metrocab taxi completion. Kettlebrook thenceforth took over from Washwood Heath. The following year saw Geoff Chater join the management team. Problems now arose for Metro Sales and Service following the demise of MCW, notably regarding warranties. Expensive litigation ensued with MCW taking over responsibility for claims and Metro Sales and Service laboured under the impression that they would continue as London area dealers. In the event they met with disappointment; Reliant turned to two new names: Exclusive in the west and Nelson Crouch in the east.

However, their hold on the company was short-lived. With property market col-lapse a major recession feature, the group sustained financial disaster and receivers (KPMG Peat Marwick) were called in. However, the labours of Geoff Chater had improved matters considerably in the business's vehicle and plastics section. They had previously suffered heavy losses but were now earning healthy profits so cab manufac-ture was still worthwhile. Assets were bought by Hoopers of Tamworth, Staffordshire, leading coachbuilders. Hoopers modified the body for improved style – new grille, redesigned lamps and bodywork protection – and several technical changes. They introduced a four-speed automatic gearbox, a larger windscreen and modern-style shaping with exterior trim updated and redesigned seating, all positively welcomed, notably by owner-drivers.

Fortunes improved dramatically in 1991; over £1.5 million worth of orders (home and export about half each) were taken at the Taxi Driver of the Year Show, opening in early September 1992. Later that month, journalists were invited to the launch of the latest variant by Hooper's chairman Peter Chowder. The principal novelties were disc brakes, first to be fitted on a London cab. Manufacturers were Girling, originally approached by Bob Parsons during the Reliant era. Winter 1992 saw Metrocab fit a new Ford engine, which boasted a new Bosch fuel-injection system offering improved acceleration despite reduced fuel consumption; carbon emission was also reduced, pleasing green enthusiasts. Acceleration was further enhanced by using a new lower-ratio differential and the most up-to-date Cosworth torque converter. Further assets included a new dashboard, extended driver-compartment storage space and improved carpeting. Ventilation and heating systems were also modernised to maximise efficiency.

Regarding provincial distribution, 1990 saw Mann and Overton's name given to the wholly owned LTI dealerships in the Manchester and Birmingham areas. This followed the arrival of Alan Bray, who had joined LTI from Metrocab, progressing through their Technical Services Division. He had subsequently been transferred to the retailing branch and in that capacity had taken over Manchester's organisation. To mark Mann and Overton's inception centenary – they had now returned to their former network distribution policy – he led a team opening a new dealership in the Bristol area, intended to accommodate growing demand for wheelchair-accessible taxis in South Wales and South-West England.

However, problems grew with the Fairway. Provincial commentators deplored the bodywork's leaks, rattles and squeaks in addition to the above-mentioned poor visibility. It was decades outdated with too much emphasis placed on wheelchair accessibility – benefitting a small number of passengers. Also other forms of disablement were neglected. A new body had been considered but by the beginning of the 1990s, nothing had materialised. Before any serious work could start, LTI had to ensure they understood demand. Autumn 1990 saw an employee of the European Commission's department on car manufacturers, John Wragg, product-definition and development expert, appointed to investigate. His initial report in February 1991, referring to UK disability, warned of future change.

LTI observed other European developments. There were several projects running initiated by specialist designers, including production of Renault's Espace, the EEC's only multi-purpose vehicle running. There were thoughts that this was adaptable as a taxi. Trials in Paris resulted in fierce opposition from both drivers and customers – 'no dependence on a vehicle from another manufacturer' was a lesson well learnt.

Thus for new Fairway running gear, LTI looked to their new 'gamma' project. GKN, (now part of DANA's USA corporation) were called in to produce a new suspension system. Their Johnston Product Design Centre in Wolverhampton saw revised chassis engineering involving new wishbones, designed with ball joints, replacing the former fulcrum pins, mounted within the coil springs, as well as telescopic dampers fitted frontally, matching those already on the rear. The Salisbury axle, known as 'Drew's Lane', originally from the Austin Westminster, was now replaced by a new GKN light commercial, hung on to the new springs. Attention then turned to braking; relying on drums all round was now deemed outdated. Also they had to be mounted on the suspension, allowing for the 25ft turning circle. Front suspension development and incorporation of disc brakes enabled A.P. Lockheed to participate in liaison with GKN. Lockheed boasted a long and excellent track record in the hydraulic-brake field and at their Leamington Spa works had developed a system involving four-pot callipers and vented discs. New drums with a self-adjustment facility were to be used for the back and there were new six-stud hubs with wider wheels offset to clear these bigger units.

Prolonged, intensive tests were conducted on MIRA's development track, including trials on the notoriously punishing rough cobblestone or 'pavé' surface before the new model was released in February 1993, as the 'Fairway Driver'. Selling at just under £20,000, the suspension (currently still of the late 1950s) was revised by GKN to incorporate all-round telescopic shock absorbers, front disc brakes and self-adjusting rear shoe brakes for noticeably improved travel (the rationale behind the 'driver' label). Additional features included two-speed windscreen wipers, electric rear-window heating and wing-mounted repeating indicators and hazard flashers; all soon became standard. Although black had been accepted as the standard colour for many years, six alternatives now became available, some vehicles being able to carry advertisements anywhere except on the boot; registration and licence numbers could not be obscured.

Most important of all, however, was disability requirement. Soon the periodically updated Disability Discrimination Act would require all taxicabs to provide appropriate facilities and LTI even consulted the organisation *Arthritis Care*, specifically their Coventry branch, to establish what equipment would suit this vehicle. The swivel seat and the extra low step were chosen.

Momentarily digressing, despite the dictum that 'you can't turn the clock back', one company, Asquith, did so. Specialising in vintage vehicles, their factory in Banbury, Oxfordshire built vans and minibuses with 1930s designs but using modern technology. One 1990 visitor saw the 'Highland' van and called over to the marketing director, Mr Crispin Reed, to the effect that only the addition of appropriately styled windows would give the appearance of a pre-war taxicab. Reed, knowledgeable in cab construction of that period, decided that manufacture of a vintage-style cab was a feasible and worthwhile bet, particularly believing that foreign buyers would be interested. A prototype of the exterior was built and exhibited at London's Motor Fair of 1991. Response was sufficiently encouraging to make a complete prototype worth building. One taxi driver was sufficiently impressed and ordered one, firing the starting gun. Manufacturers had to ensure that modern regulations were satisfied but once the PCO approved, the first licensed vehicle bore the registration L1 WED. Ten were licensed for London. However, in practice, their use was restricted to private functions.

A steel-framed GRP body accommodated four doors, five seats and complete wheelchair accessibility, all above an independent chassis. No doubt the finished product sported an attractive appearance but the PCO dismissed it for poor overall quality. A second attempt was tested during autumn 1992. Several potential customers came forward, Reed requesting a £500 deposit. There were two options (both automatics): firstly a Ford Transit Diesel engine, similar to Metrocab's but with superior compression ratio – that of the maximum to minimum piston volume available during engine strokes; secondly a Ford petrol engine. Disc brakes were fitted throughout. General Motors provided the axles and steering. The coil spring front suspension was from the Vauxhall Midi van and the rear axle was a Frontera feature hung on Dunlop air suspension.

The cab was introduced during spring 1994 at Marylebone Station, transport minister Mr Steve Norris speaking. The basic selling price was just under £30,000 with optional interior extras and air conditioning available. Reed hoped that the home market would receive up to twenty annual orders, exports comfortably exceeding that figure. Initial reception was very positive, both from purchasers and their passengers but problems soon arose – primarily with the back axle. Asquith was woefully unprepared to rectify matters and honour warranties. They were short of spares and had no direct London representative to handle problems. Garages approached showed reluctance, fearing further troubles.

But Asquith were not giving up. In 1996 trade press announcements heralded a new variant, a prototype exhibited at London's Motor Fair. A new organisation was formed, the New Asquith Motor Company, using cheap Sri Lankan labour for manufacture, hoping to sell at about £1,000 below rival Fairways and Metrocabs. The air suspension system was as before but the back was lowered for easier disabled accessibility. Sadly, financial strains prevented the plan from materialising and during winter 1997 another company – the Asquith Motor Carriage Group – was formed to take over the original's assets, reputedly leaving liabilities with investing customers. In turn, the carriage company called in the receivers before Christmas 1998.

Returning to modernity, the 'delta' project followed. A European ministers' meeting in Seville later that year recognised that with medical advances lowering mortality rates the world population was ageing and public transport needed to adjust, emphasising wheelchair accessibility. Design Research Ltd of Warwick and Automotive Engineering Centre of Birmingham University had joined forces to start the 'Hermes' project, a luxury vehicle with a hybrid gas-turbine electric power unit. The taxi version, 'delta', subsequently modified and renamed 'eta', was first exhibited at Birmingham's National Exhibition Centre in November 1993's Autotech Exhibition. The original project was largely ignored but the taxi variant, with its distinctive shape and power plant, attracted media attention. Sadly, for LTI, the technology was too advanced and complicated and the power plant was hardly maintainable in small railway-arch garages, the trade's backbone.

Thus LTI had to work on meeting demand at that level, their first problem centring on the meaning of 'accessibility', regarding floor level, door width and height. They also had to consider non-limb ailments like blindness and deafness. Contacting Warwick University, they encouraged them to take on a product development plan. Learning from the Hermes/eta work, new ideas were tabled, notably regarding front-end and rear-end facelifts. Knowing that new legislation was imminent, laying special emphasis on safety, accessibility and environmental friendliness, LTI attacked the project, concentrating on these parameters. Working on a new product necessitated compliance with European Community Whole Vehicle Type Approval (ECWVTA) regulations. Three further imperatives governed the design – the Disability Discrimination Act (DDA),

Conditions of Fitness and customer demand. Some cabbies were keen on Mercedes or BMW styles but a prototype based on them was scrapped, doors being too small to satisfy wheelchair access requirements and – more important – the icon of London's cabs, considered the greatest asset, would be missing. So work started on a hybrid, code-named delta after the above-mentioned plan but published as 'Eta/2000', attempting to sound futuristic.

This would hopefully meet all requirements to the millennium and beyond with a new body built to prevailing modern industrial standards and be universally accept-able. Not only were the elderly, sick and disabled to be accommodated but also young mothers with babies. Later Fairway models were equipped with a movable step and a nearside facing seat, which could swivel outwards and lock back into its initial posi-tion once the passenger was safely aboard. Seat edges, doorsills and interior handles were highlighted in red for the poor-sighted and automatic door locks were activated during motion. An electric sunroof and air conditioning were among optional extras. The Fairway also became the first vehicle with a rear high-level stop lamp.

By Christmas 1996, nearly 4,300 had been manufactured with three (the last run-ning on LPG) sold to the Duke of Edinburgh. Series III variants appeared in 1998 with improved styling and new seating configurations offering an option to accommodate up to seven passengers.

As indicated earlier, the British Government tackled problems in its Disability Discrimination Act (DDA) of 1995, the relevant consultative document, detailing wheelchair requirements, emerging in summer 1997. The Act aimed, in principle, to have all taxis wheelchair-accessible by the turn of the millennium (a few exemptions being granted). The principles and rationale behind this legislation were universally known but they overrode previous requirements applicable to London. As inevitably happened in this type of situation, firm resistance was rife provincially, notably where local legislation stipulated mandatory requirement that taxis be of London type. In addition to the established argument that the LTI cab was unsuitable, unreliable and lacking in appropriate service facilities, other points were forwarded. Little demand appeared for wheelchair accessibility and anyway, elderly people, fit or disabled, had considerable difficulty with Fairways. There were also problems with the taxi-card facil-ity. In practice, however, the only point impressing the government was cost.

In the new project, LTI engaged the partnership of Coventry company NGA. The first problem concerned the DDA's demand for 53in door height. The Fairway's was 6in short. In practice, only 3in were added with doors set into the roof. Then the wind-screen and driver's headroom had to be enlarged and the overall driver's cabin size increased markedly.

Then, by current standards, the Fairway lacked rigidity. In the new model, A-posts were aligned to the chassis position linking to the suspension. Further strength was added by the inclusion of a bonded windscreen, conveniently removing the risk of leaking. A full steel door was welded into place. The whole body was adaptable to left-hand drive, tooling being contracted out to local Coventry companies. The interior was completely new – seats, dashboard, hardware, trim and other fixings.

However, in certain respects, conservatism seemed justifiable. The Fairway chassis had proved itself an excellent base for 'delta'; changes would merely compromise reliability and availability of back-up services. DDA requirements demanded that wheelbases be lengthened by 3in and tracks by 2.5in. The Nissan engine had been an outstanding success in all respects but a new fuel pump was added, reducing exhaust emissions. Front suspension ball joints and the steering box were uprated, continuing the use of composite springs.

Regarding noise levels, the legal maximum was 74 decibels. The Leyland Technical Centre provided facilities to study vibration-generated noise, discovering that, whereas the Fairway chassis and body shell were linked, best results could be obtained by isolating them and attaching vibration absorbing or 'deadpan' material to the bodyshell exterior, eliminating the effect called 'body drumming'. Thus Fairways would not have met standards under European Whole Vehicle Type Approval regulations, due from January 1998, and had to go. Despite its classic shape, it had run its course and early October 1997 saw the last model roll off the production line … straight into Dorset's National Motor Museum! Conveniently this year had R registration for motor vehicles and Carbodies' resident humourist appropriately gave the cab a registration: R1 PFX.

Thus the FX series rests in peace and after a creditable innings of around four decades (although the Nissan engine and various modern technological aspects had given it a new lease of life), designs had begun to show their age. The rival Metrocab also showed limitations, notably poor build, cramped driving position, restricted visibility through the relatively narrow windscreen and exhaust-emission problems.

However, Metrocab was determined to persist with the new six-seater variant. A straight partition replaced the predecessors' dog-legged version allowing a third tip-up seat, accommodating a sixth passenger. The rear seat position could be adjusted for wheelchair admission. This idea was extended further, at least provincially, a seventh seat being positioned just behind the driver. The six- and seven-seaters were instantly successful, the first half-year's figures accounting for 30 per cent of Metrocab's sales.

Autumn 1995 saw Hoopers introduce Metrocab's Series II. The bodyshell and chassis remained but the introduction of 76PS Ford engines, first manufactured the previous January, ensured greater power and improved fuel economy. Other advances included front-end redesigning, with a new colour-coded grille and profiled bumpers, all endowed with improved paintwork. The redesigned interior sported new lights and reshaped glassware. The boot floor was depressed, leaving extra room for wheelchair ramps.

That year's Disability Discrimination Act required all purpose-built taxicabs to be wheelchair-accessible by New Year 1999. From the turn of the millennium, new vehicles would need wheelchair facility as standard. Thus, from then, proprietors of cabs like the FX4S and FX4S Plus would require appropriate conversion. Several companies had been established over the previous few years to offer this, notably Taxi Access, owned by established Licensed Taxi Drivers' Association member Mr Steve Hawes.

For conversion, hinges had to be placed enabling the nearside rear door to be opened through a quarter circle. A partition, in step form and a wheelchair ramp set would also be provided. Once conversion was complete, the £1,500 investment would legalise use for at least another two years.

There were also regulations due for specification by the Disabled Persons Transport Advisory Committee of the Department of the Environment, Transport and the Regions, known as Diptac. These would cover dimensions of wheelchair-accessible taxicabs. However, by the end of the millennium, specifications were still unpublished, leaving LTI and Metrocab wondering what to expect. Metrocab, on stage for around a decade, would need modernising or, more likely, replacement if Metrocab (UK) were to continue to, at least, run parallel with LTI.

There was one suggestion that Series II Metrocabs should be modified by dramatically increasing roof height. But the engineering involved was considered impossible, Chater rejecting it outright. Preferring to build a new model, John Dick permitted development work to start under code initials CETA – 'global' taxi. Former design head (initially of Chrysler (UK), subsequently of Austin-Rover) Roy Axe was approached to complete styling of a markedly larger model than its predecessor. A great deal was spent while Diptac kept everybody in suspense. Eventually, Metrocab gave up and scrapped it during winter 2002–03, the illustrated prototype finishing in a German motor museum owned by Dick.

Fairways may have met modern standards but the bases were on originals now thirty-plus years old. LTI thus felt obliged to start from scratch, basing new ideas on several possible candidates, notably the Renault Espace MPV. However, CR6 trials of the early 1980s had demonstrated the false economy of basing new vehicles on production lines of predecessors or other vehicles. Modifications needed would result in new vehicles getting the worst of all worlds. Also, with all the griping involved with FX4, modifying its established shape was perilous.

With the need to satisfy the stringent PCO safety regulations while maintaining the charisma expected from modern vehicles, 'delta' proved a better prospect, initial chassis faults soon being rectified. Early spring 1997 saw a close inspection by a discerning cabbie group, recognised as difficult to please.

Overall appearance and handling were impressive. The shape resembled the Fairway but LTI design director Jevon Thorpe had updated the exterior, neatly rounded several features and lowered the bonnet to slope downwards. Other popular innovations included the worker-friendly or 'ergonomically' designed driver's seat for increased comfort, informative dashboard or 'facia', walnut-styled instrument panel and car entertainment. For passengers, there were access improvements with taller and wider doors; rear seats were wider and more comfortable than before. There was an integral child's seat built into the central armrest and swivel seats were fitted with integral backrests. A power point was available for mobile phones or laptop computing and there was an induction loop for hearing aids. Disabled and poorly sighted passengers were treated to highly illuminated seat edges with grab handles and easily-operated external doors. Wheelchair access was achieved by telescopic ramps. Another novelty was a rear-window indicator, telling cabbies behind whether this one was 'for hire'.

The new vehicle was actually slightly taller and wider than the Fairway. However, with curved bodylines, larger doors, extended glass area with a deep, modestly curved windscreen and moulded bumpers at both front and rear, it appeared, if anything, smaller. It used the same running gear as the Fairway driver but had a new body accommodating five seats. Large numbers of adverse comments almost all referred to minor matters, none expressing serious disapproval.

Several names were proposed, including Fairmile but then it was suggested that TAXI with the second letter omitted should be used with the 'I' read as number one – TX1. After much poorly guarded 'secrecy' this was first displayed during 1997's London Motor Show, a fortnight after completion of the last FX4. Film star Glenda Jackson officiated as MP and junior minister with special responsibility for London Transport in Tony Blair's Labour government, .

Autumn saw its official launch when the public, attending the British Library at St Pancras, could view the product of a £20 million investment from Manganese Bronze Holdings as LTI's parent company. Two-and-half years were spent in design and manufacture. Hopefully, this would make a significant leap forward in enhancing similarity between taxicab and private saloon car. While retaining aspects of predecessors' style, it was of completely modern design.

The TX1 proved itself from 1998 as production steadily increased (initially sixty weekly then seventy–eighty by 1999); further problems were corrected as they arose. Typically, headlights caused a dilemma, balancing the need for modern appearance against necessity to minimise repair costs. Simple round fittings were chosen behind a plastic cover for convenient replacement. Similar rationale applied to moulded bumpers, which were in three pieces with separate ends. Overall technological improvements enabled service interval extension from 6,000 to 9,000 miles for less-frequent absences. A left-hand drive version was available for foreign buyers. Trials with an Iveco LPG-fuelled spark ignition engine began in summer 1996, to satisfy markets insisting on such inclusion.

From November 1997 LTI dropped the name Carbodies from their company title. It was during that month that Metrocab introduced their answer to TX1, the Series III. The new cab was first on show at RAF's Museum in Hendon, North-West London. Managing Director Mike Thurlow's introductory speech expressed hope that Metrocab's market share would improve considerably. They were already doing well, with about 25 per cent in London and nearer 40 per cent provincially, notably the West Midlands.

The Series III featured sixty-plus improvements on predecessors. Probably most important were a more efficient Ford engine, a manual gearbox operating with an improved silencer system for markedly lower decibels and a modernised starter and alternator. Resin was injected around the body for a more attractive finish. Electric windows were fitted into the rear doors. Radio speakers were now available in the passenger compartment and the new driver-passenger partition gave better visibility. Thus, drivers could watch naughty activity. The dashboard, heating and ventilating systems were all new with passenger intercom standard.

However, contrary to Chater's advice, the board had rushed, introducing the new series too early. He saw that LTI were going to take a considerable time, months at best, to get TX1 production speed up to maximum and sticking to Series II could have earned them a bigger market share during this period. As history often proved, early production hazards emerged, Metrocab finding insurmountable problems in meeting demand for their new model.

Further trouble surfaced regarding Euro 3's 2001 emission regulations. Ford FSD engines, currently used by Metrocabs, were incompliant, needing replacement. First thoughts centred around a new Ford engine – the Duratorq Turbo (gas-turbine propelled) Diesel, originally designed for their Transit and mid-range passenger cars. Sadly, failing to fit, it was rejected. It proved necessary to turn to Japan, the much quieter Toyota 2.4 turbo diesel fitting the bill, working with four-speed automatic or five-speed manual gearboxes. The model was called triple T or TTT, announced in March 2000, comfortably short of deadline. Toyota were now able to purchase and fit a front suspension and ventilated disc brakes (as for TX1) from LTI. The TTT also sported a new rear axle. A further novelty was a 'For Hire' light, featuring an LED (light emitting diode) display, improving daylight visibility.

'Lux Packs' were available, offering extras, notably chrome wheel trims, rear carpet, rich upholstery fabric or 'velour' trim, a flat-bedded wheelchair ramp and lap seat belts for rear-facing seats. The TTT was universally welcomed in the trade press.

Still considering clean air, improvements were sought. Trouble stemmed from 1952's infamous pea-souper fog, minimising visibility and causing numerous deaths through consequent road accidents and lung problems. After the Clean Air Act of 1956 matters had gradually improved. Further progress was hoped for in using LPG-fuelled vehicles, earning the complimentary title 'green'. While no specific legislation applicable to cabs existed, London's Mayor, Ken Livingstone, tried to reduce diesel emission levels. His first proposal was phasing out twelve-plus-year-old cabs by 2007. Following trade members' furious protests, 2003 saw him trying an alternative, stipulating that cab owners install a fitting to reduce undesirable chemical content of exhaust fumes: an ammonia-injection system provided the necessary effect. Firstly, cabs manufactured to August 1998 would require this equipment when presented to the PCO on or after New Year's Day 2006. Those compliant with Euro-2 regulations would soon follow.

Even this attracted stern rebuke, notably from the London Taxi Drivers' Association. While welcoming aims for cleaner air, there was no conclusive proof that older cabs were polluters. They also deplored the £2,000 cost of equipment, not yet tested satisfactorily. There was only one type available anyway. Livingstone relented, substituting New Year's Day with 1 July and making rules applicable to LTI vehicles registered prior to 16 September 1998 and Metrocabs prior to 4 December 1997. Similar delays would be applicable to cabs registered later. Nonetheless, equipment efficiency had still to be demonstrated, the matter remaining unresolved. More emission problem details appear in Appendix 21.

The TX1 was replaced by the TX2 in 2002. Similarly designed, it faced problems resembling Metrocab's, notably it's Nissan TD27 engine failing to meet Euro exhaust emission standards.

A new Ford-based engine, Duratorq turbocharged diesel, appeared, offering two clear advantages: greater torque and bhp with a new passive anti-theft system integrated into the management system. Additionally, there was full-width glass in the rear doors with the opening cleverly restricted, preventing bilkers from escaping through the window. Optional extras included CCTV, hopefully enhancing driver security, an electric seat that could be swivelled and an extra front seat.

Sadly, it proved unpopular with drivers. The engine proved disappointing with severe driveline vibrations and the mounting, designed for transverse installation on to in-line configuration, caused 'drumming' effects during various speed ranges. Additionally, electrical faults caused fires. There were also incompatibility problems for left-hand drive models. Furthermore, more than two-thirds of users needed automatic transmission requiring an engine complete with a unit compatible with the latest Euro-4 criteria. For these reasons, on 18 October 2006, the TX4 was launched, so numbered 'in tribute' to the FX4. Also, coincidentally, it used a Euro-4-compliant diesel engine. There was no TX3.

(In connection with the TX2, Hybrid Electric Vehicles (HEV's) appeared around then (technical details in Appendix 21). Canadian firm Azure Dynamics produced appropriate power units and April 2003 saw Manganese Bronze signing an agreement with them for power systems. A vehicle duly arrived in Canada two months later and was fitted with a 'G2r powertrain' for vehicles of corresponding weight range. Costs and serviceability proved vital factors in deciding whether this had a viable future).

The TX4 boasted coalescence of advanced technology and modern gadgets, all rigorously tested in wide varieties of climatic and road conditions – typically cobbled streets and sleeping policemen – over distances totalling thirty-plus planetary navigations. As LTI's new manager, Peter Shilcock, explained, this was the product of six decades' experience, three years' development and £5 million investment. Among its many attributes is the anti-locking braking system, making for smoother, more comfortable journeys. However, several taxi drivers viewed 'quiet' runs with reservations. It's important that prospective passengers easily hear the taxi coming up behind them; interesting! However, for durability, reliability and efficiency, the TX4 must be the world's most advanced taxi to date, catering for the disabled passenger as efficiently as anything yet.

Still on disability, since inception of wheelchair requirement, all cabs were equipped with approved access ramps and interior safety harnesses, securing both wheelchair and occupant. They undergo stringent annual PCO tests – similar to motor cars' MOT test but more rigorous, notably regarding safety. Testing over about forty minutes sees examiners expecting to find top-standard regulation conformity with the parameters listed in Appendix 7. With the high mileage covered by taxis, wear and tear will obviously be considerable, even on steering and suspension. No tolerance is acceptable on king pins and track rods. If vehicles fail, on the slightest fault, they must be retested until approved.

Cabs are additionally subjected to random PCO engineer spot checks; thus it is crucial for continual maintenance in top-grade condition. Thus the 'stitch in time' mentality is highly relevant and vehicles must be regularly serviced with all faults rectified immediately. While considering engineers' complaints, we also discuss customers'. Authorities usually receive up to 2,000 annually, mainly regarding refusals. Figures have gently declined recently but those received are probably scarcely more than the tip of the iceberg, most not bothering to complain. However, with the advent of email and other quick-fire communication methods, numbers will increase unless standards improve.

In particular, rules appertaining to Heathrow have changed recently. Drivers' queuing time has increased from thirty to sixty minutes; this will surely impact on complaint numbers regarding passing off unwanted fares to following cabs ('brooming') and white-knuckle journeys should fall considerably. However, drivers now have to wait two hours in a feeder park before being allowed on to a rank, only 400 cabs permitted at any time. Drivers are expected to accept any journey up to 20 miles within Heathrow's licensing area. They are particularly reluctant to cross the Thames, because of difficulty in getting return fares.

Detailing complaints, much depends on their nature and seriousness. Offences covered by Hackney carriage legislation are mostly heard by magistrates. Sadly, fears of abuse, personal investigation and court appearance tend to put many off. Court appearance is rare anyway for several reasons, primarily the seven-day process. Primary legislation requires that all relevant information be supplied to authorities within seven days of the incident. Letters take time to write and arrive; there may be inconvenience in contacting the complainant and in driver identification; the whole process could take several months without guarantee of success. Many thus decide that it's all just not worth it. With very minor complaints, the driver will usually be allowed to give his side of the story. After interview, he normally finishes with a warning or, after persistent offences, suspension.

The run up to Christmas 2003 saw Metrocab go into administration, with over 100 jobs lost. Their weekly production rate, twenty, had dropped to an uneconomical ten. Two things were deemed causative. The PCO's relaxation of 'knowledge' requirements to get prospective drivers tested successfully sooner inevitably increased driver numbers. With the slump of ten years previously still in mind, most drivers decided to keep their current vehicles rather than risk new purchases possibly proving unaffordable. Also losses sustained in the CETA project had proved crippling.

Six months' negotiations bore fruit when Metrocab (UK) Ltd found a buyer. Kam Korp Europe Ltd, Europe's division of Singapore-based technical developers Kam Korp, came to the rescue. September 2004 saw Mark Morris, acting managing director of Metrocab (UK) Ltd, announcing trade recommencement. He hoped to get TTT going by the end of that month. Owners would be provided with necessary spares, a new model becoming available in 2005. Delivery duly began in April that year, regular production of up to four cabs weekly progressing by autumn. Most purchasers were provincial.

6

Competition Arrives: 1961-Present

eturning to the 1960s – comparatively prosperous with minimal unemployment and plenty of spending money – cab demand grew considerably, the trade having difficulty in meeting it, London's numbers having slumped to around 7,000. Carbodies' manufacturing could not meet FX4 demand; authorities were not qualifying enough drivers.

The door thus opened for the taxi's biggest threat – the minicab. First raised in November 1960 by Conservative MP Mr Rupert Speir, describing taxi services as 'inadequate', notably regarding outdated design and legality, he called for a city-wide telephone service in which an easily-memorised code like TAX or CAB could be linked to all taxi ranks. He further suggested introducing smaller taxis, 'minicabs'. Replying, Home Office Minister of State Dennis Vosper discussed important points:

Firstly, minicabs would have to stand strains of continual London work, covering an annual mileage of around 40,000. The term 'minicab' would cover two groups, licensed private hire vehicles (PHV's) and illegal taxi 'touts', trying to ply for hire as 'licensed' taxis. Relevant legislation forbade private hire-car drivers accepting clients in the street or even at a rank in this manner.

Secondly, smaller cabs, tried before, having attracted little demand, were withdrawn. This presumably referred to two-seater cabs, which had never been given a fair chance. Thirdly, he still feared limited demand – manufacturers would not be interested.

There, for Parliament at least, matters rested but on 9 December, minicabs' initial inception was announced. The initiator was Michael Gotla, law graduate, advertiser and now managing director of Welbeck Motors Ltd. Welbeck sold and hired cars; he moonlighted as a private-hire chauffeur. By 1960, financed by Sir Isaac Wolfson's General Guarantee Corporation, he developed Welbeck into a flourishing business with 100-plus staff. Gotla planned to put two hundred small-car 'taxis' out during 1961. Both sexes were welcome as drivers, radio-guided by three former knowledgeable taxi drivers.

Minicab drivers were clad in khaki shirts, trousers and forage caps and their storm-trooper-like turnout earned the nickname of 'Gotla's Private Army'. The problem was legality. Minicabs were not licensed by Scotland Yard for street plying. However, Gotla did not want to count exclusively on telephone bookings. He tried to justify alternative interpretation of 'plying for hire'. All Hackney carriage Acts passed over the previous 130 years were centred around dubious distinctions between taxi and minicab, only the former permitted to ply for business on the street Gotla flouted this by encouraging passengers to hail the first minicab in sight. The driver then handed the customer his phone, which would be used to call the HQ by two-way short-wave radio and thus be provided with another minicab, hopefully arriving shortly afterwards, to satisfy the rules.

Apparently legal advice was taken, decades of taxi legislation being thrown to the winds. Cab traders were furious, insisting, rightly in practice, that minicab drivers would ignore these petty technicalities, simply getting on with the job. Big trouble rapidly approached. Cab drivers who caught minicab rivals' breaking the rules went in for bitter fighting with minicab drivers who were ready for battle.

The court authorities ruled Gotla's methods illegal. Encouraged by their success, the cab trade, more accurately the cab section of the Transport and General Workers' Union (hence TGWU), approached the government to outlaw minicabs completely. They proposed clearer and stricter laws regarding plying for hire, hopefully simplifying matters for arbitrating police.

However, no success; R.A. Butler, Home Secretary, ruled in favour of minicabs, deeming current legislation already sufficient. Nevertheless, the next two or three years saw several minicab firms successfully prosecuted for illegal touting. Minicabs – several hundred, primarily maroon Renault Dauphines and Ford Prefects – undercut taxis by charging a straight 1s (decimal 5p) per mile against taxi rates of 1s 9d for the first three-fifths of a mile, 1s 3d per mile thereafter. Thus they enjoyed the advantages of taxi work without the disadvantages – knowledge requirement, inspection, compulsory overhauls, regulated prices – while sustaining minimal authoritarian trouble.

Actually, private individuals had tried this before, using their own cars but on too small a scale for serious competition. However, it was now significant even if, according to some reports, Welbeck lost nearly £2 million. Although first to officially announce that minicabs were on the streets, two other companies had quietly beaten them to it. March 1961 had seen Carline of Wimbledon put out a dozen-strong fleet of Ford Anglias. Focusing on busy areas, like sports arenas – greyhound tracks and football stadia – and railway stations, they established ranks on private sites like builders' yards and shop driveways. They dodged 'plying for hire' charges by deeming the last cab on rank as 'headquarters'. The prospective passenger would announce his destination to the 'HQ', then be directed to the front cab, directions being radioed up the line. They considered this legal 'advanced booking' albeit the 'advance' being a few seconds. Additionally, the company planned two extra services – a credit-card option for regular passengers, under which they would be sent a monthly bill and a shared-taxi arrangement, taking three people from Wimbledon to the City for £1 15s.

Many drivers applied but Carline eliminated a proportion, citing driving ignorance and/or poor geographical knowledge. Drivers needed at least ten years' experience and were required to pass the Institute of Advanced Motorists' Driving Test – certainly creditable but of arguably dubious necessity for those spending considerable time in traffic jams. For geography, drivers needed one month's study against prospective cabbies' eighteen plus.

Secondly, there was Sylvester Car Hire, operating from Pimlico's Dolphin Square. They drove Fiat Multiplas, Fiat 600 variants in which the driver sat alongside the engine with up to six passengers behind. These were unique as the only minicabs with meters, charging 1s 6d for the first mile, 1s per mile thereafter. A fleet of Multiplas also operated from Watford but plans to expand to provincial cities like Leeds and Glasgow were abandoned.

Legally speaking, minicabs were only subject to basic motoring rules. In practice, many vehicles were unsafe and – with no explicit licence required – often driven by disreputable drivers with criminal and/or mental-hospital pasts. Abuses were common, attractive women often being offered cheaper or free rides in return for tempestuous kisses, cuddles or sexual favours. Here there was considerable fear in the taxi trade that the Conditions of Fitness might be made less stringent, making a mockery of new cabs under development. Concern was expressed in a letter to Mr Butler from Mr Welland, secretary to LMCPA. He urged Butler not to take any potentially irrevocable decision without due consultation with an advisory body. Butler responded positively, inviting Denis Vosper to chair a committee – the Hackney Carriage Advisory Committee. They were instructed to review the current Conditions of Fitness to see if smaller, cheaper cabs were feasible and whether they could be produced in sufficient numbers. Even saloon cars were possible.

Consequently work on cabs designed to meet existing stringencies – typically Winchester, Beardmore MK VIII and Birch MK 2 – was suspended, there being little point in continuing. Of these, only the latter was in the smaller, cheaper class and had, as indicated, already had its chassis rejected. However, the PCO, in two minds, clarified during spring 1961, fearing criticism if they stood firm. Beardmore, having spent a fortune on parts, etc., were also concerned and Francis Allsworth, during July, wrote to the Police Commissioner to find out more on the progress of the decision progress. The following month saw interested parties invited to state their case. Allsworth obviously supported current regulations but spoke of manufacturers' being allowed latitude to move with technological advances.

Sadly, the Committee worked like snails, many months passing before the final decision was made. With his patience rapidly running out, Allsworth wrote again to the

PCO's Mr Perrett in early spring 1962. He explained that his company was already heavily committed to producing taxis under the current rules and financiers would probably withdraw support unless guaranteed that they would, at least in principle, be kept in force. The committee eventually tried to please everybody (especially Austin) by insisting on a modest a updating of the Conditions of Fitness, keeping abreast of certain measurements and insistence on a separate chassis while retaining the turning circle and driver/passenger separation stipulations.

Also around spring 1961, cab traders' awareness of rivals started making popular press headlines. Minicabs had generally been welcomed as 'the first taxi-service innovation since the horse's replacement'. It was arguably paradoxical that minicabs received the sympathy customarily afforded to 'little' newcomers challenging big monopolies – 'Charlie Chaplin syndrome' – but Welbeck were actually the biggest fleet owners against a large number of maligned owner-driven cabs. Truthfully, however, the press tended to criticise the taxi system as a whole rather than individual drivers, described as 'good fellows'. An exception was The New Daily, a new paper itself trying to enter an unwelcoming market by emphasising public interests against a kaleidoscope of organisations. The taxi service thus 'qualified', drivers being described as arrogant, rude and unhelpful. The Daily Worker, supporting left-wing causes, was kicking the other way and published several articles written by cabbies criticising minicabs.

Such criticism divided under two headings – driver and vehicle. Since 1907, taxi drivers had to satisfy stiff tests of knowledge, health and character. In contrast, minicab authorities – with few legal requirements – made little effort, effectively welcoming anyone with a valid driving licence. While the taxi had to undergo stringent tests to satisfy the Conditions of Fitness, being regularly examined at great expense, minicabs faced no such requirements. It's ironic that failing taxis were legally entitled to operate thenceforth as minicabs! Many vehicles running as minicabs lasted barely one year. They were soon replaced and, being operated by countless independent firms, were indistinguishable from private cars.

The taxi trade reaction? Many cabbies felt that they had enough traffic problems, poor road systems, misplaced underpasses, one-way systems and 'no-left-turn' and 'no-right-turn' signs causing inconvenience. Coaches, vans, lorries and worst of all, dustcarts only exacerbated the situation. London was reputed to be one of the world's worst major cities in these respects, possibly excepting Tokyo. Initially, opinions on intruding threats varied considerably. One felt that 'they will not get far'; others: 'they must be stopped'. The latter school soon realised that this implied drastic action. On 8 March 1961 there was a 3,000-strong mass meeting of cabbies at Seymour Hall, Marylebone. General Secretary of the Cab Drivers' section of the Transport and General Workers' Union Jim Francis announced that Home Secretary Mr Richard Austin(!) Butler was allowed a few more days. Unless taxi drivers were satisfied with the proposals offered, they would have to consider steps to protect their interests. The meeting passed a resolution expressing grave distress at the threat to living standards and established a fund, each driver contributing

1d (one old penny) per week. Francis and several drivers established a Cab Trade Crisis Committee. A week later, Butler was asked in the House to make the proposed Welbeck method of hiring illegal. He replied, stating that if police thought that this constituted plying under the Metropolitan Carriage Act of 1869, prosecutions might follow.

Minicab drivers were hardly disturbed by this vague, non-committal 'buck-passing' and as indicated above, Welbeck had already ordered 800 Renault Dauphines, at £560,000, breaking the record as the largest single order placed by a British firm with foreign manufacturers. The original intention was for yellow trimming, presumably reflecting American practice but maroon, already used, was preferred as it was cheaper. The Motor Cab Owner-Drivers' Association stated that, if nothing were done, they themselves would gather evidence to start and assist such prosecutions. In practice, there were few police prosecutions but where cabbies initiated their own, they had some success. One minicab driver was fined £5 for plying and Welbeck were charged a similar amount plus £26 5s (£26.25 decimal) costs. Similar cases followed over the year but in November, one driver received two-months' jail time and a twelve-months' driving ban. A week later, an appalling incident in Brompton Road at 3 a.m. saw two cabbies hem in a minicab. The offenders received three-months' jail time and three years' driving bans. The London Cab Trade Crisis Committee called an emergency meeting and a forty-eight-hour strike, about 1,000 cab drivers observing. The following June saw the sentences commuted to £100 fines and the driving bans lifted.

Francis instructed taxi drivers not to molest minicab rivals but, knowing that feelings were running extremely high, could hardly guarantee acquiescence. War was declared and minicab drivers were soon complaining that about 10 per cent of their number – mainly older males – were attacked by taxi rivals. There were ugly scenes, many requiring police intervention. The tabloid press took full advantage (they would, wouldn't they!) thereby intensifying the conflict.

The first Sylvester cab appeared on 17 March, the company soon being swamped with orders. Taxi drivers protested furiously; the first recorded incident saw two cabbies place themselves to 'box in' a Sylvester, complaining to the police of illegal plying. The driver countered that he was seeking the address of a telephone-booked fare. A few days later, a minicab, hemmed in by thirty taxis, had to radio for help. The cabbies were booked for obstruction.

Around then, Carline tried to expand its clientele by offering *free* rides from Heathrow and major railway stations back to their Wimbledon depot. Unable to ply, they believed it sensible to generate goodwill and possibly attract new customers with journeys anyway. On realising this, cabbies again rebelled. One lady driver in her mid 20s, Valerie Atkins, was a typical victim. The Waterloo area on 6 June (D-Day anniversary) saw her surrounded and hemmed in by several taxis and calling Wimbledon for help. Police enabled her to escape. There were other similar incidents against Carline drivers as well as vehicle overturning and paint-splashing, necessitating their managing director, Mr R.W. Heath, to order private detectives to oversee potential trouble spots.

The government were reluctant to take sides but, following the Waterloo incident, Dennis Vosper seemed to side with minicabs, indicating to Parliament that they enabled wider proportions of the public – implying poorer classes – to use cabs, consistent with government policy. This was gleefully quoted by Welbeck in a full-page *Evening Standard* advertisement, their argument being that, rather than competing, they were establishing a new market. Twelve days later, 19 June saw the first Welbeck minicab take the plunge in a champagne ceremony at their Taunton Street premises with M. Guitton (French Ministry of Industry and Commerce) guest of honour. Again, the press chimed in, the *Evening News* producing a large feature exclaiming that five new minicabs would be added daily so that Christmas would see them 'part of the furniture'. Early cabs were plastered with advertisements, space being rented out cheaply in bulk so that the £75 annual return ensured an overall running profit.

In the consequent fracas, vehicles on both sides were subjected to traffic blockades, notably in key points like Marble Arch and Trafalgar Square, as well as overturning or arson. Passengers were physically pulled out of minicabs and insulted, one even assaulted. Racial discrimination surfaced when several, mostly Jewish, cabbies complained that Welbeck Motors refused to employ them, one of Welbeck's leading drivers being notoriously fascist. The best illustration was the well-publicised clash between Mrs Colin Jordan (a French 'lady' from Dior's fashion family; he was then British Nazi party leader) who took a ride with a Jewish cabbie, 'a few words being exchanged'. In fact, Welbeck were not involved but tension was already well established. The incident's adverse publicity had two serious effects on Welbeck's finances. In September, Air France withdrew their advertising. Others soon followed and with revenue worth about 1½d per mile per cab, losses proved critical. The only apparent solution, a fare increase, would compromise their competitive position. The first per-mile increment was to 1s 4d; the second to 1s 8d, implying that, for longer journeys, they out-charged taxis, defeating the object of the exercise. Two months later, Isaac Wolfson's General Guarantee Corporation withdrew financial support, selling their share to chairman R.S. Walker.

Already in October, assaults were commonplace, other tactics including squirting solder into ignition locks, punching holes into car bodywork, seat slashing and pouring foul-smelling liquids into minicab interiors. Taxi drivers also tried to disrupt minicab bookings by press-advertising cheap flat fares. A Welbeck phone number was given, leaving Welbeck inundated with wasted phone calls, obviously contributing to customers' principal anti-minicab complaint – slow switchboards.

Hundreds of fuming taxi drivers lobbied MP's, protest letters pouring into both the Home Office and Scotland Yard. The Yard received a deputation from the Transport and General Workers' Union and other relevant authorities. Worse followed when several militant cabbies turned to desperation, sending countless fake telephone calls to minicab HQ, provoking minicab drivers into illegally picking up passengers. Promptly reported to the police, they were taken to court. However, one magistrate, showing a strong sense of fair play, deemed this 'unsporting'.

Nonetheless, minicab drivers played on an equally low level. They started to pull cab-rank telephones out of their sockets and set fire to unattended cabs. The climax was reached when two taxi drivers were apprehended and jailed after chasing a minicab, forcing it to pull up against a kerb. This was considered inappropriate punishment, there being neither injury nor vehicle damage. Nevertheless, many thought this a minicab 'victory'. Police turned blind eyes to illegal minicab plying, only exacerbating cabbie-police relations, which had displayed varying degrees of ferocity since the nineteenth century. To crown it all, it later emerged that several police officers were moonlighting, driving minicabs! 'If you can't beat them …' Further parliamentary questions were asked but authorities argued that known cases were rare – offenders being severely censured – and that most officers respected instructions not to work out of hours.

Welbeck's running fleet currently boasted 250 minicabs, a further 500 being promised over the next two months. They also faced problems with high driver turnover; a typical week could welcome up to 100 new faces with two-thirds resigning or being dismissed. These were drivers either so inefficient that their income was inadequate or who were content merely to earn their minimum £8 weekly wage, spending the remaining time relaxing. Others neglected the appearance and/or condition of their vehicles and/or earned the company bad publicity with abusive and/or violent behaviour.

Strains were obviously going to increase; Mr Gotla, panicking, announced that if his scheme were successful over six months, he intended to aim for government control to be applicable to all cabs. He added that he was happy for taxis to dominate Central London if he could have the suburbs. This made little sense with most journeys, notably during rush hours, surely between one and the other. However, minicabs survived, being able to satisfy demand caused by suburban taxi shortage. The managing director, however, was dissatisfied. With Hitler-style rhetoric, he published a press article describing taxi drivers – or at least their militants – as 'a lot of sods'. He vowed to eliminate taxis completely, leaving drivers to work for him. The principal minicab operators' argument was that taxis had, to date, enjoyed a monopoly. Why could others not run cab fleets, provided they maintained reasonable standards of vehicle maintenance, driver knowledge and performance, safety and comfort? Standards, of course, were critical.

In November 1961, Gotla resigned, relocating to Worthing. However, his seeds had been planted. Over a year from spring 1961, nearly thirty new minicab companies had emerged despite the three originators all being in financial trouble. Carline received a local council notice to vacate their Wimbledon premises; the company was offered for sale. December saw Sylvester Car Hire renamed as Metrocabs, aiming to provide an inexpensive hire service at 1s 6d to 1s 8d per mile dependent on car size. Around then a complaint was made by a taxi driver against a Welbeck minicab driver plying in London's East End. He reported it to a police officer who ordered the minicab to move; it duly did. However, it returned later, the local police station becoming involved. The magistrate favoured the minicab, citing lack of evidence of illegal plying – the driver could have been awaiting radio instructions. The taxi driver's appeal was heard at the High Court in May 1962 but this time Lord Chief Justice Lord Parker viewed that the company's name and phone number, visible externally, constituted plying for hire. He directed the company to eliminate all advertising (and by January 1963, minicab numbers having dwindled to around 200, advertising had been officially banned). Within hours, all minicab drivers were contacted, being instructed to find an empty side street and remove their advertisements, leaving their vehicles indistinguishable from those privately owned.

Henceforth, it seemed that radio would be commonplace but over the period 1960–63, the number of radio-controlled cabs dropped from 2,000 to 700. The public and many journeymen were happy but many more drivers, although welcoming the possibility of keeping up with news and messages, found that they were managing without it; thus proprietors thought that radios – although admittedly invaluable in emergencies – constituted unnecessary expense. The truth was actually area-dependent. In Central London, radios were of little use. However, suburbs saw them prove their worth. But there were associated problems, perhaps describable as 'ethical'. Considerable animosity arose between radio and non-radio drivers. There was fear that cab ranks would disappear as inequitable situations could arise with a front non-radio cab superseded by the cab behind, called by radio. There was also potential trouble between radio drivers – the possibility of pushing each other off the air, office favouritism and similar. In practice, favouritism was rife anyway. Regular customers and important institutions like Buckingham Palace and Downing Street were given a priority phone number, enabling them to 'jump the queue'.

Still on taxi-driver relationships, it is very much love-hate. Regarding picking up fares, it may be pure war with no holds barred but there is no ethnic discrimination. There are regular dinners and friendly meetings, common clubbing together to raise money for worthy beneficiaries like widows and sick colleagues. If a driver breaks down, others will immediately try to help. Off the road, the main antagonism lies between the two major unions – the TGWU, primarily looking after journeymen interests – and later the Licensed Taxi Drivers' Association (hence LTDA, formation detailed shortly) for owner-drivers. Also many big garage proprietors have formed their own association and there's a subsidiary of Westminster Insurance called the Owner-Drivers' Association. Thus the trade is more fragmented than others, some drivers opting out completely as 'individualists' – the 'every man for himself' mentality.

January 1963 saw London's minicab population cut to 200 against 5,000 promised eighteen months earlier. Two more half-hearted attempts at providing cheap taxi alternatives were made. In March, 'small cab' champion Rupert Speir suggested two-seater cabs running on three wheels – effectively oriental-style 'rickshaws'. This design, loosely based on Italian Vespas or Lambretta motor scooters, was popular in the Middle East and Asia, originally pedal-propelled but later motor-driven. Modern rickshaw versions – two-seater 'pedicabs' on large tricycle frames – run in many countries.

A *Daily Express* journalist reported seeing his MP driving around Westminster in one and tried it out himself, finding that, while more manoeuvrable than the conventional taxi, it was very cold (this was April). He concluded that this was only for 'rickshaw' weather areas. Even worse here was the moped taxi 'traffic jam dodger', appearing the following year, driven by crash-helmeted young ladies, charging just under 2s per mile. *The Guardian* commented that it was worth it to put one's arms round a slim waist, even risking being soaked in the process! It failed to last a fortnight.

Meanwhile, minicabs displayed a remarkable second wind. By 1966 they were sprouting up again, some operated by reputable companies but others – sometimes described as 'fly-by-night' concerns – run by ex-criminals and other trouble-makers who lacked proper insurance, often leaving injured passengers uncompensated. Complaints of geographical ignorance abounded, taxi drivers deploring such behaviour. Minicab indiscretions reported included a driver grabbing hold of a lady's hat after receiving an insufficient tip and gross overcharging for trips from Heathrow. The commonest victims were single continental pregnant young ladies, who, having heard rumours that taxi drivers knew addresses of abortion clinics, had rushed over for terminations. Unaware that taxi drivers had to stay outside with their vehicles while hire-car drivers could tout inside the arrival buildings, these ladies could not distinguish between licensed taxis and hire cars. Cabbies were clearly disadvantaged but police could take little effective action. With customers ignorant of English currency, minicab touting and retaliatory cabbie overcharging was common. Normally, it was about £10 for the West End and £200–£300 for an abortion. But drivers received commissions from clinics, varying with pregnancy duration and the lady's ability to pay. Economic supply/demand forces were evident in their keen competition. Their level started around £15 but later settled around four times as much.

Although few cabbies offended, the whole trade was disgraced. Not only was there rivalry between taxi and minicab drivers but also between taxi drivers themselves, fights seeing losers hospitalised. One well-publicised fracas involved a lady being grabbed by a taxi driver while a rival firmly held her bag. The 'tug-of-war' was eventually settled when the first 'bought the bag' for £15. A few cabbies 'joined in the fun' by establishing their own pregnancy advisory centres, effectively acting as wholesalers while abortion clinics retailed their services. Ladies were questioned; documents were made out and having been asked how much they could pay, were driven to appropriate clinics. These were performing 200-plus abortions daily and customers, hardly given a chance for recovery, were returned to Heathrow by their original driver. Operators justified themselves by insisting that they were taking their clients to reputable clinics rather than back-street quacks. Several Sunday newspapers started investigations, not fearing to name racketeers, drivers and doctors, implying that the whole cab trade was serving the abortionists. Rumours circulated that even policemen were involved with the West End underworld, running abortions from Heathrow.

April 1966 saw the formation of the National Minicab Association, aiming to welcome reputable companies as one unit while excluding 'fly-by-nighters'. The president, Mr Frank Smith, wanted legislation requiring registration of all drivers who would then carry identification cards similar to cabbies' yellow or green badges. He also hoped for enforced regular vehicle inspection.

A central bureau for minicabs was established at Victoria Coach Station during summer 1966 but coach drivers who were TGWU members objected. Rather than strike, they organised a 'coordinated rest day', all drivers, members or not, taking the same day off. On 14 June, the modest numbers of taxis available took members to union meetings. There were a couple of altercations, the public suffering modest inconvenience, but Scotland Yard reported rush-hour traffic jams being far less prolonged than usual. Nonetheless, this modest union pressure was sufficient to force the office's closure soon afterwards.

The association could only attract about ten companies as members, three withdrawing within a year, the urge for quick profits, even at reputation's expense, proving decisive. In March 1967, 5,000 taxi drivers lobbied Parliament, complaining about minicabs operating without sufficient insurance or supervision. Home Secretary Roy Jenkins promised to receive a small deputation but cancelled at the last moment, having been called to address the House on other matters. The dispute climaxed when five militant TGWU members walked into Euston Station to find that the large car-hire firm Hertz having established a booking office, were encouraging new customers by placing attractive young ladies on the platform, handing out carnations to disembarking passengers. The incensed quintet approached the station manager, threatening to boycott the station if this continued. Misled into thinking he was up against a large union's full power, rather than five troublemakers, the manager capitulated, instructing Hertz to use more conventional advertising methods. Thrilled with their victory, the five gathered for an emergency meeting in a taxi owned by Mr Joe Toff, after which another mass cabbies' gathering was called at St Pancras Town Hall, the TGWU fully supporting the successful function.

Further positive action was called for; yet another larger meeting was called a few weeks thence at the Festival Hall. The organising TGWU taxi militants, 'ginger group', demanded formation of a breakaway union, solely for taxi drivers. The aim was to allocate a fraction of gross annual turnover, about £30 million, to pensions, improved legal aid, sickness and accident cover. Joe Toff proposed the name 'Licensed Taxi Drivers' Association'; as Public Relations Officer, he organised an enormous advertising campaign, including scantily dressed young ladies parading near Oxford Circus, handing out leaflets encouraging use of taxis rather than minicabs.

The union was officially formed in May 1967, primarily aiming to ensure that every licensed cab carried two-way radio for clear advantage over minicabs. The next few years saw it become the principal supporter of cabbies, superseding the TGWU, many drivers feeling that the LTDA better served their interests. Led by William D'Arcy, who became chairman, the union made active protests against minicab drivers' being licensed according to Maxwell Stamp report recommendations and their frequenting of hospitals and hotels. Their Festival Hall inaugural meeting attracted an attendance of 1,100, who were enrolled as members, raising a £2,000 fund. The membership increased to 4,500 by May 1971. They published a fortnightly magazine, *TAXI*, edited by well-known cabbie writer Maurice Levinson.

He emphasised the importance of hotels. Patrons often needed help with heavy baggage. Drivers were reluctant carriers, not only fearing back strain but, worse still, despite being entrusted with luggage security, not being covered by the Workmen's Compensation Act. They may have felt entitled to big tips but were often disappointed. But refusal to carry heavy cases was bound to generate a poor impression. Some hotels respected this, offering taxi drivers little perks — commissions and free meals, notably in slack seasons.

Modestly priced hotels had to be considered as important as expensive rivals. Some started life as poor hostels or cheap rooming or 'doss' houses. Also many small hotels, notably those situated near larger railway stations, accommodate couples needing a room for two–three hours, often giving the cabbie a small tip without clients' knowledge — maybe an expensive way to be unfaithful but cheaper than divorce. It is mistaken to think that the posher the hotel the richer the customer and the higher the tip. The rich are not necessarily the most generous. In Australasia, for example, tipping is non-existent and visitors from there consider the practice impolite here.

Sadly, this union's formation led to serious friction with the TGWU. Both tried for better working conditions but faced authorities unwilling to combat the illegal activities of minicab rivals. Their population continued to increase, albeit primarily with part-timers, up to the 20,000 mark, easily outnumbering 13,000 cabbies. Cab trade unrest intensified and eventually the authorities felt obliged to intervene. On 15 July 1968, the London Cab Act technically abolished minicabs. Legislation had been suggested in November 1965 but the effective Bill only reached the parliamentary agenda two years later, a further nine months elapsing before enforcement. Now it was illegal to use words *Taxi* or *Cab* on vehicles or in advertisements unless they referred to those licensed. Theoretically, this even applied to vehicles carrying a capital-bound passenger from the provinces but in practice, it was accepted that drivers could not be expected to obscure signs on entering the London area. However, on completion, the driver was liable to prosecution if he procured another fare.

The Act was not universally respected, and the first firm prosecuted was Dial-a-Cab (Minicabs) Ltd, fined £10 for illegal advertising in February 1969. From March, the minimum fine for first offenders was £20, subsequent offences costing £50. Henceforth, minicab advertising virtually disappeared although London telephone directories still displayed advertisements from thirty-plus companies. In this Act, the Home Office also included legislation on another crucial point. There were years of public complaints about drivers either refusing to travel beyond 6 miles or, where they acquiesced, grossly overcharging for long trips, typically to Heathrow, the blue touch-paper jour-ney for driver-passenger conflict. Pre-1968, rules stated that normal fares applied for 6 miles but then it was open to negotiation between the two parties. Average quotes were £2.50–£2.75; however a newspaper survey of thirteen journeys from London's West End revealed a range from £2.25 to £3.50. Worse still, return journeys were overcharged more heavily – £4 to £6 plus.

Drivers pleaded that the odds against their picking up another fare when returning – time and petrol lost – justified doubling the fare. They felt further cause for com-plaint with plain-clothed hire touts frequenting arrival lounges, procuring fares before travellers reached taxi ranks; cabbies had to respect local by-laws forbidding entry. They had already struck, protesting at this injustice, in May 1966; exactly two years later, an intruding cabbie was asked to leave the building and arrested. This incident again pro-voked strike action but both stoppages were short-lived. Another cabbie disgraced the trade when, according to the potential 'victim', he threatened to bomb a private-hire tout's home.

The Act terminated the bargaining facility, requiring all distances within the London Metropolitan Area to be meter-registered. Drivers were entitled to double fares but only over distances exceeding 6 miles. With prices prevailing, there was inconsistency between meter fares and those agreed between the British Airports Authority and the TGWU. Worse still, the Owner-Drivers' Radio Taxi Service accused several hotel porters of abusing the situation, indulging in blackmail by insisting on 10s tips for providing a driver with a fare. If the driver refused, they would call private hire cars or minicabs.

Dishonest drivers also indulged in Asian immigrant 'trading'. Countless people arrived at Heathrow, predominantly Indians and Pakistanis, who came from their respective countries or as refugees from Idi Amin's Ugandan dictatorship in East Africa. At best, they had a few coins but were charged up to £40 for trips to the Sheffield, Birmingham and Manchester areas where waiting relatives were blackmailed into paying up or facing the police. Usually, victims dreaded police involvement, especially at this delicate stage. Matters would, at worst, be reported to the PCO with little prospect of drivers getting into trouble. Heathrow is governed by the Airports Authority Act, 1965 and associated British Airports Authority by-laws into which relevant sections of Hackney Carriage Acts and Deputy Commissioner's Cab rank legislation are incorporated. However, enforcement is the responsibility of the British Airports Authority Constabulary rather than the regular police. Those in charge are neither professionals nor answerable to Scotland Yard, leaving legislation hopelessly ineffective.

Situations could arise seeing many passengers wanting cabs but no cabbie being allowed to remain in the airport, except on authorised ranks, with 'For Hire' signs on. Even if hailed, he was strictly barred from accepting. Thus drivers had to switch signs off after dropping fares and immediately leave the airport precinct – legally 'private property' – without new passengers.

Three ranks were monopolised by two gangs of spivs, a local group from Hayes, the 'Hayes Mob' and another from London, the 'Quality Street Mob'; it was extremely difficult for outsiders to participate. Worse still, these spivs exercised legal rights to refuse any passenger wanting to travel over 6 miles towards the West End unless they looked like paying a good tip. Police apparently sympathised with the criminals, the vicious circle continuing.

Several drivers threatened to boycott the airport when the new regulations were enacted but most decided not to try. They still had to face threatening private hire touts until late summer 1970, when 'rescue' came from a most unexpected quarter. Fear of hijacking by Arab terrorists forced government authorities to send countless extra police to the area and the touts beat a hasty retreat. That gave a breathing period for several months but from May 1971, as surplus police were withdrawn, back came the touts. The LTDA threatened a boycott if they were not removed and added that similar action would be taken at Cromwell Road Air Terminal unless touts were similarly treated. Most touts, however, had seen enough by mid June.

However, hotel porter conflicts resurfaced in August when doormen were accused of accepting bribes from minicab firms to favour them against licensed taxis. Allegedly a leading minicab name had thrown a champagne party to entertain leading hotels' head porters. They were promised a £50 tip if they called the appropriate minicab company whenever guests needed transport for long journeys. Cab drivers retaliated by planning to boycott those hotels (apparently playing into enemy hands) and two, the Clifton-Ford and Churchill, were excluded for three days by the LTDA. However, before further trouble materialised, the TGWU cab section received an undertaking, signed by many leading hotel owners, that cabbies complaining of 'stolen' work would receive an immediate sympathetic hearing.

However, the LTDA still deplored police blindness to minicabs. Early 1972 saw twenty members lay out a 'challenge' by taking private cars to the Piccadilly area and plying for hire. The police ignored it, even with the extra 'carrot' of vehicle signs explicitly indicating their violation of authority. The drivers went further still, marching into the local police station, requesting prosecution! No luck – police ignored the Act. The Home Secretary admitted that the number of prosecutions for illegal hire plying were negligible compared with those suffered by cabbies for offences under Hackney carriages legislation. Cabbies were on a hiding to nothing. One incident epitomised the whole situation. A cabbie approached an unoccupied pedestrian crossing, reasonably feeling entitled to proceed at normal speed. At the last moment, a pedestrian, standing on the middle island, showing no interest in crossing, shot out in front of him, waving his arms furiously. The driver slammed on his brakes, only to have the pedestrian spit in his face. The driver spat back but the presiding woman magistrate was unimpressed, suspending him and fining him £50 for failing to stop and unruly behaviour. The driver thus lost a month's wages – the magistrate stated that he was lucky not to lose *three* months' – and faced the possibility of further PCO action, typically additional suspension. That same week saw a minicab driver brandish a knife at a taxi driver to face a 'crushing' fine of … £2!

Still on legality, history has seen police officers emerging, typically from Bow Street Station to Trafalgar Square, with the express purpose of ensuring that taxi drivers obey the law to the letter, descending mercilessly on offenders. Once the sixties were reached, more relaxed attitudes were adopted and blind eyes would often be turned to minor infringements of the hopelessly outdated Hackney Carriages' Act. Also, with modern heavy traffic, catching offenders was more difficult. However, with the driver leaving his vehicle unattended, even to answer a call of nature, there has been no let-up. Regarding cases that have gone to court, magistrates' attitudes have varied. Before the Second World War, they were very intolerant, subsequently taking a more lenient view before tightening up again, notably as inflation and the affluence of the sixties and seventies enabled drivers to pay stiffer fines. Their justification rests on cabbies' being paid professionals and therefore expected to be exemplary in their observance of the Highway Code.

This is perhaps logical but cabbies spend a far longer time on the road than anyone, except perhaps other professional drivers, therefore being more likely to face trouble. Also drivers continually have to pull up to pick up or set down passengers where *they* want it, the elderly, sick and disabled needing special consideration. Drivers could also manage without little pettinesses like having to wear badges in a conspicuous breast position – particularly unpleasant on hot and/or humid days.

This period saw two new potential threats. London Transport's introduction of the 'Star Bus' system, linking Aldwych to Paddington Station, passing through the West End's 'Magic Circle' to transport late-night theatre and restaurant patrons to major car parks. Shortly afterwards, a minibus service enabled local residents to call a central office to arrange pick-up and travel between Hampstead Garden Suburb and Golders Green Underground Station, primarily for shopping and travel to central London. There were fears of extensions to other areas.

Autumn 1971 saw a meeting at Seymour Hall protesting the illegal plying of minicabs and the adverse effects of VAT. This would cost £2–3 per journey which could not be passed on to passengers without violating Home Office fixed tariff rules although it was permissible to write off £200 (10 per cent of the current new taxi price). The trade was also incensed by VAT exemption for rival forms of transport, like buses and coaches.

Disruptive plans brought several minutes' cheering and clapping, after which central London was brought to a halt by the dumping of countless cabs around Piccadilly Circus. A further protest was staged in a heavily supported 'slow drive' down Bayswater Road, past Marble Arch and into Oxford Street and Holborn with full-power audio-visual effects from horns and headlights. The issue, however, came to a head with disharmony between the two unions. Peace might have been restored when both received invitations from the Treasury to attend a meeting to put their case forward but the TGWU leaders refused to meet their LTDA counterparts. Thus the 'meeting' was conducted in two sessions, the government probably surmising that it was wise to ignore the internal trade dispute. But, as the old saying goes, 'If you ignore something, it does not go away' and discord was intensified at a TGWU meeting at Central Hall, Westminster, when the chairman declared that there would only be trade unity if and when all LTDA members joined the TGWU.

Cabbies' prospects brightened in July 1972 when the Home Office, under the 1968 London Cab Act, exercised the right to increase the compulsory distance (applicable exclusively to Heathrow) from 6 to 20 miles. Thus spivs could no longer be choosy but had to accept fares to the West End, even the City. This came into force early the following month but outside the Metropolitan area, drivers retained rights to refuse or bargain on meter charges.

Returning to Frank Smith's legislation, this resurfaced years later following the Maxwell Stamp report. (Arthur Maxwell Stamp was a merchant). The Home Office had established a committee to undertake a complete survey of both taxicab and private-car hire trades around London, to consider their respective roles and make recommendations regarding current and proposed legislation and statutory controls needed for safe, efficient running.

Following three years' work, the eight members' report was published in October 1970 but none had intimate trade knowledge. They mistakenly assumed three forms of taxi service – licensed, minicab and private hire. In fairness, this was not necessarily inconsistent with Hindley's report assumptions; this discussed only two: luxury private hire and licensed taxi. In those days, minicabs did not exist as such but there were unlicensed operators or 'encroachers of rights' or 'interlopers' (minicabs' pre-war equiv-alent), which, in Hindley's opinion, were non-existent. A problem thus arose for taxi proprietors in that, if minicabs were recognised by Maxwell Stamp, i.e. given respect-ability, then any journeyman not wishing to buy his own cab could opt out of taxi driving, turning to minicabs, thence being free of many restrictions, controls and answerability to Hackney Carriage Office inspectors. Further, it might be more profitable to drive minicabs than taxis, resulting in minicab numbers increasing, swamping taxis out.

Twenty-two thousand private hire drivers working for a variety of firms were detailed – ranging from reputable old-fashioned limousine hire companies, to 'fly-by-night' concerns, operating from one room with desk and telephone, agents for owner-driven minicabs. These were arguably unworthy of description as 'companies', there being obvious concern regarding safety and insurance as well as driver com-petence and trustworthiness. The Metropolitan Police Commissioner confirmed that significant numbers of private-hire drivers had criminal records. Regarding licensed cabbies, there was far less criticism, main problems centring around Heathrow. The earlier mentioned regulating Act, although passed in 1968, had not yet been enacted. However, taxi design was heavily rebuked, notably engine and braking performance, limited vision and cramped driver space.

Recommendation that minicabs be allowed licence under less stringent rules than Hackney cab regulations amounted to cab-trade condemnation. The principal prob-lem, infuriating cabbies, was police relationships. Rules, applicable to cab drivers, were inapplicable to others and the inequity extended even further. Even if it was argu-ably fair that several police officers (must be trained drivers) became taxi drivers on retirement (if you can't beat them … again!), it seemed grossly unfair that many serv-ing officers supplemented their incomes by driving minicabs outside hours. Typically an officer pinched a prostitute for soliciting, picking her up in his minicab the next day! 'Yesterday is history …' as the old song goes.

Still on sex and crime, years ago, police were strict towards indecent exposure of genitalia and couples misbehaving in taxis; nowadays almost anything goes. Legislation such as the Street Offences Act technically pushed prostitutes off the streets but in practice trading continues. Available young ladies legally congregate in pubs and clubs hoping to meet male customers. Alternatively, male representatives solicit on their behalf, advertising services as 'massage', 'language lessons' or similar. Many prostitutes have no car and use taxis to reach clients' homes, hotels or nightclubs. Additionally, instances have seen lady passengers fancying their cabbie and invited him in 'for a drink'. They would then strip, hoping he would succumb to temptation. Regarding serious criminals, underworld members often use taxis as a 'safe' way of travelling – they might be easily identified using an owned or stolen car. Strangely, to avoid trouble, they tend to tip generously, seldom bilking drivers. Pickpockets and petty criminals, however, are more likely offenders.

Returning to the committee, it primarily recommended that taxis and hire cars should come under jurisdiction of a new independent authority established by the Greater London Council (GLC) but not considered part of it. The GLC had sug-gested, two years earlier, that, as they had already gained control of London's buses and Underground system, extension to taxicabs seemed obvious. Taxi drivers, offered no board representation, disliked it. One member represented consumer interests (the Consumer Council would have liked more) and taxi representatives felt that this should, at least, be balanced by their trade. The new body was 'The London Taxi and Hire Car Board'; financial arrangements are detailed in Appendix 19.

The union happily accepted most of the report but rejected about a fifth, particularly incensed about taxes levied on licences and plates. The LTDA were more aggrieved. While welcoming an established central rank-linking control point, they described it as 'the only ray of sunshine'. They objected to taxis and private hire operatives being organised under one roof while stringencies were enforced only on taxis. One obvious example was the fare system – taxis strictly regulated with private hires left to their own discretion, fare-fixing deemed to 'stifle competition'. William D'Arcy added that if, consequently, private hire proved more profitable long-term many cabbies would switch, dramatically reducing numbers. Already one of the two major radio-taxi opera-tors, the Owner-Drivers' Radio Taxi Service, was using private cars as fleet 'extras'. Private hire legislation came in towards the millennium (brief details in Appendix 15).

The first serious attempt at regulation came with the 1976 Local Authorities (Miscellaneous Provisions) Act. Paragraphs gave local provincial authorities discretion to lay down rules demonstrably appropriate locally. Typically, no vehicle specifically designed and built as a taxi could be hired privately. This popularly offered taxi/limousine advantages without incurring the costs of Rolls-Royce or Daimler to the private-hire trade in provincial areas, where licensing authorities deemed capital-applicable regulations unnecessary. A sizeable income would be lost immediately, Carbodies complaining bitterly regarding FL2 sales. Cries fell on stone-deaf government ears. They insisted that vehicle design identified it as a taxi, the public being confused if it operated in another capacity – there would be temptation for illegal plying for hire. That was curtains for the FL2 and for Austin, both it and the FX4 had run their course. After forty years, 75,000 having come off the assembly lines, it faded out over winter 1997–98, having passed through stages of FX4R, FX4S (from 1987, accommodating an extra passenger, five in all), Fairway and Fairway Driver but the overall shape survived throughout as a recognisable feature – LTI's backbone.

Nowadays, owner-drivers expect to pay around £28,000 but dependent on choice of TX1 or Metrocab and extras included, prices can vary by £10,000. Economically, it pays to exchange a vehicles biannually to optimise resale and minimise maintenance costs, likely to rise for ageing vehicles. Advertising can earn up to £500 per annum, helping with maintenance payments. Currently, more than a third of cabs are radio-controlled for which owner-drivers pay installation fees of £500 plus a monthly subscription, around £100, which is obviously a considerable outlay but probably worthwhile, radio contact being the route to extra work and possible advertising.

Satellite navigation, 'satnav', is now commonplace. Once standard, the necessity for 'knowledge' will be questionable; if it disappears, established drivers will feel aggrieved when newcomers walk in with minimal effort. Possibly the industry will have to move with the times.

Looking at the future, designers have specified new parameters to match supply to demand, detailed in Appendix 18.

Volvo, based in Göteborg, Sweden, have entered the taxi field, interested since the UN Environmental Conference, Stockholm in 1972, aimed to satisfy modern needs. Volvo's three most important parameters are safety, versatility and action diversification, specially emphasising sick/disabled needs.

The proposed vehicle is spacious despite greater compactness, with its short front and overhanging rear. These features make for maximum driver vision and a tight turning circle. Maximum safety is achieved with 'Volvo's safety-cage principle':

a) The whole internal occupant area is surrounded by heavy-profile members, hopefully absorbing the bulk of any shock on collision.

b) Front and rear sections are designed as 'crumple zones' expected to absorb impact energy.

c) Doors (central locking and warning lights) and vehicle flanks incorporate 'built-in' protection using tubular steel bars. Heavy-duty rubber moulding runs along the flanks at a height deemed optimum to reduce heavy-traffic damage costs.

Additionally:

a) Safety belts are replaced by an adjustable padded cross-bar, anchored to the body, which the passenger pulls down in front of himself, ideally positioning just above waist-height. It folds back against the roof when not required but when used, serves as a pleasant arm rest. Experience indicates passengers prefer this.
b) The slightly convex floor has five cross-bars, also steel, as reinforcements.
c) Engine mounted well ahead of driver for maximum protection on collision.
d) Bumpers, front and rear, designed for maximum impact-absorption, comfortably satisfying the 5mph crash-impact requirement.
e) Dashboard deeply recessed well ahead of driver to ensure minimum distracting reflection in sunny conditions.
f) Driver comforts included, of which most innovative is control design for minimal risk of inadvertent misuse. Controls of similar nature are grouped, typically: lights left and windscreen washers etc. right.
g) Other controls are shaped variously according to operation manner: pulling, twisting, flipping.
h) Fuse box, with automatically resetting fuses, behind driver's seat.
i) Steering wheel has collapsible or 'crumple' zone, yielding on collision.

Germany's Volkswagen, based in Wolfsburg, have also joined futuristics, arguing that vehicles are excessively wide and low with excessive fuel consumption and emissions. Criteria are under five headings:

a) safety, comfort, manoeuvrability;
b) ease of passenger entry/exit, accommodation;
c) compactness, good ratio between overall length and space;
d) high standards of drivability and comfort; and
e) running economy, minimal emission.

New vehicles aim for improvement:

a) Four passengers accommodated, each in single seats, three facing forwards, the fourth backwards; leg-room improved on predecessor sedans; baby carriages and wheelchairs accommodated;
b) Passengers carry hand luggage, folding restraining device and capacious boot accessible, both internally and externally, for larger baggage items;
c) Seats have adjustable backs, fitted with armrests, integrated head restraints; covers for optimum ventilation, durability and slipping avoidance; lap-type belts fitted.
d) Bullet-proof wall, separating driver and passenger fitted but with intercom. Wall fitted with window for easily viewed taximeter; transfer device for passing fares.

e) Regarding seasonal temperatures, vehicle has dense, noise-absorbing interior mate-rials and gasoline-powered auxiliary heating system for midwinter when engine is switched off; air conditioning for hot days.

f) Large sliding doors fitted both sides for ease of entrance/exit; obvious safety factor – passengers always board/leave vehicle on kerb side; more commonly used right-hand door electrically operated by driver with automatic extending running board for comfortable stepping on/off.

g) Minimisation of driver fatigue is significant safety factor. His seat, accessed from left, equipped with three-point retractable safety-belt system. Controls designed for user-friendliness. Visibility improved by absence of front hood and seat elevation above road-surface level.

h) For extra safety – many drivers' crash injuries stem from steering wheel and column, special safety steering-control system – collapsible support placed connect-ing the driver's end of steering wheel to padded dashboard; connection folding at pre-selected position on collision, absorbing a proportion of the impact, hopefully reducing injury seriousness and minimising degree of wheel or dashboard entry into driver's compartment. Any protruding design edges also padded. Driver and pas-sengers are above level of expected collisions.

i) Deformation element placed immediately behind front bumper, absorbing energy in head-on collision. Four stiff longitudinal beams placed behind, attempting to pre-vent driver-cabin collapse, irrespective of impact angle. Longitudinal door beams hopefully transmit side-impact forces through vehicle frame, thus damping damage, maintaining cabin's configuration.

j) Fuel consumption and air pollution figures compare favourably against traditional vehicles. Internal combustion and electric motor hybrid offering advantages of both systems in cohesion: no exhaust fumes when operated solely on motor; range only limited regarding fuel-tank size.

The Italian contribution: Milan-based Alfa Romeo, offers similar ideas.

A recent PCO-approved London taxi is Mercedes' Vito Traveliner. Manufactured by Mercedes-Benz, sold in London by KPM-UK Plc, LTI dealers since 1989. This is based on the Vito van, used provincially as a wheelchair-accessible taxi and minibus for some years.

With the oil price skyrocketing continually, electric taxis are appearing. The Peugeot E7 boasts prospective running at one-seventh petrol's cost while accommodating six or seven passengers.

Appendices

APPENDIX I
TAXICAB LANGUAGE

Appearance	knowledge student's periodic PCO oral examination
Bilk	cheat driver – fraud – leave without paying
Bill	cabbie's licence
Blue Book	book including list of runs for memorising
Broom-off or brooming	pass unwanted job to next cab
Butterboy	newly licensed driver (Turpin Engineering used to run yellow cabs; Turpin ran 'knowledge' school)
Cage	Cab area reserved for passengers
CO	Carriage Officer (PCO examiner)
Cock and hen	male and female passengers
Cole Porter	Cabbie working long hours (Night and Day)
Clock	taximeter
Double clock	fare over 6 miles
Doubling up	sharing cab with partner, typically day/night
Droschke	German light open horse-drawn cab
Droshky	Polish-Russian equivalent
Extras	Modest additional charges: extra passengers, luggage, or public holidays
Farmer Giles	piles – occupational hazard
Feeder	subsidiary rank from which cabs queue for main rank
Flagfall	hiring charge
Flounder	alternative slang for cab
Flyer	airport job, typically Heathrow or Gatwick
Four hander	job involving four passengers

Full flat	cab rented for the week
Green badge	applies to driver licensed to work throughout Greater London
Gypsy	American unlicensed cab
Hail or Flag	stop taxi for hire
Half flat	weekly rental in partnership
Hickory	rhyming slang for clock
In and out	return journey
Kipper Season	February–March period – quietest in trade year, tradition-ally ends late March, Ideal Home Show opens
Knowledge	detailed geographical study of Greater London area
Knowledge Boy	student (either sex!)
Legal	exact fare without added tip
Linkman	hotel/club doorman
Little people	Cabbies' name for minicab drivers
Minicab	private hire car – telephone booking for short journeys
Mushes	owner-drivers (French *marche*, need to plod on)
On point	first cab on rank
Orbiting	refusing fare, then going to back of short queue at rank, hoping for better fare next time
Overhaul	repairs need to ensure passage of test for annual licensing
Passing	submission of cab for inspection for licence issue
Plate	licence plate visible at cab rear
Punter	passenger
Rails	major railway stations
Roader	job outside Metropolitan Police District
Roasting	spending considerable time waiting on rank
Scab	minicab driver illegally touting
Set	accident, commonly collision
Shoful	Yiddish: fake or imitation
Shtumer	Yiddish: hoax telephone call
Stepney	spare wheel (early tyre company)
Stop note	rejection notice issued to proprietor of cab deemed unroadworthy
Tout	see Scab
Unders	mechanical vehicle undercarriage parts steam-cleaned on overhaul before PCO presentation
Vet	American unlicensed cab
Wangle	manoeuvres taken in PCO driving test
Whitecoat	former PCO senior vehicle examiner
White knuckle journey	journeys from Heathrow which drivers attempt to com-plete within one hour

Wind-up	minicab's Shtumer
Yard	PCO
Yellow Badge	cabbie licensed to ply in restricted suburban areas
Zieger	Russian for meter, indicator or pointer

APPENDIX 2
PRIVATE-HIRE LICENSING, FACILITATED BY PRIVATE HIRE VEHICLES (LONDON) ACT 1998.

Under provisions, licensing was introduced in three stages:
1) operators in 2001
2) drivers in 2003
3) vehicles in 2004

Regarding Transport for London, mayor's responsibilities:

Appointment of board, 8–15 members expected

Chair meetings or appoint suitable deputy

Set TFL budget on existing services

Decide on general TFL strategies

Approve fare scales

Fund new services and schemes

Regarding taxi services he also:

manages the Greater London Authority network;

regulates taxis and private hire vehicles; and

helps co-ordinate dial-a ride and taxi cards.

Stringency applying to cab roadworthiness is tighter in London than provincially; therefore, many 'aged' substandard cabs can migrate to provinces pre-retirement.

APPENDIX 3
METROPOLITAN PUBLIC CARRIAGES ACT 1869

METROPOLITAN PUBLIC CARRIAGES ACT 1869
(32 and 33 c. Vict 115)

HORSE CAB-DRIVER'S LICENCE

I, having been appointed by the Secretary of State to grant cab-drivers' licences under the Metropolitan Public Carriage Act 1869 hereby license …
residing at …
to drive horse cabs

This licence is subject to compliance by the licensee with the provisions of:

(a)   The Metropolitan Public Carriage Act 1869 and the London Stage and Carriage Act 1907 and
(b)   any order made thereunder by the Secretary of State relating to horse-cab drivers including any regulations contained in such Order and the Acts relating to Hackney carriages in force at the time of the commencement of the Metropolitan Public Carriage Act 1869.

The licence shall have effect from …

And shall continue in force for three years unless sooner revoked or suspended.

Photo

Date of issue

Signature of licensee

Fee 3/-

Abstract of laws re drivers and conductors of public carriages as relevant to taxicabs within Metropolitan Police District and the city of London and its Liberties.

Definition of Metropolitan Police District altered between Acts of 1829 and 1840 (extended beyond Westminster and defined parishes in Middlesex, Surrey and Kent). Commissioner required assurance for £1,000 or unlimited amount for protection of public and third-party claims.

Painting on cab stating number of persons to be carried.
Penalties re overloading but 1 or 2 under 10 years of age count as one adult
Tickets for hirer display on breast penalty 40/- rules re loss or mislay or forgery
Delivery of licence and plates
Persons under 20 not to conduct alone
Taximeter to bear seal or mark approved by commissioner
Breaking or tampering with seal or mark of meter itself
Delivery of lost property to police station penalty 40/-
Penalty for breach 40/-
Check string or wire – renew periodically penalty 20/-
Adverts not to obstruct passengers' light, view, ventilation, etc. penalty 40/-

Not conveying person suffering from infectious disease or corpse of deceased from such disease; penalty 10 pounds. After offence, disinfect notice penalty 5 pounds cost of disinfection recoverable from causer.

Do not clean or dress a horse in a public place or clean or repair a carriage there; penalty 40/-
Horse has to be fit; penalty 40/-

Reckless driving, wilful bad behaviour or language: penalty 3 pounds or up to two months' imprisonment
Compensation up to 10 pounds similar for abusing police 5 pounds or jail
Plying for hire outside designated places penalty 20/-

Obstruction or loitering
Feeding horses publicly other than by corn from bag or hay from hand
Demanding or taking more than legal fare penalty 40/-
Refusing passengers or reasonable luggage penalty 40/-
Refusing to drive 6 miles or one hour or at not less than 6 miles per hour

Also mentioned were:
Rules regarding act of hiring
No smoking if passenger objects; penalty 20/-
Fines regarding bilking.

Additional laws relevant from 1930s onwards

Licence plate carries licence number surmounted by lion, unicorn or crown, symbol changing annually.

Driver must wear his identification badge on left breast both when at work and when appearing in court, be that as accused or witness.

No parking outside the General Post Office.

The meter must be set in motion as soon as the taxi is hired and must be switched off on journey's completion. Drivers must not tamper with the seal on the meter, put on by the police after annual maintenance.

The driver is expected to keep his verbal and body language clean.

The driver must be prepared to carry a reasonable amount of luggage.

The driver must not carry more than four passengers.

The driver must give up lost property to the authorities within twenty-four hours. Although few members of the public are aware of this, the driver is not obliged to stop when hailed; however, if he does stop, he is under an obligation to take his passenger at least 6 miles.

Modifications to keep in line with larger taxis:

All taxicabs carry a licence plate showing licence number and how many passengers it can legally carry, normally four but may be five or six.

APPENDIX 4
CHAPTER TITLE NEEDED

POLICE No. 17

CERTIFIED FIT FOR PUBLIC USE

RICHARD MAYNE The Commissioner of Police of the Metropolis

HACKNEY CARRIAGES may be hired by TIME or DISTANCE at the option of the Hirer, expressed at the commencement of the Hiring; if not otherwise expressed, the fare to be according to Distance.

FARES BY DISTANCE
Within a Radius of FOUR MILES from Charing Cross

If Hired when STANDING ON A STAND, for any Distance NOT EXCEEDING a Mile } 1s

If Hired when NOT STANDING ON A STAND, for any Distance NOT EXCEEDING a Mile } 6d

For any Distance EXCEEDING One Mile, at the rate of Sixpence For every Mile, and for every part of a Mile not completed

If Discharged beyond a Radius of FOUR MILES from CHARING CROSS – For every Mile or Part of a Mile beyond such Distance } 1s

If stopped by the Hirer, for every Fifteen Minutes 6d
Two Children, under the age of Ten Years to be counted as One Adult Person

EXTRA PAYMENT IN ADDITION TO ABOVE FARES – When more than Three Persons are carried Inside a Hackney Carriage, any distance NOT EXCEEDING a Mile or more than Two Persons any distance EXCEEDING a Mile, one sum of Sixpence shall be paid for the whole hiring in addition to the above Fares for each Person above the number of Three or Two in the respective cases herein mentioned.

FARES BY TIME

One Hour, or Part of an Hour
2s
For every Fifteen Minutes or less beyond One Hour
6d

Each Person above Two, the whole Hiring
6d
Two Children, under the age of Ten Years to be counted as One Adult Person
EXTRA

If the Driver is required to drive more than FOUR MILES
an Hour, for every Mile or Part of a Mile above FOUR MILES EXTRA   } 6d

PAYMENT FOR LUGGAGE – When more than Two Persons shall be carried Inside
The Carriage, a further sum of TWOPENCE for every Package carried
Outside the said Carriage is to be paid in addition to the above Fares.

Distinction between fares for different types of cab from 1908

Hansom Cabs	1s for first mile 6d for each subsequent mile Waiting time 2s 6d for the first hour and 8d for each subsequent quarter hour.
Taxicab	8d flagfall (hiring charge) for first mile (or ten minutes) and 2d per quarter-mile (or 2½ minutes)

APPENDIX 5
LICENCE

DRIVER OF CABS

32nd and 33rd Victoria Cap 115

LICENCE

No. . . . .

Dated the   day of   One thousand nine hundred and . . .

To
of

to act as Driver of Cabs propelled by mechanical means known as Renault Unic Panha
and none other for one year unless this licence is sooner revoked or suspended.
By order of His Majesty's Principal Secretary of State.

THIS LICENCE is issued subject to the conditions of 32 and 33 Vict. Cap 115 and of
all orders made by His Majesty's Principal Secretary of State in pursuance thereof
and if not revoked, suspended or renewed, must be delivered up at this office on
the   DAY OF   19....

PHOTO of licensed person   Signature of licensed person

APPENDIX 6
COMMITTEE MINUTES

The Committee comprised several parliamentary members:

George Russell MP Under Secretary of State of Home Department
(Henry Cunynghame assisting)
Edward Bayley, John Burns, Thomas Lough, Charles Whitmore.

Also one non-member:
Francis Hopwood CMG Board of Trade Assistant Secretary (Railway Department)

Their brief included:
Considering whether changes are appropriate to:
    Grant of drivers' licences
    Amount and disposal of cab plate revenue
    Jurisdiction regarding complaints by and against cab drivers
    Relations of cab owners and drivers with railway companies
    Tariffs
    Cab stands and shelters
    General service conduct

Committee met twenty-three times, interviewing Home Office, New Scotland Yard, Police Court representatives, cab proprietors, drivers, railway companies, etc. Comparisons made with provincial cities and abroad. Majority of suggestions urged stricter discipline.

Discussed quality of cab inspection – bribery accusations proved largely unsubstantiated and/or allegations broke down. Found common evidence of inadequate horse inspection and unsanitary conditions in cab yards. Discussed proposed driving tests, age limits – possibly 16; in practice entrants rarely under 17. Drivers proposed 21; police and comparable cities abroad recommended 18. Also discussed reissue to offenders and those not using licences for some time.

Recommendations to eliminate loafers or butterfly loafers, i.e. those without desire for regular work or disciplinary respect. Additionally considered number limitation – public safety, fairness to applicants – finding Central London's excessive; ratio of drivers to cabs (12 or 14 to 10) was also considered as were:

Amount and disposal of plate revenue:
Recommended abolition (regarding Hackney carriages) proposed by cab proprietors to government.
Lost property charge should fall to owners.
Finance for shelters and covered standings for driver/horse benefit.

Complaints:
Drivers complained of delays re hearings, often feeling obliged to plead guilty rather than face heavier fine for court time-wasting. Impression that drivers were treated unfairly; proprietors agreed. Resentment at bracketing with criminals.
Hope for removal of temptation to crawl and ply; more serious offences included drunkenness, abusive behaviour, equestrian cruelty, assault.
Bilking: distinction between three categories: The fare who:

1) Disappears
2) Refuses to pay or knowingly underpays
3) Refuses genuinely (driver's mistake or wilful overcharging)

There were combinations and, during the days when fares were paid largely in coins, a well-known trick was giving countless small coins of insufficient total, disappearing while driver counted.

Recommendation that third category be referred to police.

Regarding others, Committee opposed power of arrest, going to nearest police station to ascertain bilker's name and address.

Suggestion that driver be empowered to insist that fare has sufficient funds – unpopular, driver fearing 'distrust' might jeopardise tip.
Suggestion of Sir John Bridge and others that driver be empowered to demand name and address of fare – refusal or falsehood resulting in 40/- fine.
Another made regarding fines and/or jail for fares bilking.

Discussions regarding debt recovery problems; reference in Jurisdiction Act, 1879, that cab fares be recoverable as civil debt proved too cumbrous to be worthwhile. Recommendations made for provisions as Act's predecessor – commitment to jail until fare paid.

Further discussions involved cabbie-railway company relationship, notably privilege system – currently governed by agreement between railway companies and owners, drivers' opinions ignored.

Drivers argued the system:
  a) gave undue preference to privileged drivers leading to frictions with outsiders;
  b) did not secure best cab, horse or driver for stations;
  c) caused congestion, empty cabs rushing back to stations after depositing fares; and
  d) rarely worked anyway – privileged cab supply frequently failing – outsiders entered, causing congestion.

Also legal doubts: recommended adopting system like that applicable at Waterloo and others of the London and South-West Company whereby all cabs satisfying inspectors were admitted (1d fee).

Note was taken of some conditions, applicable to convenience of public as required at railway stations.

1) As cab standing-room at arrival platforms is necessarily small and as passengers arriving with luggage are prevented from choosing cabs; essential that cabs allowed into area be of good quality with well-behaved drivers.
2) Essential that sufficient numbers be available.
3) Mistakes regarding luggage were inevitable; rectification facilities vital.

Report concluded that privilege system enabled conditions to be met reasonably but still room for improvement regarding lost luggage.
Also recommended that privilege system's irritation be removed – drivers allowed to bring passengers to stations but not take them away; discussion regarding possibility of railway stations' being declared 'public places'.
Regarding tariffs and prices, little cause to alter existing fees – 6d up to a mile within current law.
Suggestions made included:
Available method whereby drivers can advertise readiness to take fare – optional with right to remove. Committee keen.
6d per mile be made standard during business hours 10 a.m. – 6 p.m. or 8 a.m. – 10 p.m.
6d fare be introduced in congested districts within different radii e.g. a mile of given point
Pre-1869 law be restored i.e. minimum fare for cab taken off stand be 1/- but crawling from street 6d.

Committee not keen – would encourage crawling.

Opinions of drivers regarding the 6d fare divided; suggestion it be optional.

The Committee now considered adoption of taximeter – distance-measuring machine but *guide*, not absolute calculant of fare.
Other similar machines enabled owners to check driver performance. No specific machine recommended but hope to find reliable one.
Suggestion of two-class cab classification – committee not keen following bad foreign reports.

Biggest contention – conflicting evidence (because of conflicting central area, suburban drivers and public interests) arose regarding four-mile radius. For public, radius extension would be advantageous, not only because they could travel additional distance at 'inside' rate of 6d per mile but also because of present anomaly requiring those entering the circle from outside to pay at 1/- per mile throughout. Large numbers currently outside circle would then be 'included' on extension.

Central drivers (who rarely left their radius) were indifferent but welcomed extension to places like Hammersmith where, on depositing one fare, they would likely get another. Suburban drivers opposed but Committee deemed it hardly damaging. There would be benefit from increased demand from outside radius. Also short fares locally would still be charged at 1/- rate. Furthermore, for journeys beyond radius, 1/- per mile still charged on crossing boundary.

Regarding cab stands and shelters, more shelters needed. Committee re-emphasised that shelters be taken over by revenue-funded public authority.

Regarding general service conduct, consideration regarding:

a) liability of cab drivers:
   Existing law provisions bearing heavily on proprietors –
   1) Had to appear before magistrate if driver convicted of offence.
   2) Faced unlimited liability to pay fines and rectify luggage losses; also complaints regarding short notice.
   Proprietors claimed limited liability.

b) Consolidation of Hackney Carriage Acts

   Committee expressed hope to simplify drivers' relevant handbook.

c) Transfer of control from Home Office and Scotland Yard to London County Council

Following recommendations:

1)   numbers of staff: inspectors, police, controllers be increased;
2)   inspectors be knowledgeable in car technology and animal matters;
3)   cab registration and stable inspection;
4)   Sub-letting be forbidden;
5)   Drivers' age limit be raised from 16 to 21;
6)   Applicants for drivers' licences be examined for driving knowledge;
7)   Licence for driver should contain spaces in which proprietors should insert
         a)   periods over a week during when drivers were not working;
         b)   cause of leaving;
     also, on renewed licences, details of serious offences in last two years.
8)   Failure to use licence for considerable proportion of a year and conviction for serious offences should, unless exceptional circumstances e.g. judge's recommendation, debar renewal right.
9)   Carriage tax (15/-) be abolished;
10) First non-serious offences dealt with by cautionary notices rather than summonses. No summons granted unless accompanying deposition of facts supplied.

11) Act passed regarding recommendation on bilking (Cunynghame memo);
12) Privilege system be abolished at railway stations but companies be required to make regulations subject to approval for cab admission and supervision. Power reserved to Secretary of State to permit exceptional arrangements in travelling public's interests.

Two committee members unhappy, arguing that 'open' system is impractical; also that, if privilege system were abolished, privileged drivers — a large steadily increasing respectable body of men — will lose work, railway companies employing their own drivers and vehicles (evidence confirms)

1) Radius be administrative area of London minus Plumstead. Drivers should not be compelled to drive considerable distances beyond certain late hour except towards home. Area be divided into districts, distinguishable by cabs' carrying various coloured lamps.
2) Some small standings for 2–3 cabs only be placed in crowded thoroughfares away from larger neighbouring standings. Standings should be sheltered.
3) Proprietors should be relieved of liability to pay fines of drivers or produce drivers in court except for offences wholly or partially attributable to proprietors.
4) Proprietors' liability for lost luggage be restricted to 10/- except on owner's declaration.
5) As legislation necessary to fulfil above recommendations, if adopted, opportunity be taken to consolidate statutes and fulfil changes recommended regarding badge-wearing etc. The consolidating act should empower Secretary of State to decide periodically on relevant offences and penalties.
Other recommendations could be fulfilled under current law.

Signed by H.H. Asquith Secretary of State

APPENDIX 7
PUBLIC CARRIAGE OFFICE REGULATIONS FOR CONSTRUCTION AND LICENSING OF HACKNEY MOTOR CARRIAGES

a) Vehicles' condition inspected at New Scotland Yard.
b) Must demonstrate compliance with relevant motor acts.
c) Drivers must produce regulation and maker's certificates, indicating vehicle's safety.
d) Also produce certificate indicating no machine design alteration since last inspection.
e) Chassis clearance at least 10in.

f) No undue skidding.

g) Regarding chassis springs, distance between outsides of rear springs minimum 40in.

h) Similarly regarding front springs, distance maximum possible, at least 32in.

i) Centre wheel track: minimum 40in.

j) Turning circle maximum 25ft (still stands), particularly problematic to new manufacturers of front-wheel drive vehicles. Adapting existing vehicles difficult.

Metropolitan Police Regulations for Construction and Licensing of Motor Cabs in London.

Main points summarised:

a) Steering: wheel on offside

b) Braking: specification of nuts, bolts and pins

c) Turning circle: 28ft parallel lines, 25ft diameter, for U-turn ease, even in narrow street.

d) Tyres: specification

e) Suspension: specification

f) Fuel tank: under bonnet, protected from collision damage; cut-off device available

g) Electrics: interior lighting; insulation of all electric circuits from exposure to water, oil and petrol; fuse protection; batteries placed out of danger

h) Exhaust pipe: shielded from inflammable material; fumes directed clear

i) Fire appliance: carried for easy use

j) Body: dimensions — overall width including wing mirrors maximum 1.755 metres; overall length maximum 4.575 metres. Dimensions important regarding cab rank size and capacity, hotel pick-up points, popular buildings and allowance for traffic flow in congested London; floor curvature, doors and doorways — to open at least 90 degrees; unrestricted opening across doors minimum 75cm. Height of doorway minimum 120cm and maximum height of door sill above ground level 38cm when cab unladen; inside passenger compartment: minimum clearance of 1.3 metres between floor and roof, minimum distance between facing seats 42.5cm, minimum distance of 66cm in front of removable cushion or 'squab' of forward-facing seats when no other seats are fitted; gentlemen able to travel comfortably in top hats; all occasional seats must be automatically tipped-up when unused and minimum 40cm in width and 35.5cm in depth and 4cm apart; boot lid hinged at top; steps.

k) Passenger seats: upholstery, spacing out

l) Driver's compartment, compulsory off-side door

m) Passenger — driver communication

n) Windows: at both sides in rear and easily openable/closable by passengers

o) Heating: demisting, defrosting

p) Glass: toughened (British standards)

q) Door fittings: double catches of approved type throughout

r) Fare table and number plate: easily visible

s) Floor covering: easily cleaned and non-slip

t) Luggage: carrying and securing with improved type of roof guard

u) Horn: approved deep tone

v) Taximeter: approved design

w) Taxi sign: standard type

x) Radio apparatus in driver's area

y) Maintenance details

z) Certificate of Insurance (1934 London Cab Act)

APPENDIX 8
HACKNEY CARRIAGE LEGISLATION

NOTICE

TO DRIVERS OF

HACKNEY CARRIAGES

By virtue of the Act 13th and 14th Victoria, Chapter 7, entitled
"An Act for Consolidating the Office of the Registrar of
Metropolitan Public Carriages with the Office of Commissioners
of Police of the Metropolis and making other provisions in
regard to the Consolidated Offices."

I .... commissioner of Police of the Metropolis, do hereby appoint a Standing for
THREE HACKNEY CARRIAGES at QUEENS SQUARE, BLOOMSBURY

On the South side of Queen's Square, Bloomsbury, alongside the railing
round the garden enclosure.

Horses heads Eastward.

Provided that no Hackney Carriage shall be suffered to stand across any
Street or THOROUGHFARE, or opposite the end of any Street or Carriage-way,
or upon any place where Foot Passengers usually cross the Carriage-way.

Signed

Metropolitan Police Office   The Commissioner of The Police of The Metropolis
New Scotland Yard SW1
       11th April 1894

APPENDIX 9
DISTRICTS

In the early days of horse-drawn cabs the PCO divided the administration area into ten districts, specifying two dozen cab-inspection places — some very basic, typically market areas.

After moving to the Metropolitan Police building, Lambeth Road in 1927, more up-to-date facilities for cab inspection were provided in more 'private' police station back yards. Districts were now reduced to four, each having several inspection or 'passing' stations.

District 1: Lewisham, Croydon, Lambeth
         2: Caledonian Road, Ilford
         3: Kilburn, Finchley
         4: North Fulham, Richmond, Ealing, Kingston, Sutton

1950s: passing stations reduced to four, one per district:

    1: Lambeth Road, only one with comprehensive facilities
    2: Caledonian Road — poorest facilities, lacking ramp or pit, making underneath inspection extremely difficult, well-nigh impossible for FX4, ground clearance being markedly less than predecessors'.
    3: Kilburn Police Station — destroyed by 1940 Blitz; site remains put to some use; one rain-protected inspection bay
    4: Walham Green Fulham, two protected pits

Twelve districts of Public Carriage Office administration:

Rochester Row
Camberwell
Peckham
Hunter Street, St. Pancras
Harrow Road
North West Fulham

Paddenswick Road, Goldhawk
Bow
Kentish Town
Brixton
Richmond
Golders Green

APPENDIX 10
STATISTICS

Cabs in London (nearest 50 in each case), except with low numbers:

	Horse hansom four-wheel	Horse	Motor	Total
1903	7500	3900	(1)	11400
1904	7000	3950	(3)	10950
1905	6850	3900	(19)	10750
1906	6500	3800	100	10400
1907	5900	3900	700	10500
1908	5100	3750	2800	11650
1909	3300	3250	3950	10500
1910	2000	2700	6400	11100
1911	1050	2300	7650	11000
1912	550	1800	7950	10300
1913	400	1550	8400	10350
1914	250	1150	7250	8650

Horse-drawn cabs had greater dominance provincially. Surveys in ten major cities: only Bristol, where motor cabs outnumbered horse-drawn cabs by about 5:1, and Liverpool saw horse-drawn cabs removed from the table's top.

Number of new cabs licensed in London early in the first half of the 1920s:

1920	211
1921	506
1922	793

1923   973
1924   959
1925   287
1926   383

APPENDIX 11
METERS

Bruhn's Taximeter Company operated from Holborn's Gray's Inn Road, introducing a new variant, with a drum counter replacing the disc. (The company was absorbed into (German) Kienzle Company, who marketed 'Argo' meters through Lucas Service branch (UK) Ltd.) Numerically, the most successful meter produced by Swedish firm, Haldex, marketed in London by Halda Ltd, Brandon Road, York Way. First examples designed 1898; although the company's formal constitution was not UK established until 1911; meters fitted from 1907. Several foreign police authorities, weights and measures etc. departments interested, notably Warsaw and Moscow. Fiats (Bologna) and British Motor Cab Company switched to Halda meters for their 1,000-plus entire fleets. That year, agreement struck between seven companies to hire out meters on agreed terms but never respected. Between wars, Haldex parent company suffered financial strife; only kept afloat by English support. Following post-1929 Wall-Street-Crash depression and resultant shockwaves, matters worsened when annual rental charge per meter was dropped from £7.50 to £4.25 and company might fhave faced bankruptcy. By 1937, 'Halda 'membership' had dropped to 900 but this proved low point ('nadir') of company's experience. By the Second World War's outbreak, number exceeded 1,000, demand still increasing. Nevertheless, of seven signatories, only two survived beyond 1945.

Later, two new companies arrived, Metropolitan Fare Registering Company and Bell Punch. Metropolitan was off-stage by 1975; that year saw Bell Punch acquired by Halda. Another company, British Taximeter, was taken over by its German supplier. 1960 saw arrival of MK 8 electric model and Halda now had the competitive edge; it could reclaim top position held fifty years earlier. By 1976, over 22,000 were used, mainly rented; markedly increased PCO workload; obliged to follow every meter's progress — failures, repairs, retestings, changes to new vehicles.

APPENDIX 12
COMPETITION

There were 14 entrants for 1898's competition, 13 electrics and one gasoline:

Four Kriegers (including one open Victoria)
Six Jeantauds (including one hansom)
One Jenatzy (Belgian)
One Bersey
One Brouhey and
Gasoline Peugeot

All, except those bracketed, were motorised four-wheelers, driver sitting ahead of passengers in a closed body. Tested for features like speed, climbing ability, gradients and braking. Peugeot proved impressive against electric rivals regarding acceleration even at expense of smell, extra noise, vibration and unwanted heat accumulated on hot-weather long journeys. Battery longevity test: Jenatzy proved winner with 105km, just ahead of Kriegers (just under 100km) and Jeantaud Hansom, just under 87km. No clear-cut overall winner.

The following year, 1899, saw vaguely similar entries but now electrics had improved overall speed, Panhard Hansom was deemed fastest. Unwanted heat problem solved by placing engine under driver's box, away from passengers.

APPENDIX 13
DISTINCTION BETWEEN TWO-AND FOUR-SEATER CABS

	Two	Four
Minimum clearance (in)	8	10
Minimum track (wheel-wheel width) (in)	48	52
Minimum tyre diameter (mm)	760	810
Maximum length (ft)	14	14
Maximum breadth (ft/in)	5'9"	5'9"

APPENDIX 14
REGISTRATIONS OF AUSTINS AGAINST OTHERS

Competitiors included Beardmore, Morris Commercial and Unic KF1s (only being sold to 1933). Figures to nearest 10.

Year	Austin	Rivals
1930	270	270
1931	400	240
1932	310	200
1933	830	130
1934	1110	300
1935	1180	340
1936	880	310
1937	660	100
1938	210	90

APPENDIX 15

Cab legislation is partly down to:
  London cab orders from Secretary of State under Metropolitan Public Act, 1907
  Direct provisions through parliamentary Acts
  Regulations by Commissioner of Police under statutory powers

The relevant Acts are:
  Hackney carriage Acts passed since 1831, including:
  London Hackney Carriage Acts 1831, 1833, 1843, 1850, 1853 (2)
  Metropolitan Street Act 1867
  Metropolitan Public Carriage Act1869
  London Cab Act 1896
  London Cab and Carriage Act 1907
  London Traffic (Miscellaneous Provisions 1934 and amendments thereto)
  Road Traffic Act 1937
  London Traffic (Parking Places) Consolidation Regulations 1941

Following example, published in 1937 but still referring to an 1850 Act.

Regarding private hire, first major Act: 1998 Private Hire Vehicle Act, regulating relevant operations for the first time. Also Private Licensing London Act that year. Three hundred applications were received but by October 2001, all private-hire operators required licensing; drivers' licensing began in 2002.

Outside London, legislation varies with area size and local authority judgment. Since April 2005, all private hire vehicles in England and Wales must be licensed.

NOTICE

TO DRIVERS OF

CABS

By virtue of the provisions of Section 4 of the London Hackney Carriage Act, 1850 I, the undersigned, Commissioner of Police of the Metropolis, do herby appoint a Standing for FIFTEEN HACKNEY CARRIAGES at HIGH HOLBORN, W.C. and do make the following Regulations with regard to the Boundaries for the same, viz.:-

In centre of roadway, commencing at a point 15ft East of the refuge opposite the Prince's Theatre, and extending Eastward as far as necessary for fifteen cabs.

Front of cabs towards the West.

Provided that no Hackney Carriage shall be suffered to stand across any Street or Thoroughfare, or opposite the end of any Street of Road-way, or upon any place where Foot Passengers usually cross the Carriage-way.

	Signed
Metropolitan Police Office	The Commissioner of The Police of The Metropolis
New Scotland Yard SW1	
6th November 1937	

APPENDIX 16
LICENSING 1970

	Taxis licensed during 1970	New cabs licensed that year
Austin FX4D (automatic)	961	230
Austin FX4D (synchromesh)	7124	1168
Austin FX4 (petrol)	640	80
Beardmore	125	
Winchester	139	33
Metrocab	1	1
Total	8990	1512

APPENDIX 17
TAXI ORGANISATION ECONOMICS

Taxi organisation economics in three possible set-ups:

1) Employee-driver: drives vehicle, company owned, usually paid on commission basis; key element: employee-employer agreement: employer guarantees driver minimum hourly wage and payment of Social Security Taxes, payroll taxes, other benefits. Commissions range from 43 to 50 per cent but with addition for fringe benefits – effectively over 50 per cent of drivers' revenue.

2) Lessee-driver avoids above employee-employer agreement, deeming driver 'independent contractor'. Driver pays lessor a daily, weekly or monthly fee. Option to contract firm for services like fuel, maintenance, dispatching and advertising.

3) Owner-driver, owns cab, therefore no fee, otherwise like lessee arrangement. One special case, however, single taxi firm, often deemed 'independent' or 'owner-operator' existing in many cities, displaying very different operation. Driver, notably if he does not belong to cooperative dispatching set-up, dependent almost exclusively on street-hail business, concentrating on 'high-density' areas, airports and hotels. These operators rarely join the International Taxicab Association, seldom answering questionnaires; thus little known about numbers, entry, withdrawal rates and finances. However, they commonly form local associations to earn benefit of discounts from buying fuel and tyres in bulk and to establish cooperative dispatch services. At one extreme, organisations may be fragmented with cabs of different colours and working under different names. At the other, close co-operative ownership.

These are not always clearly distinguished; firms could have feet in any two or all three camps. But over time, more tended towards ownership or leasing for economic reasons, saving of Social Security contributions, hospitalisation and Workmen's Compensation schemes and Unions. Also firms need to keep long records, which is expensive.

APPENDIX 18
SAFETY

Design specification points regarding safety:

Luggage accommodation
Seating, main and supplementary
Head restraint
Arm rest
Smoking: ashtrays and restrictions, fire, gas emissions
Electrics, power, lighting, signals, warning lights re. open doors etc., and heating
Door entrance and exit height and width
Security
Safe deposit for fares
Driver vision and sun visors
Bumper design
Audibles: hooter and alarm

APPENDIX 19
FINANCE OF LONDON TAXI AND HIRE CAR BOARD

	£
Taxicab licence per annum	21
Taxi driver's licence initially	10
addition on triennial renewal	5
Annual Hire Car licence	3
Hire car operator's licence, renewable triennially	21

Discrepancy between cost of taxi and hire car licences accounted for by extra expense of cabs' more stringent test.

Additional annual charge, £2.50 payable by drivers for rank telephone use; TGWU considered this impertinent.

APPENDIX 20
CABMEN'S SHELTERS IN THE LONDON AREA

Chelsea Embankment SW3 – near Albert Bridge junction

Embankment Place WC2 – near Players' Theatre

Grosvenor Gardens SW1 – western side of north gardens

Hanover Square W1 – north side of central gardens

Kensington Park Road W11 – outside house numbers 8 – 10

Kensington Road W8 – near junction of Queen's Gate SW7

Pont Street SW1 – near Sloane Avenue junction

Russell Square WC1 – north-west corner

St George's Square, Pimlico SW1 – north side

Temple Place WC2 – opposite Howard Hotel

Thurloe Place Kensington SW7 – opposite Victoria and Albert Museum

Warwick Avenue W9 – near tube station

Wellington Place NW8 – near Lord's cricket ground

Pictures from Russell Square Shelter, known as 'Emirates', frequented by Arsenal supporters. (Author's Collection)

APPENDIX 21
FUEL

Diesel Emission: Early diesel engines tested by PCO examiner: observed smoke while engine revved up; applicable to 1970s.
From mid April 1995, cabs required to undergo smoke tests at MOT Stations; approval presented on re-license application.

Diesel's advantages over petrol engines: greater longevity and economy, producing almost negligible carbon monoxide and hydrocarbon levels. However, later experimentation revealed release of nitrous oxide and carbon particles: potentially health-hazardous.
Problem attacked by combustion chamber modifications and revised injector design. Only proved effective on direct-injection engines like Ford FSD; disappointment for indirect injectors like Nissan TD.

Liquid petroleum   An Iveco petrol engine was adapted to run on LPG in TX1 cab but
Gas (LPG)   failed to meet required standards, proving very uneconomical. Further localised problem exists: governing authorities for road tunnels like Dartford and Mersey refuse gas-powered vehicles.

HEV technology   Hybrid Electric Vehicles work from petrol- or diesel-driven electric generators. During running, engine releases minimal exhaust gas for benefit of scarcely 10 per cent of petrol pollution and greater fuel economy. Further advantage: efficient battery charging.

Index